The Presence of th

The Presence of the Feminine in Film

By

Virginia Apperson and John Beebe

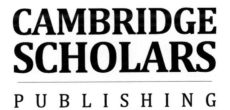

CAMBRIDGE
SCHOLARS
PUBLISHING

The Presence of the Feminine in Film, by Virginia Apperson and John Beebe

This book first published 2008. The present binding first published 2009.

Cambridge Scholars Publishing

12 Back Chapman Street, Newcastle upon Tyne, NE6 2XX, UK

British Library Cataloguing in Publication Data
A catalogue record for this book is available from the British Library

ISBN (10): 1-4438-0513-0, ISBN (13): 978-1-4438-0513-1

In memory of John Apperson, Jr. and Patricia Eloise Beebe

TABLE OF CONTENTS

ACKNOWLEDGEMENTS

This book would not have come into being had there not been the idea for a Jungian film festival, to be named "Psyche and Film," in the mind of Nonnie Cullipher, the farseeing Executive Director of Journey into Wholeness. After Nonnie approached the two of us with the idea, we came up with our own title, "The Feminine in Film." Under both titles, and with the help of Fran Cronenberg, at that time leading the Commission on Spirituality of the Episcopal Diocese of Alabama, the conference took place in Birmingham, Alabama, May 18-21, 2005.

We extend warm thanks to the conference participants; their enthusiastic response affirmed our hunch that the topic is an important one. We didn't realize that we would be making what had occurred in Birmingham into a book until several months later, when we were contacted by Nonnie with the news that a new press in England had written her a letter about the possibility of making a book that drew on the themes of the conference. In the writing, our ideas have developed, evolved, and found new roots. What hasn't changed over the past three years has been the vision that it was possible to say something in these pages not just about the image of woman in movies, but also about the image of the feminine in all her many cinematic guises using the tools of the working analytical psychologist in the investigation of films. We have therefore to acknowledge, first of all, C. G. Jung and all the Jungian analysts who went before us to enable us to recognize "the feminine" in imaginal material. Some are named in these pages, but many cannot be. We have to thank our analysands, as well, for showing us both the vitality and the necessity of such an approach in the practical understanding of products of the human imagination.

More than a quarter century ago, John Beebe hit upon the idea of showing and discussing films to allow a public audience some access to how a Jungian analyst thinks about the imagination, and John has been lecturing, writing and publishing on film ever since. Many of his film reviews have appeared in *The San Francisco Jung Institute Library Journal*, and some of these have been included, with a few revisions to adapt them to the present context, here. This journal, founded by John, is now published by the University of California Press under its new title, *Jung Journal: Culture and Psyche*, and John continues to write about movies for its present editor, Dyane Sherwood. We thank her, the *Library Journal's* previous editor, Steven Joseph, and the constant Mary Webster, who for many years was the Assistant to all of this journal's editors and thus the very first person to see and comment upon John's reviews. As editors, John and Mary both fell in love with Jane Alexander Stewart's review of *The Silence of the Lambs*, which with only a few changes is reprinted here. I am very grateful to John for bringing this remarkable piece to my attention, and to Jane for being willing to make a guest appearance in our book.

For articles of John's included here that come from other journals, we want to thank: guest editor Harvey Roy Greenberg, for the special issue of the *Journal of Film and Popular Television* on "Psychoanalysis and Cinema" in which John's essay, "The Notorious Postwar Psyche," first appeared, Andrew Samuels, guest editor for the Symposium: Post-Jungian Thought, in the August, 1996 issue of *The Psychoanalytic Review* in which John's essay "Jungian Illumination of Film" first appeared and Nancy Cater, the editor of *Spring Journal*, who commissioned the article that became "The Eye at the Heart of the World" for her special issue on "Cinema and Psyche." We are also grateful to the editors of books in which essays of John, reprinted here, first appeared and were improved by their editing: First, Nathan Schwartz-Salant and Murray Stein, editors of the Chiron Clinical Series, who asked for the essay that became "The Anima in Film," in their 1992 volume, *Gender and Soul in Psychotherapy*. This essay was selected by the Parisian analyst-editor Aimé Agnel, a veteran of the French film industry as well as a wonderful writer on Ford and Hitchcock, for a 1995 issue of the *Cahiers Jungiens de Psychanalyse* entitled "*Cinéma : une approche jungienne.*" The essay came out again in the seminal book *Jung and Film*, edited by the English analysts Christopher Hauke and Ian Alister. John's essay on *Marnie* developed out of a weekend on "Healing in Film" at the C. G. Jung Institute of San Francisco during which *Marnie* was shown in full, was refined by presentations of clips from the film at the C. G. Jung Institute Los Angeles, and at Luton University in England (for a program organized by Luke Hockley), and then became a talk given as part of a panel John organized for the 2001 Congress of the International Association for Analytical Psychology, whose Organizing Committee was chaired by Ann Casement and Programme Committee by Robert Hinshaw. These close friends and colleagues of John's have always supported his work on film, and with their encouragement he invited the Cambridge analyst Ian Alister and the distinguished author and screenwriter Diane Johnson, to join him in discussing "The Interpretation of Film as a Psychological Art." His essay on *Marnie*, "Hitchcock's Opposing Personality" was originally written for the Proceedings Volume, *Cambridge 2001*, which Robert Hinshaw brought out through his Swiss publishing house, Daimon Verlag, in 2003.

The people to whom John and I have to be most indebted in writing a book on this topic, however, are our mothers. Not only did they first introduce both of us to the feminine, but to film as well. In John's case, Patricia Beebe held him at the age of 18 months to see a Bob Hope movie. She was a budding movie critic when John was an infant, starting him on the path of evaluating and analyzing a film. "See!" she used to say to him, when they sat together looking at a movie in a theater (which was usually twice a week throughout his childhood). Barbara Apperson's capacity to be entertained by film, still to this day, is truly something to behold. It has always been a treat to sit by her side watching a film, her peals of laughter delighting my brothers and me, sometimes more than Peter Seller's antics. More than anything else, my mother gave me the best gift a mother can give her daughter, a firm foundation in the feminine.

Three other women, among so many, stand out as having influenced my interest in pursuing the interface between Jungian ideas, broader cultural issues, and film—Sonja Marjasch, Linda Leonard, and Ingela Romare. Each in her own way has taught me how to marvel at the creative psyche's ability to effectively mobilize the stagnant parts of our lives. Their outright refusal to settle for the status quo has helped me to look beneath the surface and experience movies' transforming potential. Others that have supported this endeavor include members of the Atlanta Jung Society, the analysts that comprise the Georgia Association of Jungian Analysts, Mary and Martha's Place, Don Kalsched, and Annette and Jim Cullipher – they have all helped me to find my voice. Thanks go to the Center for Women at Emory University for supporting a briefer version of the Alabama Film Festival and to Cary J. Broussard and Women on their Way's generous support of that event. Jessica Teal is the enormously talented film editor who created the montage of film clips. So many have believed in this project as it has taken shape; would that I could name every single person! I am grateful for my family and friends' patience with my absences during the book's creation. My thanks go especially to Cynthia Williamson, Kitty Deering, Rebecca Gurholt-Sands, Anne Sterchi, Alicia Franck, Vivian Lawand, Ann Pequigney, Tricia Brown, Perry Hooks, Eugene Pidgeon, Cynthia Smith, Jeannie Dubose, Margaret Baldwin, and Germaine and Charles Williams. I am appreciative of Timmen Cermak's correspondence around the development of his concept of *echoism*. John has named Elizabeth Osterman, the first analyst to tell him that film was the medium through which he could really make his contribution to analytical psychology; David Brown, with whom he saw many movies in the 1970s when it was possible, thanks to the nostalgia boom, to see the entire film canon at revival houses; Barbara McClintock who invited him to give his first film seminar at the C. G. Jung Institute of San Francisco, and Holly Reppert, Heather Tarnas, Barbara Berman, Aaron Daniels, Eric Giegerich, and Baruch Gould, who kept that tradition going, with the strong support of the Chairs of Extended Education there, James Yandell and then Thomas Singer. John has often told me how much he has valued the counsel of Adam Frey, with whom he has shared more conversations about movies than with anyone else and who has lovingly critiqued progressive drafts of the essays in this book; among many other movie-loving friends that have also read his work and helped to shape the way John sees film. He wants me to mention particularly Bill Berkson, Antoine Faivre, Millicent Dillon, Anthony Grudin, John Harbison, Diane Johnson, Victoria Nelson, Scott Paul, Judith Rascoe, Hans Stahlschmidt, and Marina Warner, Fredy Wäspi, as well as his colleagues in psychological film teaching, Angela Connolly, Joseph Henderson, Geoffrey Hill, Francis Lu, Christopher Hauke, John Izod, Don Fredericksen, Linda Leonard, Don Williams, Scott Feaster, Jim Palmer, Kirk Schneider, and Patricia Berry. Among professional filmmakers, he deeply appreciates his (usually all too brief) contacts thus far with Peter Ammann, Peter Bogdanovich, Phil Cousineau, John Dahl, Tom Noonan, Jim Lantz, Guy Maddin, Billy Frey, Naftali Rutter, Nathaniel Dorsky, and Sean Tate. There is not room enough to name the published film critics and historians who have influenced him over the years, but for direct personal communications on issues related to this book he is very grateful to Stanley Cavell, Lutz Bacher, Dudley Andrew, and V. F. Perkins.

In the end, though, John and I are analysts, and it is our clients who have kept us grounded in the process of looking and listening for psyche. I can't speak for John, but when I wondered if what I was working on in these films had any legitimacy, I simply listened to my patients' stories and was reminded of how much help the feminine still needs from us in our world today.

In the course of producing this book, Ursula Egli, our editorial assistant, has been steady, dependable, eagle-eyed, and even cheerful through and through, giving this book its final order and coherence and its index. Another talented contributor and feminine spokeswoman extraordinaire, acclaimed artist Gail Foster, allowed us to use for the book's cover her charcoal sketch *Step Forward,* an image of exquisite feminine energy arising from the depths that catches the spirit we have tried to convey in *The Presence of the Feminine in Film*. Many thanks go, too, to Gail's husband Tom Swanston, who has been unsparing in his backing of this book. Finally, everyone we have had the pleasure to work with at Cambridge Scholars Publishing, including Dr. Andy Nercessian, Amanda Millar, Carol Koulikourdi, and Vlatka Kolic, has been remarkably responsive and endlessly patient.

John has only occasionally alluded to the role his own anima must have played in guiding him to his understanding of film, but as a woman I can feel how important she is to him. My own inner figures have been steady anchors as well. But finally, as a woman analyst writing about the feminine, I want to speak about my two great male allies in this process. John Beebe has not only been a marvelous writing partner, but as my editor he has gently guided me, while at the same time setting the bar high. My greatest champion throughout this writing venture has been my husband, Pete Williams. It hasn't hurt that he is a great fan of John's as well. Pete is one of the truly great defenders of a feminine sensibility. He has been a pillar in the background of this book, making sure that what is here is not only readable, but real.

Virginia Apperson

PREFACE

JOHN BEEBE

Trained first as a medical doctor and then as a psychiatrist, I came of age as a psychotherapist by learning to attend to my dreams. I recall, for instance, one I had in my early thirties in which a strong male figure kept exhibiting his sexual prowess, until the good-sport woman under him finally said, "I can't keep up!" Clearly, the masculine figure was outstripping the feminine one in my dream, and that indicated to the analyst I was seeing at the time a state of imbalance. But what exactly did "masculine" and "feminine"—the major signifiers of these unknown people in my dream—mean? I was in analytic training at the C. G. Jung Institute of San Francisco at the time, and had already read a lot of Jung. Simply to turn to the language of archetypes, however, and say, "My shadow is stronger than my anima" was no longer helpful to the enlargement of my consciousness. I had to develop my own way to understand the qualities that my dreams were assigning to male and female figures. I had to wonder, in what did their masculinity or femininity reside?

It is Jungian to look for a public, cultural analogue to any private psychological experience. In addition to working out my personal associations to the figures in my dreams, I hit upon the idea of looking at movies to see what they thought "masculine" and "feminine" were. I saw quickly that though movies invariably betray a level of cultural anxiety, including the commercial concern to supply a fickle public with dramatizations of issues already on their minds, so that they will be motivated to sit through the movie, culture (including the sophisticated American culture of post 1970s feminism) could not explain everything I was seeing at the movies.

I decided to try to let the movies themselves tell me what masculine and feminine were, by engaging in a series of meditations on films. This book does not pretend to record every possible nuance of the feminine, but it does record many significant ways that the feminine can present herself in a movie. Although it collects work I have done over the past three decades to promote the Jungian depth psychological study of film, I am fortunate on this occasion to have my viewpoints paired with the extraordinary sensibilities of Virginia Apperson. Virginia trained as an analyst in Zurich and has watched first hand in a variety of clinical settings, from the hospitals of her original training as a nurse to the consulting room of her private analytic practice in Atlanta, what terms like "matriarchal" and "patriarchal" (to name just one of the pairs of opposites the reader will encounter frequently in the essays of our book) actually mean for people in significant distress. We are grateful that the psychologist Jane Alexander Stewart, from the heart of the film industry in Century City, has consented to let us reprint her classic essay on "the feminine hero" in *The Silence of the Lambs*.

Such a patchwork approach, relying on materials from films chosen almost at random, may seem to some readers naïve, tendentious, and even backward. But it has enabled Virginia and me to turn our attention to a series of themes disclosed to us by films that have already grown familiar. The topic areas we have developed do not exhaust the possibilities of the feminine. Nor should we pretend that all emotion and image belongs to her. Particular movies, however, establish a presence of the feminine in film that goes well beyond both the depiction of women's lives and the fantasies men have about women, the topics that have dominated film studies in recent years. Everyone recognizes that film has become our culture's most cherished medium for the exchange of images and ideas. What has not been sufficiently appreciated is that both the content and the process of such exchanges invite the feminine to come forward, and that she has often managed to accept the invitation. Virginia and I have sought to redress that imbalance of recognition by offering our readers ways to notice her presence.

FINDING THE FEMININE IN FILM

CHAPTER ONE

O SISTER, WHERE ART THOU?

VIRGINIA APPERSON

The archetypal feminine! How do we begin to describe her essence? As we try to bring her into focus, two crucial points must be kept in mind: she certainly cannot be captured by a simple, clean, "masculine" definition, and she does not just belong to women. Since by her very nature, she leans towards the obscure and elusory, we inevitably (and quite naively) rely upon a rudimentary summation of her fundamental nature. We remember her in the same way that we recollect most anything—by focusing on what is familiar—the feminine in our mothers and grandmothers, our sisters and playmates, our teachers, girlfriends and wives. This inclination to source the same resources is a bit lazy where the feminine is concerned and distracts us from discovering her other talents. Furthermore, as the more single-minded masculine has taken center stage with the rise of the West, his solar brilliance has eclipsed and condescended to her lunar reflection, and we are simply left with a stereotypical packaging of the feminine.[1] Such a narrow take on the feminine offers a sense of comfort and order to a patriarchal sensibility. In this climate, women have a hard enough time fostering a full-fledged relationship to their femininity. For men, the situation is even more dire, because when a man shows an inclination towards his own feminine side, he is too often treated with disdain and considered an embarrassment to the male gender. The dreary result is that much of what is most remarkable about the feminine has been mislaid, along with a more companionable masculine. Lifting the lid off of Pandora's Box brings chaos to our normal way of thinking and reinforces a longing to get back to the safety of our typecast routines.

Until we go to the movies. It is in the cinema that it is socially acceptable for the feminine to morph and contort and blossom in the many different variations of her potential. Anyone who is halfway paying attention can easily access this feminine repertoire for the price of a movie ticket. So as we search for our "lost sisters," women, as well as men, have a phenomenal opportunity to discover secreted aspects of their femininity, if they dare to be engrossed by the compelling force fields that they encounter on the big screen.

In the twenty-first century, film is our most available, yet still provocative, form of fairy tale. This multifaceted medium dishes up scenes that not only vividly recreate common experiences, but also introduce us to alternative ways of being. With its visual and auditory power, film has the capacity to confront our lives, illuminating the best and the worst of ourselves, both personal and collective. Moreover, its emotional impact defies the old standards that have guided us, challenging us to reflect on what it is in a particular film that is stretching us right out of our comfort zones. Indeed, films can carry us forward to regions beyond our wildest imagination, rendering images that expose and counter our psychological status quo. Few fully take advantage of such an opportunity, preferring to passively sit back, relax and opt for entertainment and diversion over psychological growth. Watching film "at such a distance" only permits the film's sway to be mildly felt, rather than sinking past our surface defenses. Nonetheless, any viewer who chooses has the prerogative to allow a film to work its profound magic, letting the film speak to what so longs to be redeemed inside. Outgrowing our past and becoming worthy of our future is truly a heroic task. Rarely does anyone decide to change without a prod from pain and suffering, since it is our anguish that typically demands therapeutic assistance. So, in addition to more traditional psychotherapeutic approaches, studying film is worth adding to a healing regimen.

The feminine's difficulty competing with the masculine is a theme in the unconscious that Jungian analysts are encountering with alarming frequency in their work with dreams. Establishing a more balanced relationship between the masculine and the feminine has proven to have far-reaching therapeutic consequences. Film provides just the right accompaniment to analytic endeavors because it helps us image the feminine's successes and failures. On the screen, we can plainly see the propensity towards masculine over-development, which has led to a conspicuous unevenness on the playing field. In particular, when a scene in a film moves us (like when a strong affect occurs in a dream), a quite crucial question should be asked: "what deeply entrenched imbalance is being compensated?" There really is no better tool than film to help us incarnate and visualize the dynamics that re-occur not just between men and women, but more specifically between masculine and feminine energies.

The Jungian analyst Ann Ulanov sums up quite beautifully our challenge of establishing the feminine on par with the masculine when she writes about a "human project" that literally impacts the entire planet:

> The wholeness of every individual revolves around the axis of a fully developed polarity of maleness and femaleness....The polar structure of the psyche is the source of its energy and the matrix for its fulfillment. Libido, the life energy which is generated from the tension of the polarities, flows from one pole to the other, thereby differentiating the ego from its nascent unconscious state and effecting the emergence of those distinct elements whose reconciliation makes wholeness possible....Thus, in becoming whole we must grow into a conscious relationship to the masculine-feminine polarity within us....
>
> If a man fails to develop his relation to this feminine element in him, he suffers at least a partial diminution of being and at worst, a serious mental illness....[T]he concern of many women with what a woman's nature is and with what a relationship with a man should be may be considered as concrete expression of the urge to recover to consciousness the neglected feminine pole of the central masculine-feminine polarity. Seen in this way the struggle for women's "rights" is not a part of a political platform for women but a human project concerned with all of us as persons (1971, 164-166).

And so we embark on this cinematic journey, rummaging around for the discarded bits and pieces of the feminine that might help her hold her own for such a truly and life-giving "human project."

The Feminine and the Masculine

Before further imagining how film might assist with this worthy balancing act, let us rephrase our original question: "Who really is the feminine that we propose men and women alike might find in the cinema?" Recognizing her resistance to being apprehended, here is a go at some of her distinguishing qualities. She is deeply rooted in nature, the animal and instinctual world. She is the cycle of life, death, rebirth with all the exuberant spontaneity and morbid suffering that are part of the vicissitudes of life. Rather than denying the emotional, affective realm that is inherent in our human nature, she feels her feelings without shame or apology. She wails; she rages; she squeals with laughter; she gyrates; she laments; she erupts. She can be a mess. She takes her time. And she can, also, be as impersonal, detached, ruthless and unrelated as a tsunami or a drought. She contains us in her womb; she nurses and rocks us against her

Fem.

bosom. She bleeds; she boasts of her softness and roundness. She does not need to know; she lets us be. She drives us crazy with her desires and moods. When she embraces alterities, unimagined options sprout. She is an ugly, smelly hag, a giggly girl, a fertile field, a juicy tomato, an overflowing breast, and the crazed mare that has been separated from her foal.

Given the outrageousness of some of these traits, it is not hard to understand why the feminine has been denigrated in our hyper-rational culture. Her gifts do not accord with our modern day demands. The masculine, as we know him, is focused, competent, accurate, reliable, and his purposeful drive jibes perfectly with our needs. We choose him to quarterback because he has little trouble proving his superiority to the feminine as a way of consciousness.

Notwithstanding his enormous talents, the masculine may require a longer glance from us to explain the reasons we have privileged him in the West and to elucidate why we are beginning to tire of him. In contrast to the mysterious feminine, the masculine is pretty cut and dry. He sees the world quite simply—in blacks and whites—not the befuddling grays. His linear approach supports competition and power and divisiveness. Aggression and authority come quite naturally, sometimes for good, sometimes for evil. Logic and facts become the only things that really matter. Task-completion, action-orientation, the bottom line—these are what inspire and motivate him. Time is not wasted on the little things. He protects and guides; he procures and commands; he has all the answers. The intellect is his home. He growls and orders and dares to leap tall buildings with a single bound. He is a rapacious and promiscuous Zeus, a visionary and dynamic entrepreneur, a vicious tyrant, a scavenging predator, a vigilant father and a steadfast husband.

But wait! Hasn't feminism effectively taken on the flagrant pedantry and misogyny that such masculine privilege has so famously flaunted? Isn't his power base steadily losing its grip as women come into their own? A truly honest answer reveals quite the opposite. Though present political correctness makes it easy to romanticize and idealize feminine traits, when it comes down to employment, we all too often find the masculine a more efficacious hire. Our preference for simple solutions supports the masculine standard of judgment about her ungovernability, and so we hop into bed with him before we even know it. He is the ruling principle of our modern consciousness, and the principle of the ruler in the sense of how things are measured. Precisely because she is so imprecise, as well as elusive to measurement, the archetypal feminine gets marked as beside the point—the point being to get things right, create structure and maintain stability. Her natural ambiguity remains a problem to our unequivocal minds. Her comfort in the depths of the unconscious and with catty ways makes her even more suspect, justifying our refusal to take her seriously. As a consequence, equality is merely a mirage.

Archetypes and Film

How can an entertainment medium like film begin to address such a fixed paradigm where the feminine gets short shrift? The answer becomes clearer when we consider the care with which films are made. At the center of the production of a memorable film is a director. The director does not control every effect, as the auteur theory would have it, but his (and increasingly hers) is the shaping consciousness at the center of things, enabling the meaning of the finished product to cohere. A good director approaches the work of filmmaking in a fashion similar to that of a Jungian analyst approaching psychotherapy. They both know they are drawing upon the energy of archetypes, the cheapest yet most valuable and abundant currency available to any creative entrepreneur, to enable them to do their jobs. The word archetype comes from the Greek *arche,* which takes us back to the beginning of time, the source, the very nuclei that are common and shared by all of humanity. *Typoi* are the innumerable and nuanced impressions that through history have given this ancient core shape and image (Moon 1991, viii). With the freedom to pick from an endless supply of characters generated from the archetypal field, the director is able to break away from stereotypical roles that determine what a mother or father, husband or wife, daughter or son should be or do. Like an analyst who counts on the symbolic world to provide answers when a client is stuck, whether or not a film works on a psychological level is dependent upon the director poring over the archetypal prospectus and shaping the characters so that the archetypes can deliver something more than what the viewer already knows.

The Archetypes at Work

A film director's job is to tell a compelling, captivating and credible tale. The Jungian analyst's job is to tap into the archetypal possibilities that lie within their analysands' dreams and neurotic symptoms, helping them discover that which blocks them and that which will lead them into a more meaningful existence. With a shared reverence for image, the movie director and Jungian analyst carry a confidence that this instrument that they most rely upon, the archetypal image, "is a living, organic entity which acts as a releaser and transformer of psychic energy" (Edinger 1972, 109). Without the symbolic possibilities found in the many layers behind the image, neither could do their job. Without the vitality of the symbolic, there would be no growth, no dynamism, no effective movement, no transformation, no redemption.

In an analysis, this evolution occurs when an archetype is recognized, when the symbolic image is seen behind a symptom. For example, a faultfinding figure in a dream reminds the dreamer of the constant criticism she experienced whenever she spoke up in her family and that left her chronically dispossessed of her own authority. What is different in the dream, however, is an adorable, but impudent little girl who scoffs at the attacks and slights of the dream "Critic," refusing to be disenfranchised. This young upstart gives the dreamer a tangible example of not only how to survive future vitriol, but the hope of thriving in the face of it. Such knowledge can help her in the future, as long as the dreamer remembers "to borrow" the cheekiness expressed by her dream companion. Encounters with caustic people will likely still be painful, but now the dreamer has something more substantial with which to work. Instead of perpetually feeling isolated by external (or internal) judgment, she can strike a brand-new posture to the once self-limiting critique. Like the filmmaker who develops certain characters to enhance and enliven and move the movie's plotline, Jungian analysts rely on compensatory archetypal images that act as catalysts, breathing life into the tattered scripts upon which their clients have repeatedly relied. This only works, though, if a relationship is established between the client and the image: the presumptive and carefree dream parvenu who has so much to teach.

To further help the uninitiated reader get a feeling for what is meant by the dynamics of an archetype, let us take a closer look at how a relationship with the mother archetype (the first archetype that any of us encounter) might evolve. We discover the archetype of Mother through our experience of (or failure to experience) our personal mothers. For all of us, that experience begins in the womb, and for most of us continues throughout infancy and long beyond. Rarely are people indifferent to their experience of their mothers. As much as we keep hoping that our personal mothers will fulfill all of our needs, no mortal mother can fit that bill, which is finally contained not in our actual mothers, but in the mother archetype itself (perhaps the "inherited" image in Jung's collective unconscious for which there is the most incontrovertible evidence through such common experiences of fantasy, emotion, and expectation, of her universal importance). So how do we move beyond our experience of a personal mother and make use of the archetypal mother?

To better understand this process, let us suppose the reader had a mother who was a homebody, a cook, an introvert. You may have preferred one that yelled at the ref, taught you how to socialize rather than bake, and openly discussed the political issues of the day, rather than how to harmonize with your surroundings and work quietly behind the scenes. The archetype that fuels your discontent is simply more inclusive than the mother you happened to have. If received, this "other mother" archetypal energy becomes an effective change agent in your life helping you to grow in ways that your personal mother simply did not know how to facilitate. As inspiring as this option sounds, however, since our original experience of mother is so familiar and the alternatives utterly foreign, we refuse too often these archetypal urges, reducing and limiting the archetypal mother to our personal mother. It is hard to believe that there could be another way because the old way is so deeply ingrained. In such a case, the conservatism of the archetype is at play. Most of us live in a tension between longing for something new and a desire for the comfort of the status quo. Maybe, this is why we covet others' experiences of parents and are at the same time offended by them.

Since each of us channels the mother archetype in such a partial (and partisan) way, looking past a version of mother with which we are identified and making room for other kinds of mothers in our lives requires considerable faith that there is something to the archetype beyond our experience so far. Such trust is not for the faint-hearted. Part of growing up is accepting our parents for who they are, graciously receiving what they gave us and taking responsibility for how we live from here, and it is really that process that opens us up to the possibilities of the larger archetype. (Much easier said than done!) When we grasp that our mothers are simply mortals and will never be able to completely fill the Great Mother's shoes, the payoff liberates us from being limited to our childhood experience. Once we can venture beyond the family system and issue an invitation to other aspects of Mother that might suit our present purposes, we are ready to learn from the vast reservoir of cultural images that can instruct our widening perspective.

Archetypes, Analysis and Film

Since what we first know about Mother is fairly specific and concrete, it can be difficult to envision how to break the mold unless we have at hand alternative images. As we search to find an image of mothering that will satisfy our psyches' demands for wholeness, we encounter characteristics of Mother in all sorts of places. One place where unanticipated maternal qualities reveal themselves is in the therapeutic relationship, especially if the analyst is female. A "mother transference" arises with a surprising energy that is really more like a primal bonding that is experienced for the first time rather than something transferred from earlier experiences. A similar maternal charisma can be exerted by a teacher, a nurse, a celebrity, a neighbor—each one offering their own flavor of mother. Even a particularly nurturing male can become the incarnation of the mother archetype for us. As already mentioned, an archetypal approach to dreams can be enormously helpful when customizing a maternal experience that complements our original experience of mother. Bodywork, ventures into nature, great literature, theatre—really, participation in any of the arts—are avenues to find more of what one is looking for. Each way offers up its own value. The reason John Beebe and I are featuring film as a therapeutic tool is because of the particular energy the picture show lends to the process of personal development. A film, when we go out to see it, visually commands attention. It is meant to overpower us, to take us off our beaten paths. As we let it in, a film widens our narrow ego consciousness time and again. We are drawn out of ourselves and have an opportunity to grow something new from the film's expansiveness. Since the shift from being affected by a symbol to being transformed by it requires psychological muscle and heft, it makes a lot of sense to let film's unparalleled and deliberate bigness help us along.

Just look at this small sampling of movie mothers from which to choose (or reject). In *The Sound of Music*, Mother Superior believes in Maria's potential.[2] As *Mommie Dearest*, Joan Crawford sadistically destroys her daughter's spirit.[3] Mother Nature, having toppled the *Titanic*, shows off her capacity to generate "the perfect storm."[4] On a humbler, but equally provocative, note from mother earth, Scarlet is inspired by a lowly radish (everything else is *gone with the wind*) to turn her life around.[5] *Being Julia* entitles a woman who prefers her identity as an actress over that of mother.[6] A fairy godmother—a magical mother—converts pumpkins and tiny mice into coaches and fine steeds, while an ill-willed stepmother tries to cram her daughters' not so dainty feet into petite slippers.[7] As a wicked witch attempts to usurp the feminine realm, the temporarily motherless Dorothy is forced to grow up.[8] *The Hours* move slowly as we watch the quiet desperation that eats at the heart of an unmothered mother.[9] An orphaned cub is adopted by a bear whose protective instincts are keen and well-attuned to the cub's vulnerability,[10] while *Mrs. Doubtfire* returns love to a household that has been devoid of a motherly spirit.[11] On the conventional side of the archetype, weekly TV reruns provide steady comfort to our culture as June Cleaver[12] and Aunt Bea[13] remain indefatigable in caring for their families.

These characters quite efficiently engage the viewer with the personal and collective range of what we might call Mother. Renditions of movie mothers, like the archetypal mother, are endless and irreducible to a simple description—one single image will never satisfy our longing for more. Savvy moviegoers understand that entering a theatre opens their psyches up to an inexhaustible panorama. They allow the symbolic archetypal image in and feel its affective heat. They wonder about what has been stirred and evolve its energy by reflecting on what is being awakened inside. For example, if the scene works on our behalf in *The Sound of Music* when the Mother Superior sings "Climb Every Mountain," it is because we imagine a positive mother standing by us in our darkest moments and giving us the courage to move into the struggle, rather than running away. The inspiring energy that comes out of such a spiritual mother fills the hearts of every person sitting in the movie theatre, and at least for a split second, they believe in themselves and their own actuating ability. Why not bring that conviction home with you? Why not remember that kind of encouragement in the face of dark times? Her vote of confidence is there for the taking, but requires accountability and connection on the viewer's part. Such a Mother cannot do Her life-enhancing work by Herself; She needs to be treated as a legitimate life force that deserves to be related to and reckoned with. C. G. Jung encouraged the development of an active imagination, as opposed to a passive one, which means an ongoing dialogue with your very own Preeminent Mother who lives on even after the picture show. But remember, if we leave her on the screen, her innervating power will become null and void.

A Montage of the Feminine

Throughout the course of this book, which records how two Jungian analysts have come to see the feminine with the aid of film, we will be tracing the cinematic history of the feminine. Our intent is to use films' "feminine" tactics to help us uncover how the rejection of the feminine has taken place. More important, our movie selection will also show innovative ways to reinstate her. As a way of setting the stage for the chapters to follow, here is a montage of familiar film clips to help the reader start to appreciate how films can expose the nature and dynamics of the feminine. We encourage, you, the reader, to take your time as you "watch" this set of well-known sequences again with us. Let yourself imagine that each clip has something personal to say to you, that it is intended to awaken something inside yourself. Consider what the never-been-taken-seriously lass, the infernal vixen and the shrinking violet (among others) have that you need.

The first clip reveals a haughty Bette Davis standing mid-way up a staircase. She is clearly taking a stand and practically growls these cautionary words at us: *Fasten your seat belts. It's going to be a bumpy night.*[14]

In 1950, the seat belts Bette was referring to were still mostly on planes, but the message to the audience is the necessity of preparing one's self by buckling up when faced with the feminine who has had just about enough. Davis's restless character insists, if we are going to ask that films give room for the feminine to do her thing, then we had best be prepared to accept some pretty significant turbulence; so hold on. With this premonitory advice, we go on to meet more of the feminine, perhaps a bit more prepared for the inevitable disturbance that comes with Her movie message.

Now the scene changes from the seasoned and starting to be cynical Davis to Shirley Temple as the feisty and refreshing "Little Colonel."[15] Beneath her frilly crinoline, Shirley embodies a pint-sized tigress. She refuses to be cowed by her military-minded grandfather's gruff and dismissive authority. Determined to have the last word, she defiantly flips the table on which their game of toy soldiers resides. In his very own parlor, the Senior Colonel faces his first defeat, and we marvel at the mighty ingénue's victory.

Like the Davis clip, this one has reverberations in our minds, which lead to questions. How did the little Colonel manage to defeat the big one? Doesn't she know that a young lady is to be seen and not heard, at all times deferential to grandfather's experienced mandates? Why is she freer to oppose him than we would be? What has kept her spirit from being broken? If this was a therapy hour, we would have to ask, "When did you last glimpse your own audacious and curly-headed cadette?"

Next, the camera zooms in on the saintly convent Sisters who gather and deliberate musically on how "to solve a problem like Maria." They tell us (through Oscar Hammerstein's lyrics) that their clerical charge is a "flibberti-gibbet, a will-of-a-wisp, a clown." We hear about her disgraceful escapades: tree-climbing, stair-whistling and waltzing to mass. The Sisters remind us that this novice, Maria, must be fixed, regulated, and contained. Above all, she must learn not to be, but to "behave." But how, they wonder, "do you keep a wave upon the sand or a moonbeam in your hand?" Then a door slams, and with a frantic rush of feet, we see Maria herself, late, *again*, for vespers. We know that in the face of this disturbing evocation of untamed feminine potential, the perplexed and static Sisters have met their match!

This is probably the ultimate image of patriarchal expectations ruling the feminine world. We all recognize the stringent self-righteousness from within that wants to bind and break our spontaneous feminine mettle. But like Bette Davis's Margo Channing and Shirley Temple's Little Colonel, Julie Andrews's Maria cannot be hushed up. Though Maria briefly tries to fit herself into their rigid expectations, her true nature refuses to be eradicated. Her instincts have not yet been squelched. She understands the real profanity and sacrilege of selling out to conformity. And we all like her and want to see more of her. The therapist is required to ask, "When is the last time, in nun-like fashion, you scolded your own irreverent whims? What was the price you paid?"

Now the scene on the screen abruptly changes to a London town home. Professor Henry Higgins, accustomed to being in charge, is telling us in a clipped, masculine sort of talk-singing, how vexed he has become since allowing "a fair lady" into his life.[16] Irritably begging to resume his monotonous routine, he muses, "Why can't a woman be more like a man?" Skulking down the stairs, interrogating his housekeeper, blasting the phonograph's cackle and babble, gibber and jabber of women screeching, his ruminations help to justify his disgust of the other sex. His circular reasoning descends into the final narcissistic question at the core of his downward and regressive spiral: "Why can't a woman be more like me?"

The therapist wonders, "Does this cut, too, take you to a familiar place, where the masculine is at its wits' end because He has started to lose control?" We recognize that Higgins's very impatience and intolerance is starting to release an emotional, affective expression in spite of the masculine's heavy-handedness. Provoked by the flower seller within, a disturbing energy is starting to disclose and differentiate itself. We all know that masculine side of ourselves who wants to throw her to the wolves, while at the same time being fascinated by her disquieting presence.

The collage takes yet another turn: switching to the soot-smudged chimneysweep Bert chatting with the spit and polish banker Mr. Banks.[17] "It's that Poppins woman!" They decide that the new nanny is the culprit; it is she who caused Banks's settled life to turn on its head. Bert commiserates, but with a twinkle in his eye, when he considers how inconsiderate it has been of Mary Poppins to expect a man of such prominence to take time out for his children. Her insistence that he give each of them a spoonful of sugar—what rubbish!?!? But look closer, the camera skillfully captures evidence that Bert's mischief is seeping through the armor with an exquisite shot of Banks's puzzled face—a turning point in the film when the all-knowing male starts to second guess himself.

It surely is hard to argue with Mr. Banks's sincere concerns. Our lives are demanding. As his name suggests, someone must pay the bills, and in his world that is usually a man. Similarly, rules must be observed, order maintained, also "guy things." The irony is that the ingenious Mary Poppins understands decorum and responsibility as well as anybody, and yet she can also dance with the children over the rooftops of London or frolic in the fields on her merry-go-round steeds. Julie Andrews's Poppins, both controlled and unsectarian, brilliantly conveys another profound truth about the feminine: that the feminine is inclusive of opposite qualities. Unlike the masculine, that prizes separating distinctions, as far as the governess is concerned, everyone loses if we are bound by an either/or existence. The therapist naturally asks, "Wouldn't you love to have a tablespoon of that?"

The montage cuts back to the cogitating Professor Higgins's humbug, as the masculine desperately tries to maintain his turf. "Let a woman in your life!"—and one's peace of mind and sense of propriety go down the drain. He wants us to know, emphatically, that there is a very simple solution. "*Never* let a woman in your life!"

As if he, or we, had a choice.

Now an African-American family is gathered round a table for Sunday dinner. We are watching a scene from *The Color Purple*.[18] Albert commands from one end of the table, his father from the other. Celie, Sophia and Sug are scattered amongst various and sundry family members. Albert's pomposity strikes Celie's last battered nerve. In a split second, a carving knife is brandished in Celie's irate hand. Sophia awakens. Their voices will no longer be muffled, and their newly discovered signature color of rule, purple, at last prevails.

Celie, finished with being the butt of Albert's reproaches, takes her own charge and preempts the possibility of any further disparagement. Sophia snaps out of her stupefied state. This is the power of the feminine. The therapist unequivocally asks, "Dare you find a similar élan within yourself to finally upstage the tiresome tyrant in your life?"

Our collage of film memories has moved to its final scene: *Breakfast at Tiffany's* Holly Golightly, the ultimate "anima woman"—the feminine in her most unconscious expression, as a mock-elegant gamine, living in service of the moneyed, elite masculine.[19] This is woman as a quintessential chameleon whose next move is always contingent upon a man's fancy. In this scene, though, she finally gets a glimmer that there is another way. Now that much of her persona is gone, her chum Paul finally gets through to her that he wants her, loves her, just as she is. Something is awakened in Holly by his sincerity, his desire and his goading. But first, she must find the cat—one of the oldest symbolic expressions of feminine essence, perfectly mirrored in Audrey Hepburn's feline grace—before she can be fully present to love him or herself. In a downpour, she rushes towards the cat that she had just callously tossed from her life. As if to underscore that a feminine path to wholeness has finally been found, the montage fittingly concludes with one of the most transcendent of all popular songs, "Moon River." [20]

The therapist reminds us that Johnny Mercer's lyrics did not fail to appreciate the feminine, a realm we might all aspire to "cross in style someday." Aren't we all "out to see the world"? Yes, but only if we let ourselves look! We can start with motion pictures. The screen bears witness to the feminine in ways that are impossible to refute. And our lives are better for it.

References

Beebe, John (1992). *Integrity in Depth*. College Station: Texas A&M University Press (original hardbound edition).

—. (1995). *Integrity in Depth*. New York: Fromm International (paper edition, with corrections).

Edinger, Edward (1972). *Ego and Archetype*. Boston: Shambhala.

Moon, Beverly (ed.) (1991). *An Encyclopedia of Archetypal Symbolism, vol. 1*. Boston: Shambhala.

Teich, Howard (1993). "Homovision: The Solar/Lunar Twin-Ego." In Robert H. Hopcke, Karin Loftus Carrington & Scott Wirth (eds.), *Same-sex Love and the Path to Wholeness*, 136-150.

Ulanov, Ann Belford (1971). *The Feminine in Jungian Psychology and in Christian Theology*. Evanston: Northwestern University Press.

Wiley, Lee (1971). "Moon River," (music by Henry Mancini, lyrics by Johnny Mercer), track one on the reissued *Back Home Again*, compact disc ACD-300, © 1994, Audiophile Records, New Orleans, LA.

Notes

[1] Even the equation of solar with masculine and lunar with feminine is stereotypical. John Beebe cites Howard Teich (1993), who "has proposed that we should see solar and lunar, lights that have conditioned our view of gender, not as metaphors for the genders, but as perspectives in both masculinity and femininity" (Beebe 1995, 91). That is, solar and lunar "are dimensions that modify gender, appearing as polarities within both masculinity and femininity" (Beebe, 1992, 91).

[2] *The Sound of Music* (1965). Screenplay by Ernest Lehman. Directed by Robert Wise.

[3] *Mommie Dearest* (1981). Screenplay by Robert Getchell. Directed by Frank Perry.

[4] *Titanic* (1997). Written and Directed by James Cameron.

[5] *Gone with the Wind* (1939). Screenplay by Sidney Howard. Directed by Victor Fleming.

[6] *Being Julia* (2004). Screenplay by Ronald Harwood. Directed by István Szabó.

[7] *Cinderella* (1965). Teleplay by Joseph Schrank. Directed by Charles S. Dubin.

[8] *The Wizard of Oz* (1939). Screenplay by Noel Langley, Florence Ryerson, Edgar Allan Woolf. Directed by Victor Fleming.

[9] *The Hours* (2002). Screenplay by David Hare. Directed by Stephen Daldry.

[10] *The Bear* (1988). Screenplay by Gérard Brach. Directed by Jean-Jacques Arnaud.

[11] *Mrs. Doubtfire* (1993) Screenplay by Randi Mayern Singer. Directed by Chris Columbus.

[12] *Leave it to Beaver,* TV-Series (1957-1963). Written by Joe Connelly et al. Directed by Norman Abbott et al.

[13] *The Andy Griffith Show*, TV-Series (1960-1968). Written by Jack Elinson et al. Directed by Bob Sweeney et al.

[14] *All About Eve* (1950). Written and Directed by Joseph L. Mankiewicz.

[15] *The Little Colonel* (1935). Screenplay by William M. Conselman. Directed by David Butler.

[16] *My Fair Lady* (1964). Screenplay by Alan Jay Lerner. Directed by George Cukor.

[17] *Mary Poppins* (1964). Screenplay by Bill Walsh. Directed by Robert Stevenson.

[18] *The Color Purple* (1985). Screenplay by Menno Meyjes. Directed by Steven Spielberg.

[19] *Breakfast at Tiffany's* (1961). Screenplay by George Axelrod. Directed by Blake Edwards.

[20] John Beebe suggests Lee Wiley's 1971 recording of the Mancini/Mercer song as the rendition that most powerfully reveals its scope and depth.

CHAPTER TWO

JUNGIAN ILLUMINATION OF FILM

JOHN BEEBE

Film as a Medium for Realization of the Unconscious

The medium of film is peculiarly suited to psychological analysis because it is perhaps closest of any art form to the natural process by which the unconscious chooses to make itself known—by visualizing itself in motion, as in dreams. A starting place for the understanding of film may be found in C. G. Jung's statement, "One does not become enlightened by imagining figures of light, but by making the darkness conscious" (Jung 1954b, 265). From its beginnings in the first films produced by the synchronistically named Lumière brothers 100 years ago, cinema has seized the opportunity to render visible what formerly had been dark to conscious representation, the movements of individuals in their lives over time. Cinema has grown up concurrently with psychoanalysis, and as close siblings nurtured on a common zeitgeist, the two share a drive to explore and realize the psyche.

The greatest filmmakers seem to have grasped almost instinctively the potential of the medium to represent aspects of the unconscious directly as if it were a regular part of reality, even as Freud demonstrated it to be in *The Psychopathology of Everyday Life* (1901/1960). Jung spoke of the "figures" of unconscious life, and in a well-realized movie these figures often insert themselves as characters, complicating the scenario as they interact with one another and with the characters that represent more conscious attitudes. In *Scenes from a Marriage* (1973), for instance, Ingmar Bergman illuminates the unconscious life of his protagonist couple by introducing a second couple with whom they have dinner. This shadowy, dysfunctional, quarrelsome pair would be poorly drawn if the depiction of actual people were intended, but viewed as inner figures they come across beautifully as the animus and anima. They tip the audience off to the unconscious dynamic that lurks below the gracious surface of the primary couple.

In film the unconscious may also be depicted as a particular place to which the protagonists travel, such as Vietnam in *The Deer Hunter* (1978) or the Land of Oz in *The Wizard of Oz* (1939). There the protagonists can discover the full measure of the conflict hiding in the conscious situation introduced at the beginning of the film, and perhaps also the key to make things different. North Vietnam is not depicted in a politically correct way in *The Deer Hunter*, but showing sadistic Vietnamese officers torturing the American protagonists effectively conveys the underside of the young men's relationships in the United States. Similarly, like a great healing dream, or a psychotic crisis that actually leads to psychological improvement, Dorothy's sojourn in the Land of Oz offers the appealing but fragile Judy Garland—ever at risk for being "blown away" by disorienting affects or situations—a chance to confront and deal decisively with her shadowy object-relations—to slay a witch mother and unmask a false father—and to manifest a new potential for relatedness. Through the bond to her loyal friends in Oz, the feeling of being at home is established within.

The Relation between Conscious and Unconscious in Film

The relationship, in *The Deer Hunter,* between the young steelworkers' Pittsburgh suburb and Vietnam, or, in *The Wizard of Oz,* between Dorothy and her alternately charming and terrifying Oz acquaintances, forms a new kind of paradox for the understanding of works of art, because imagery depicting a conscious standpoint is directly juxtaposed with visualizations of the realities and potentialities of the unconscious itself. Rarely in other art forms are conscious and unconscious elements given such equal emotional weight by being viewed within a common frame. Today it is more common for students of film to draw upon Lacan's formulations, but I have found Jung's emphasis on the reality of the psychic image and the necessity for an articulation of the ego's engagement with the unconscious well suited to the explication of this artistic phenomenon. As a "visionary art" (Jung 1930) cinema finds its genius in the play between the conscious and unconscious signifiers in its semiotic.

Film critic Andrew Sarris (1968) has argued that concern with the conflict between the conscious depiction of a theme and the subjective emotional meaning for the director of the images that occur in the storytelling is the hallmark of an *auteur* film. Before Sarris, Siegfried Kracauer (1960, 36) pointed out that in films there is often a tension between the "realistic" use of the medium to document and the "formative" use of the medium to provide dreamlike imagery. This strain is not evenly balanced in all films. A film like Attenborough's *Gandhi* (1982), for instance, may seem like nothing other than the re-creation of an historical reality, whereas a stylized film like Polanski's *Chinatown* (1974) is entirely dreamlike, peopled by figures charged with erotic, hostile and repressive potential.

In the psychological analysis of a movie, its documentary aspect may be usefully taken as a gloss for what Jung spoke of as the conscious or ego "standpoint" toward a situation; the dream aspect would then correspond to the attitude of the unconscious. I believe that the most interesting films deal with the interaction of the documentary with the dream level, and that the practice of making movies inevitably involves the director in what Sarris (1968, 37) describes as "a very strenuous form of contemplation" of the movie materials, which is quite similar to what Jung (1954a, 204) called "active imagination."

Active imagination, a self-chosen meditative, visionary daydream through which an individual makes direct contact with unconscious figures, may also be compared to what the Kleinian analyst Wilfred Bion (1962, 36) called maternal "reverie," through which the mother takes an active responsibility for the affective state of the child by imagining the child's needs and brooding within herself on how best to meet them. In active imagination, one engages with the needs of the unconscious figures and enacts the ego's own desire to handle the internal objects with integrity. This can take the form either of a fantasy dialogue with the unconscious figures, or more strategic efforts to control or overcome them: the result is not unlike a movie scenario. Such reverie or active imagination is inevitably part of the *auteur* director's work from the first shaping of the scenario to the final editing process.

It is not hard for the psychological critic to find evidence within *auteur* films themselves for the processes involved in creating them. In Victor Fleming's *The Wizard of Oz*, for instance, Dorothy, as played by Judy Garland, goes well beyond Baum's character in the children's novel. As a human befriending a trinity of imaginary figures—the Scarecrow, Tin Woodman, and Cowardly Lion—who comically personify unconscious anxieties about ego strengths, Fleming's Dorothy becomes an image of psychological commitment to the archetypes that are being explored, the personal connection that makes the director's engagement with his materials vital.

The creative capacity to engage with unconscious materials Jung (1916) calls the transcendent function, and this function is symbolized in

the movie as the yellow brick road. Following the yellow brick road—that
is, feeling and imagining the relation to the unconscious—Fleming was
able to animate the unconscious materials of the scenario, bringing
intelligence, heart, and courage to the picture, thus substantially increasing
the integrity of the creative product. The goal of the transcendent function,
according to Jung, is the realization of the self, a central value symbolized
in the *Wizard of Oz* by the Emerald City. There the vulnerable ego and the
powerful unconscious manage to come together and are even revealed to
be aspects of one personality, in the figure of the humbug Wizard who
exhibits both the grandiose pretensions and the realistic limitations of the
visionary artist. The Wizard, with his magic lantern effects, is like a film
director, at once in control and not in control of the ultimate impact of his
images.

Film as a Medium for the Creation of Consciousness: The Example of *Schindler's List*

As Jung was radically optimistic about the healing possibilities of the
self, so audiences, like Dorothy and her friends off to see the Wizard, seem
to approach movies with the expectation of a miracle, hoping for an
extraordinary effect upon the state of their minds. Often enough this hope
is disappointed, and yet there are films which induce an unexpected new
consciousness in many who view them. The occasional dispensation of
this miracle may be why film viewing and criticism have become such
important activities within our culture: in addition to wanting to be
entertained, the mass audience is in constant pursuit, as if on a religious
quest, of the transformative film.

One such film is *Schindler's List* (1993). Steven Spielberg's movie
was audacious in taking on the Holocaust, a subject long considered off
limits to representation in art because the gravity of the material almost
always overcomes any effort to contain it. One recalls that the representation of human subject matter all but disappeared from serious art for
nearly a generation after the events of World War II, which led Jackson
Pollock, among others, to, in Joseph Henderson's (1987) words,
"detonate" even "the archetypal image" which had held sway previously in
the surrealist movement. This is not to deny the persistence of realism as a
continuing stream in art, but rather to convey how irrepresentable the
spiritual "caesura" (Lacoue-Labarthe 1990, 41) of the Holocaust and the
"hole" in history (McCarthy 1961, 4) of Hiroshima appeared to be to a
generation of artists concerned with defining how the meanings of World
War II should be recorded.

As one of the handful of visionary directors who have been able to reach a mass audience, Spielberg is an American *auteur* in the lineage of Griffith, Capra, Welles, and the later Hitchcock. For an artist with his reputation for popular entertainment to make a film about the Holocaust was risky. But Spielberg redeemed himself, even as Schindler did in his transformation from wartime profiteer to savior of a group of Jews who otherwise would have perished, by producing a commercially successful film which actually increased the capacity of the public mind to hold the events of the Holocaust within a coherent frame. A healing film, *Schindler's List* works therapeutically against those tendencies in the psyche that would dismiss this dark chapter in the history of the West.

One need not look in *Schindler's List* for a character who represents our conscious attitude toward the Holocaust, for the simple reason that we have essentially not had one. The work of the film is to create the necessary consciousness to hold the events of the Holocaust, which are as bewildering to the naive viewer as to the little girl in red seen running, nearly uncomprehending, through the Krakow ghetto during its liquidation.

One way to appreciate the way this film works on the viewer is to recognize it as a trickster work of art (Beebe 1981). Such a work usually has a trickster character, like Schindler, as its central subject, yet is itself a trickster in the way it continually reverses its audience's expectations and yet commands a fascinated acceptance of its authority. Such works are often about survival. (Compare Hitchcock's *Psycho*.)

The film is not so much about the Holocaust per se, which it never quite shows us, as about surviving the Holocaust, even as the audience survives the viewing of an also very painful film. In fact, *Schindler's List* moves unexpectedly toward becoming almost comedy, in the sense of Dante's *Divine Comedy:* it has a happy ending that takes us to the edge of Paradise itself, so that it is finally about being led through and out of Hell rather than getting stuck in it.

A way to amplify[1] the trickster element in *Schindler's List* is to consider the film's effect on its viewers as a kind of alchemy. The alchemical trickster, "the soul of the metals" (Jung 1948, 198), at once responsible for the success and elusiveness of the strange, underground Renaissance science of gold making, was the wily Mercurius—Hermes, god of merchants and thieves, gone to military Rome where he became a darker god. One could scarcely find a more apt mythologem for the figure of the movie's central character, the war profiteer, Oskar Schindler (Liam Neeson).

In the first factory Schindler buys on the cheap from Jews, an enamelware company, we watch as a circular sheet of metal is stamped into the form of a cooking pot and coated with enamel. The pot itself echoes the all important alchemical symbol of the container, which operated as the sacred vessel in which materials of opposite nature could be united in what the alchemists called the chemical marriage, their name for the mysterious process of chemical combination. Jung saw in the sequence of cooking reactions (called "operations" by the alchemists), a metaphor for the progressive consolidation of the self. I would say that what was being consolidated was, more precisely, integrity, exactly the process that we follow in the story of Oskar Schindler.

The strategy of *Schindler's List* is to follow the process through which Schindler is bound to the Jews in what amounts to a sacred marriage, his fate linked inextricably to theirs. For the alchemists, that elements of unlike or opposite nature could enter into a combining relation with each other was an object of reverent awe. For us, watching *Schindler's List*, the "work against nature" is the degree to which Schindler, who sets about to capitalize on the Nazis' mischief, courting their officers—even physically resembling, in an eerie way, the Hauptsturmführer Amon Goeth—is nevertheless driven to pledge his troth to the Jews and eventually to save his own integrity.

Progressive stages in the development of Schindler's engagement with the Jewish people turn on his encounters with particular Jewish women. There are, for example, the young woman who asks him to accept her parents into his factory, the Jewish girl who brings a birthday cake to him, Goeth's kitchen maid, Helen Hirsch, and the Jewish women, separated from their own men, whom Schindler rescues from the jaws of Auschwitz. This trickster is forced to react to signifiers of the anima.

Toward the end of the film, we see Jewish men forge a ring from gold melted down from the bridgework extracted from the mouth of one of the Jewish workers. Schindler places the ring on the fourth finger of his left hand, and the Jewish women surround him as he breaks down to embrace his own shame at not having done more for the Jewish people. The audience's willingness to suspend disbelief and enter the film's theme of the possibility of integrity as acceptance of "one's infinite responsibility to the other" (Levinas 1989, v; Beebe 1992, 33-4) is galvanized by this current of marriage symbolism.

In alchemy, tricksterish ebullience is an attribute of mercury, and the mineral associated with the extreme suffering of nature is salt, the incorruptible ingredient in tears. When in a stage of the chemical marriage mercury and salt are brought into profound combination, the resulting product is *Luna* (Jung 1963, 59; McGoveran 1981, 250-253), the earthly representative of the feminine moon, which for Jung (1963, 146) symbolized the capacity to reflect and feel and imagine in the midst of the dark nights of the soul. It is this construction of *Luna*, Jung's "feminine principle," which the symbolism of marriage between Schindler and the Jews seems to betoken. As we watch the gradual shift in Schindler's consciousness from his initial, awkward flirtations to his final willingness to enter a virtual marriage contract with the Jewish people, dedicating himself to the survival of 1100 of them, the alchemical symbolism has the uncanny effect of guiding us to accept the pull on a mercurial, mercantile nature to engage with the salt of human suffering so as to produce a new, more intensively reflective consciousness that as audience we can participate in as we imagine and feel the events of the Holocaust.

 Luna is associated with the metal silver in alchemy while *Sol*, Jung's "masculine" principle, is associated with gold (Jung 1963, 92 and 130). Spielberg's choice for the body of his film is black and white, which returns us to the silver screen. It is precisely the creation of the luminous light that alchemists knew as *Luna* and which Jung has described as the less familiar feminine principle of consciousness, that distinguishes *Schindler's List* from conventional attempts to document the Holocaust. This is a film that allows us to reflect in a related way upon a moral catastrophe as D. W. Griffith might have done, outside at nightfall on a snowy evening. Like moonlight, the view is indirect: the Gorgon's head is seen reflected on Athena's shield. The effect is to enable us to hold in memory what might otherwise be too painful to endure. This was the perspective that eluded the painters after World War II who knew instinctively that they dared not approach the religious mystery of so much suffering through the pitiless north light of their studios.

 Jung's works on alchemy were composed during the period in which the terrible events of the Holocaust were happening, and his emphasis in these writings was on the need for emotional experience to be contained and reflected in a lunar way, rather than interpreted and defined.[2] A generation later D. W. Winnicott became the spokesperson within psychoanalysis for the importance of maternal holding, as opposed to the fatherly capacity to interpret, in the metabolism of psychological experience. We continue to look to psychoanalysis as the cultural institution which enables individuals to hold painful affects like mourning and shame. This capacity is developed in the viewer who is gripped by *Schindler's List*, a poignant reminder that moviegoing can be a containing, as well as entertaining experience, and even a healing rite of vision.

References

Beebe, John (1992). *Integrity in Depth*. College Station, TX: Texas A & M University Press.

—. (1981). "The Trickster in the Arts." *San Francisco Jung Institute Library Journal* 2(2): 22-54.

Bion, Wilfred R. (1962). *Learning from Experience*. London: Maresfield Library.

Freud, Sigmund (1901/1960). *The Psychopathology of Everyday Life*. In J. Strachey, ed. and trans. *The Standard Edition of the Complete Psychological Works of Sigmund Freud*, 24 volumes. London: Hogarth Press, vol. 6.

Henderson, Joseph (1987). Personal communication.

Jung, C. G. (1916). "The Transcendent Function." In H. Read, M. Fordham, & G. Adler, eds. *Collected Works of C. G. Jung*, vol. 8. London: Routledge. Princeton: Princeton University Press.

—. (1930). "Psychology and Literature." *Collected Works*, vol. 15.

—. (1948). "The Spirit Mercurius." *Collected Works*, vol. 13.

—. (1952). *Answer to Job*. *Collected Works*, vol. 11.

—. (1954a). "On the Nature of the Psyche." *Collected Works*, vol. 8.

—. (1954b). "The Philosophical Tree." *Collected Works*, vol. 13.

—. (1963). *Mysterium Coniunctionis*. *Collected Works*, vol. 14.

Kracauer, Sigmund (1960). *Theory of Film*. New York and London: Oxford University Press.

Lacoue-Labarthe, Philippe (1990). "The Caesura." In Heidegger, *Art and Politics* (C. Turner, trans.). Oxford and Cambridge, MA: Basil Blackwell.

Levinas, Emmanuel (1989). Preface (by Seán Hand). In *The Levinas Reader*. Cambridge, MA: Basil Blackwell, v-vi.

McCarthy, Mary (1961). Letter to the Editor of Politics, [1946, following the publication of John Hersey's *Hiroshima* in *The New Yorker*]. In *On the Contrary*. New York: Farrar, Straus, and Cudahy.

McGoveran, Patrick (1981). "Application of an Alchemical Model to Milieu Functioning." *Journal of Analytical Psychology*, 26: 249-260.

Samuels, Andrew (1995). Letter to *London Review of Books*, 17(10) (25 May), 4-5.

Sarris, Andrew (1968). "Toward a Theory of Film History." In *The American Cinema*. New York: E. P. Dutton, 19-37.

Notes

[1] In reference to this term, Samuels (1995) has recently pointed out that "...Jungian analysis involves linkages being made between the material of the individual patient (dreams, fantasies, transference projections, and so forth) and so-called 'amplificatory material' drawn from myth, legend, art, and literature.... The procedure of amplification is not as odd as it sounds to modern ears when one considers a possible parallel with contemporary psychoanalytic practice wherein the here and now of the clinical interaction is, so to speak, 'amplified' by reference to infantile and other early or primitive mental and emotional processes held to be inaccessible to the patient's consciousness in the session itself. There always seems to be this need in analytical therapy to turn up the volume, make things that seemed a bit thin more ample, convert one kind of material into another kind, and to establish that individual experience has shared elements—cultural, social, political—in it."

[2] This emphasis informed Jung's reflections on the problem of evil in *Answer to Job* (1952), which was his deepest response to the Holocaust and to his own blindness, at an earlier period of his development, to the reach and power of the Nazi shadow.

AT RISK

CHAPTER THREE

MAD

VIRGINIA APPERSON

Wide Sargasso Sea
(1993). Directed by John Duigan.
Screenplay by Carole Angier, John Duigan, and Jan Sharp.

Long curious about Mrs. Rochester, "the madwoman in the attic" in Charlotte Bronte's *Jane Eyre*,[1] the post-modern novelist Jean Rhys wrote her masterpiece *Wide Sargasso Sea* (1966) to investigate what could have led up to the tragic confinement of Mr. Rochester's wife at Thornfield. In this prehistory, the woman who became nineteenth century fiction's most unpresentable wife is Antoinette Cosway, an exotic young woman from an aristocratic Creole family in the West Indies that over several generations has lost its money and its moorings. While she is still a schoolgirl, Antoinette is married off, like chattel, to Edward Rochester, the second son of English landed gentry, a young man who is strongly motivated to secure a wife with property to provide him the financial footing that primogeniture has denied him. Antoinette, in turn, marries for—she is not sure what—because that is what young girls do. The just post-slavery culture in which the couple settles to live is a hostile one, an environment that does not bode well for union. Antoinette attempts to engage Edward in the land that she loves, but gets stuck in an unreal role: half tart, half babe-in-the-woods. Initially charmed, then increasingly disquieted by his wife's Caribbean ways, Edward reverts to his English family's authoritarian posture in dealing with her. Although the two of them do make attempts to transcend their incompatibility, they ultimately fall into the worst of male-female scripts: she to hot feminine sulkiness when she feels him pull away from her and he to a cold, patriarchal insistence on ignoring her outbursts of feeling. Soon he is listening only to his own desires and ambitions. Although Edward treats Antoinette as if she has done something really wrong (it is this judgment that eventually drives her crazy), it is made clear by the film that her essential psychological crime is nothing more than a deep longing to be considered.

This calamitous tale has been poignantly captured on the big screen by director John Duigan. The film closely follows Rhys's novel to reveal the morass of the feminine's suffering in the face of masculine incomprehension. The movie opens with the sea spinning in a kaleidoscope of sparkling colors, seaweed swirling in mandala-like shapes, and a light dancing mysteriously through the dark waters. As a backdrop, foreshadowing the heroine's descent into madness, the Sargasso Sea represents an eerie and enigmatic oceanic womb, the feminine in her most undifferentiated yet also multifarious mode. Within these deep waters exist elements that have long been feared and rejected as maladaptive, displeasing, and too independent. Though this grand and munificent sea sets the stage for the heartbreaking story, its vital role as a fertile matrix for deep transformation is tantalizingly downplayed. The central motif of maritime largesse becomes an undistinguished and remote background presence, whose lack of development and realization in the film ironically anticipates Antoinette's fate.

The Sea of *Sargassum*

Before proceeding to a close look at the film to discover more of Antoinette's story, we should linger just a bit longer over the neglected body of water that supplied Rhys with her title. The real Sargasso Sea seems boundless in its expanse. Geographers designate the Sea as a massive body of water placed smack dab in the middle of the Atlantic Ocean: it encompasses a two million square mile area between the West Indies and the Azores. It has exceptionally clear blue, warm and ultra-salty waters that extend three miles to the bottom of the ocean. *Sargassum* is Portuguese for grape, but in this context the *sargassum* is berry-like seaweed that floats in clumps the size of small islands just below the sea's surface. The result is something like a moist desert—rain is rare, the waters are windless and stagnant, and the air around them is thick, humid, and wickedly hot.[2]

The Sargasso Sea, like an ancient heart enabling a sluggish circulation, serves as a catch basin, an organic holding environment, for the entire Atlantic Ocean. This is the result of a slow-moving clockwise rotation within its waters. Plankton, tiny crabs, shrimp, and octopi all survive the current's seductive downward pull by clinging to the protective seaweed, without which they would sink through abysmal depths to die of starvation on the Atlantic floor. This particular sea, however, is not simply a festering *cioppino* produced by a last gasp, monotonous struggle for existence. There is a perverse vitality that makes this prison also a womb. In this mysterious world between worlds, eels from Europe, the Mediterranean and the United States meet to mate, to produce offspring and to return to their ancestral seas—a remarkable feat of reproductive and self-renewing migratory instinct that demonstrates the ebb and flow of life at its most exuberantly natural. Though eels for the most part cause land creatures to recoil, these snakelike fish are extraordinary role models for resilience—emblems of the right way to participate and to thrive in Mother Sea's seemingly pointless, chaotic and regressive pull.

The apparently wishy-washy world of the Sargasso Sea has developed a long and infamous history as a devouring trickster, with maps pointing out its sordid dangers dating back to early Greek times. Deemed by those who have actually traversed it as an indelicate body of water throughout, the Sea has long been regarded with suspicion by its toilers, who view it as an especially uncanny hotbed with a harsh fate lying in wait for those who manage to reach its symbolic center. Tales of ships pirated by ghosts, of mayhem inflicted by savages, and of men entrapped in the tangled seaweeds have for centuries frightened the most seaworthy sailors. Further heightening a traveler's anxieties are the legendary mishaps of ships (and even planes) being gobbled up without a trace in the Bermuda Triangle,[3] an area that overlaps the Sargasso Sea. The conclusion most often drawn about this particular body of water is that once entered, she never lets her guests escape.

Taken symbolically, however, the wide, clotted sea is laden with a plethora of divergent meanings. It is a self-contradictory, ambivalent domain representing the "inexhaustible vital energy" of the Great Mother, who both generously bears new life and inconsiderately "swallows everything" (*The Herder Symbol Dictionary* 1978, 167). Water, long understood by analytical psychology as a symbol of the unconscious, is that first mother who frustrates us with her fluid evasiveness, yet recurrently entices us with her enormous promise. Because the mother is always archetypally of two minds about letting life proceed, her maritime image here evokes a transitional force that has potential to do us in, but also to act as a go-between mediating between our conscious selves and the dangerous depths. The eels that come to spawn in these precarious waters have perhaps the right appreciation for the complexity, sacrifice and reward that are all to be found in the Sargasso Sea. For those willing to honor her, the Sargasso offers a realm of fantastic opportunity. Mankind, however, has made the mistake of classifying this oceanic realm as a cesspool, an irregular graveyard—mirroring the contempt that is often directed at the difficult female body with its murky mysteries.

The film masterfully captures this basic aversion to the feminine. Edward Rochester's instincts, like those of all patriarchal voyagers since antiquity, have been warped by a prejudice against the matriarchal to such an extent that they are blind to the Sargasso's charm, despite Antoinette's appreciation for her island world and her care in sharing its finer points with him. Not grasping or not caring that the Sea's mystical waters could serve as a fairy bridge between his privileged, sophisticated England and Antoinette Cosway's Caribbean island routine of lazy mornings, fantastical imaginings, and sensual and embodied emotions punctuated by dance, the ungrateful Edward refuses to entertain any enduring respect for this uterine domain. Though the surrounding sea is vast enough to contain the couple's contrary perspectives and complex enough to tolerate Edward's resistances and to melt his defenses, the young man is so set on mastery that he is not prepared to deal with such an unexplored frontier. Instead, his brief glimpses of the steamy Sea merely ignite his ambition to return to England, taking Antoinette with him, as soon as he can afford to.

The movie works because we are all, nowadays, a bit like Edward. We have long lost touch with eelish instincts; we are ignorant of the energy that exists in the oceanic world of the Great Mother. Even our analytic sophistication works against us: we have been schooled by the psychological authorities of the past century to flee the Great Mother's uroboric clutches. The standard psychoanalytic counsel, both Freudian and Jungian, has been to "grow up" and responsibly separate from our actual mothers, and how can we quarrel with that? Leaving mother and infancy behind is a necessary step in adult development. However, if we abandon Mother altogether in the name of individuation, we leave too many treasures behind in the unconscious. In order to appreciate the feminine values contained in this largely uncharted Sea, we have to loosen our stereotyped psychological take on the Mother world. C. G. Jung should be read as one of the first depth psychologists to assist with this endeavor. His essay on the mother archetype emphasizes three essential and intertwined characteristics of the Mother that most other psychologists, even sadly, his own followers, have managed, destructively, to obscure by trying to tease them out from each other, in a masculine, evaluative way: "her cherishing and nourishing goodness, her orgiastic emotionality, and her Stygian depths" (1954, par. 158).

To the degree that we still live in Edward Rochester's psychological world, we want to identify the "cherishing and nourishing goodness" motif found in the Great Mother archetype as her one defining and definitive attribute. (The American Mother's Day celebrates this cherry-picking approach to mother's psychological legacy.) For the most part, we care very little for (and know even less about) "her orgiastic emotionality and her Stygian depths." Emotions and depth tend to disturb the Anglo-Saxon ideal of appropriate self-containment—by that standard, these aspects of the Great Mother are much too extravagant, complicating, and finally self-indulgent to be cultivated.

Though it is easy to pretend Edward Rochester's arrogantly disciplined nineteenth century world is no longer ours, he actually holds the perspective in which most modern men and women have been raised, and he is the figure with whom it is easiest to identify. We have been groomed and tutored by the same masters as he to believe that reason and discipline where emotional life is concerned are the keys to success and survival. (Read any self-help book that you can buy in an airport, and you will find the ideology that Edward carried with him to the New World.) The overwhelming message is that affects are messy; we need to get over them, plan our lives not to arouse them, and take our antidepressants when despite our best efforts they get out of control. A hundred years ago such emotions were explicitly associated with a woman's "wandering womb" and considered "hysterical." Have we made much progress? Today women free themselves from the stigma of being looked down on as simply "feminine" by evincing their own masculine qualities. The problem with this kind of progress is that the female sex, just as much as the male one that we criticize for a lack of emotional intelligence, is losing touch with a balancing feminine perspective.

We have lost our ability to appreciate the feminine when she presents herself as disconcertingly chaotic. Jungian psychology recognizes that this tendency to reduce the feminine to forms of dysphoria and dyscontrol bespeaks a major flaw in our culture's attitude toward the psyche itself. In *The Feminine in Fairy Tales*, Marie-Louise von Franz explains the impasse that results:

> All the well-meaning charitable enterprises in the world are built up on a *Weltanschauung* that does not take the dark side of Mother Nature into consideration....At one time nature and her dark side were in harmony, but [for centuries we have only invested in] the one-sided light attitude.... There was no realization that a further evolution was necessary...an awareness of the dark side (1993, 41).

Another Jungian analyst, Edward Whitmont, has commented on the common resistance to incorporating essential aspects of the feminine because we cannot fit them into our current conceptions of what is appropriate to value:

> Today, we believe in human rights. But by and large, we still limit their definition to biological, social and political standards. We are largely unaware of their psychological implications and give little value as yet to individual feeling needs. For the sake of social conformity with the masculine ideal of bravery, we still repress and teach our children to repress their subjective feminine sides, their affects, feelings and neediness. Thus our culture collectively…represses rather than sensitively integrates the Goddess's realm of birth, death, and the tides of inwardness, moods, and emotions. Likewise, it represses Dionysus's domain of desire, joy, aggression, and destruction. This results in a widespread sense of depersonalization, frustration, resentment, hate, incapacity to love and insensitivity to the humanness of others and of self. Primeval envy, greed, and destructive hostility increasingly dominate the scene. We have not yet confronted the paradox of the need for individual authenticity versus the demands of social ethics (1997, 12).

Jungian analysts have been succinct and persuasive when delineating the archetypal problem that underlies the patriarchal spirit of Western culture, whose colonizing shadow side is so bleakly depicted for us in the scenario of *Wide Sargasso Sea*. They make us see that the psychological shortcoming of patriarchy is a chronic undervaluation and suppression of the "unbecoming" side of the feminine. Contemporary men and women, in their desire for a well-managed existence in which to pursue their measure of personal happiness, reject the world of the Great Mother as chaotic, diffuse, and poorly defined; in this way, they miss out on its splendor. Like Edward, most of us living today fear and mistrust the sultry power of the Great Mother's emotional potential. She is forced as a consequence to remain on the sidelines of our efforts to develop ourselves, in a highly suspect, undistinguished role, at best a tolerated spectator to our psychological lives, while the rest of the cast of complexes that make up our psyches are kept ignorant and skeptical of her "no man's land."

   While most psychologists were going along with the cultural trend that led modern people to turn away from the Great Mother's eccentricities, Jung continually wondered about the loss to wholeness entailed by so marginalizing the feminine:

> What has become of the characteristic relation of the mother-image to the earth, darkness, the abysmal side of the bodily man with his animal passions and instinctual nature, and to "matter" in general? (1954, par. 195).

Jung understood that the psyche actually needs the Great Mother's capacity to nurture, contain, embrace and bear new life. This is more radical than at first glance it appears. As a psychotherapist specializing in states of possession by the unconscious, Jung fully appreciated the necessity of learning to outgrow the Great Mother's devouring clutches, but he was deeply concerned with the irreparable damage that can be done to the psyche when the individuation process gets stalled at the point of trying to separate from the mother realm. Such an attitude toward the Great Mother fixes the ego at a stage of walling off vital aspects of the feminine simply to keep a tighter control on life.

Wide Sargasso Sea tells the story of just such an impasse, created by a young man's suspicion of the Great Mother world, but Edward is only one of the characters in the movie who squirm in fear of the strange Sargasso Sea. The scenario introduces us to a number of persons, female as well as male, who would cede this realm of the feminine to a masculine authority. Many of their deeds result in undermining Antoinette's very sanity, which depends upon her positive relation to the environment in which she grew up.

Eels, which are among the most peculiar, perhaps, but also most hardy of the creatures that thrive in this maritime environment, have something that Antoinette lacks and that Edward can not fathom. They represent symbolically some of the most ancient, chthonic, primitive aspects of all our selves. Eels' sinuous movements connect us to our own lost instincts, our sexuality, and the uncanny authority of the mother goddess. When honored, these creatures heal; when despised and threatened, they discharge their poisons. With their eerie, autonomous movements, eels remind us how effectively the Great Mother functions when she is free from masculine attempts to control her natural abilities.

Within the Sargasso Sea, eels oscillate in the deep ocean waters, well below the reach of any possible conscious attitude. Edward is horrified by such sea "gremlins" and frightened by the extreme world that they must inhabit. The implication is that though his desires are quite as strong as Antoinette's, his superstition and his ignorance prevent him from carrying on with his passion for her. Because of his phobic response to the Great Mother, he is deprived of the archetype's mitigating balms that could assist in assuaging his misgivings. Therefore he cannot relate in a healthy way to Antoinette's exotic, sweltering, untamed wilderness any more than he can continue to make love to her body; rather he becomes hostile, cold and calculating, bent on building a detached empire where only the civilized ego can survive.

The feminine is never granted the authority to stand up to Edward and prevail in this film; so she becomes inflamed and hysterical. That is to say, the entire feminine world of the film seems to go mad, and Antoinette's madness is just a special, though very poignant, instance of that. Antoinette's madness is surely an eruption of the feminine, and it is not hard to see that in this rigid, masculine set-up she will wind up in the attic, with all the other things we don't know what to do with.

The depiction of the unraveling of the marriage is one of the most sorrowful stories ever told. Like a case study, it follows two inadequately mothered souls attempting (and failing) to break out of their family-bound fates. The film is painful to watch, because it asks us to contemplate how the feminine potential of any promising relationship can slip through our hands. To take the film seriously, we have to leave our self-contained lives and enter zones of the feminine that we have forgotten. When we do so, we quickly learn that the experience can be both repellent and exhilarating. In the end we can not wait to get out of there. At the same time, we know that we will have lost something irrevocable, if we leave the Sargasso Sea behind.

The Divisions of the Father

The movie opens on an image of the bottom left quadrant of the Sargasso Sea and proceeds to float the viewer into the frame of reference that Antoinette brings to the picture, which is the over-ripe island paradise of her childhood world. Here grotesque marine life is brazenly marketed on the docks; brilliantly colored flowers miraculously thrive under the scorching rays of the tropical sun, and jet black, muscular, half-naked bodies of the newly freed slaves aimlessly display their sluggish and languorous habits of immodesty and abandon. The native lifestyle is juxtaposed against the pale, overdressed, fretful, domineering, self-righteous white colonialists' routine.

Antoinette's island home had become segregated as soon as her father's gentrifying kind landed, and although the revolution has brought at least a measure of political equality between the races, it has not really changed the basic class distinctions that are encoded by color. The contrasting priorities between the colonizers and the colonized are made even more apparent when the two groups are placed side by side on screen. It is clear that the "masters" are still unabashed about enforcing their dominance over the original inhabitants wherever they still can. The film therefore becomes a tapestry woven out of opposing threads: white versus black, rich versus poor, immigrant versus indigenous, English versus French, legitimate versus bastard, son versus daughter, husband versus wife. The former of the terms, within each of these polarities, tries to assert its superiority over the latter, but in most cases, it is the latter categories that have the last laugh. The lack of parity between the opposites should be laid at the door of colonialism itself, which guarantees that those who have come as uninvited guests will insist on indoctrinating and taming, rather than incorporating and including. An uneasy tension between masculine and feminine is at the root of all the conflicts dramatized in the film. We are witnessing, psychologically, a deeply split world that cannot function as a whole; one in which even its warring opposites become alienated and fragmented parts. The movie is haunted, like a person with a neurosis, by possibilities lost. A concerned Jungian analyst called in to consult in such a situation might say that the clues for the cure must be found in the archetypes trapped in the core of such a neurosis. This solid matrix of transformation, envisaged in the wide Sea's imposing structure, would be sufficiently resilient to withstand the violent ruptures occasioned by contradictory ambitions, if only it could be accessed. Visually, the impressive charisma that the beautifully languid ocean grants to the ambience starts to wane relatively early in the film. Our hopes for healthy resolution of Edward's restlessness are soon pinned on Antoinette (played by the sensual and naturally aristocratic Karina Lombard); she is vital, intelligent, lovely, and we count on her to provide the necessary counterbalance to Edward's masculine insistence on hegemony.

With her poised verve, Antoinette, protégée of the underrated feminine realm, seems when we first encounter her more than equal to the task of retaining a feminine authority. The daughter of a Creole woman, she has a fresh, dark bloom that makes her seem like a natural product of this primeval world. Barely out of her teens, she is already aware of the suffering and incongruities of life. She is handicapped, however, by the other side of her heritage, because she is the daughter of an English aristocrat, and so is like Edward in being a patriarchal child. It is when acting as the good father's daughter that she resorts to the power plays that lead her to abandon her island consciousness. Psychologically, her identification with her dead father's entitled ways has begun to obscure her aboriginal sensitivities. As a symbol, for the audience as well as Edward, of an anima that has lost its grounding in the mother, and instead is unstably supported by the father, Antoinette represents a forsaken daughter that I believe we can identify within every man and woman raised in a patriarchal system. Certainly hers is the fate of the anima when deprived of any masculine benefactor who can respectfully nurture and

defend her feminine perspective. This is what, with mounting dismay, we
feel is missing in Edward Rochester, who is given every reason to want to
care for such a wife.

Antoinette, for her part, envies the uncompromising cheeky spirit of
the recently freed servant women. These shadow sisters bring spice to the
film: they carry some of the Great Mother's impertinence, about which
their patriarchal mentors know nothing. Antoinette tries to emulate her
servants' confident self-containment in that regard, but she can never
make it stick. Her father world has taught her too well that she needs to
rise above, separate herself from, and disidentify from the primitive. There
is no model for a white woman to integrate such crude and sassy aspects.
This prejudice precludes the blossoming of any effective feminine agency
in Antoinette. We watch helplessly as Antoinette attempts the native ways,
then the colonial ways, and eventually abandons both by becoming a
madwoman that neither side respects.

Edward does not mean to be inhumane, but when he realizes that his
power is unchecked, he becomes guilty of astonishingly cruel unconscious
aggression against the feminine. Once the marriage is contracted, Edward
receives the patriarchal power denied him in England by primogeniture
and now has inordinate sway over Antoinette's world. He does what he
has been trained by his upbringing to do—colonize—and he does it well.
Such a successfully imperialistic man is not going to be interested in ever
again partnering with his wife; his marriage is simply the proof of his
power to get what he wants on his terms. The most shocking sequences in
the film are the ones in which it becomes obvious that Antoinette's desires
have become essentially irrelevant to him. A human truth is brought home
by them: unbridled masculine energy, cut loose from any felt obligation to
develop its anima potential through relationship, simply becomes disloyal
to the feminine. It is this dynamic that leaves good daughter Antoinette
without her expected masculine protector.

The Black Sheep

Faced with such a catastrophe in the life of a patient, Jungian analysts
often try to discover what has happened to the mother's protection.
Antoinette's widowed Creole mother, Annette ("Nettie"), is no real help to
her daughter because she herself is torn between her affection for a natural
island existence and the comfort she takes in a pampered standard of
living. In a regressive attempt to create a luxurious artificial routine, she
turns her back on her native heritage and flirts her way into a second
marriage with the well-off Mr. Mason. No sooner are these two married,

however, than a dark and unsavory character from her past emerges, as if out of nowhere, in the still of the night. He is Daniel Cosway, who alleges he is Antoinette's half brother. Antoinette's father, it develops, had bedded many a slave girl, and at least one of these girls bore a son, the depraved Daniel, a fitting rejoinder to the polished persona behind which Antoinette's father had hidden his philandering. Psychologically we can say that because Father Cosway was unwilling to relate to the feminine respectfully and consciously, an undermining counter-being was created: Daniel Cosway is a wretched shadow figure, a sort of Caliban who has steadily become more resentful and vengeful. Again, we are shown a home truth: once an excessively patriarchal standpoint has been taken up, it is not uncommon to find a sniveling, discarded derivative crawling around nearby demanding its due (one thinks of Gollum in *The Lord of the Rings*[4]).

Daniel's mission in life is malice. He wants to expose the shame-filled secrets of his father's world and to make his more socially acceptable half-sister Antoinette bear the brunt of his revenge. In the midst of his transgressions, however, Daniel offers her one of her greatest opportunities in the film for transformation. By exposing their father's escapades, the interloper, like the intruding stranger that sometimes appears in a woman's dreams to compensate her conscious attitude,[5] gives Antoinette a chance to wake up from her patriarchal fantasy of being the perfect daughter to a perfect father. This was precisely her conscious attitude: if Antoinette could have seen her father for who he was, this insinuating brother would have posed little threat. It is because she has not realized how corrupt a colonial system can be that Daniel has power over her; he personifies the insight she needs to have. Like Lucifer, he is the light bringer, coming unbidden to tempt her like a complex perception she has not managed to integrate. As Jung writes:

> A complex can be really overcome only if it is lived out to the full. In other words, if we are to develop further we have to draw to us and drink down to the very dregs what, because of our complexes, we have held at a distance (1954, par. 184).

As the depiction of a dark unconscious process in Antoinette, Daniel, who is not unlike a little rodent, represents a shadow complex that is gnawing away at her soul. In analysis, the usual reaction to experiencing the presence of such a complex in oneself would be similar to Antoinette's initial reaction toward Daniel—to regard the complex as coming from a sleazy part of the self, to see it as regressive, feeding on psychic garbage, and to regard it as unworthy of consideration. The patient would usually want to refuse to grant it an audience and would resent an analyst dwelling on it. Like anyone invested in maintaining the persona (and hers is replete with privilege and propriety), Antoinette has little psychological readiness to receive such an intruder. Unfortunately for her, her unconsciousness of how to deal with people like him becomes Daniel's wedge into her soul.

A very young woman like Antoinette desperately needs masculine guidance, but it should be guidance that, as always in the best education, mirrors her own innate gifts, motivating her to listen to her own imagination and to trust her own instincts. The ideal tutelary spirit would come from a father who is invested in the development of his daughter's special talents because he is already secure in his own anima development, rather than from a father who is unconsciously asking his pretty, smart, original daughter to develop his anima for him, by learning to cultivate his tastes and manners and sacrifice her own. Such a fairly protective masculine spirit is absent in *Wide Sargasso Sea*. What we find instead in the film is an incessant question posed with increased urgency as Antoinette's animus emerges, unsupported, to lead her into madness: Without paternal and fraternal safeguards, what choice does the feminine spirit have but to devolve into its own chaos?

The Fire in the Background

Antoinette's marriage to Edward comes at the end of her adolescence in the aftermath of the defining event of her early youth, when unreconciled cultural tensions have culminated in a shocking conflagration. The colonizers that have so efficiently and successfully separated the dark-skinned from the light-skinned, the supposedly bad from the "respectable" good, and the robust from the more vulnerable, have slowly lost control of the island. The hostile ex-slaves have gained enough freedom to be dangerous. Their resentment and fury, which have been aimlessly seething for quite a while, find a target in the ostentatious Cosway mansion, which during Antoinette's adolescence has become the stage for her mother's ambitious second marriage. This compound of the persona, reconstructed by Antoinette's new stepfather, is dealt a blistering blow when the fed-up servant staff sets it aflame.

The torching of the patriarchal compound is the first of two fires in the film that mark turning points in Antoinette's life. We have to ask: what is fire? Obviously, fire brings warmth and purification; cooks food and boils water; illuminates, enlivens, and transforms. Fire is a basic image of archetypal energy, and perhaps the most basic symbol of the dynamism of archetypes, for it has an intensely disruptive side—especially when its passionate energies are not handled with respect. Jung has spoken of the "Luciferian virtue" to be found in fire, the most volatile of the four elements of ancient natural philosophy. The unexpected virtue to be found in a tempestuous and inflammatory inferno is its capacity to be an agent for change, a way to bring a stagnant life situation to an end.

To better understand fire's incendiary merits from the standpoint of its meaning as a symbol of unconscious emotion, we need to appreciate that emotion's rousing energy is born of conflict—conflict that if successfully negotiated could carry us forward to greater consciousness, but if not resolved can destroy us:

> Conflict engenders fire, the fire of affects and emotions, and like every other fire it has two aspects, that of combustion and that of creating light. On the one hand, emotion is the alchemical fire whose warmth brings everything into existence and whose heat burns all superfluities to ashes.... But on the other hand, emotion is the moment when steel meets flint and a spark is struck forth, for emotion is the chief source of consciousness. There is no change from darkness to light or from inertia to movement without emotion (Jung 1954, par. 179).

Fire's virtue, when effectively handled, is the potential healing power of emotion itself, often identified as an aspect of the feminine, seen for instance in the flaring up of feminine rage at overoccupation by the masculine.

Feminine fire, whether channeled through indignation or desire, is the inconvenient catalyst that drives the story in *Wide Sargasso Sea*. Fire is linked to "the orgiastic emotions" peculiar to the feminine; the cold fury of the masculine, which we see in Edward Rochester, seems in the film to come from another source, and to have another goal. It is axiomatic in Jungian analysis that in order to effectively conserve the transformative potential of the feminine, we must first be moved out of our patriarchal ego comfort zones by emotion—to change in psychotherapy we need to feel the burn of the archetypal energy that is trying to re-equilibrate our sickly system. Jung warns that if we turn our backs on the heat of emotion, eventually an even more violent and finally toxic frenzy will build in the unconscious, ultimately leading to pathological destructiveness, rather than forging the union of opposites, which a more contained fire could have lit the way to.

Relying on the "cherishingly good" side of the feminine does not prepare us for such fiery expressions of her nature when they emerge. In *Wide Sargasso Sea,* the torches carried by the ex-slaves have been lit by tiny smoldering embers of resentment, the consequence of longstanding lack of attention to the feminine on the part of the colonizers. Not heeding their servants' feelings in the transition to a post-slavery time, the colonizers have occasioned much anger.

The unmanageability of the fire compensates the masculine attitude of bland, blunt reasonableness that is constantly being put forth in this film by the colonizers, who throughout the film manage to obstruct every healthy outlet for the feminine, whether ardor, irritation, sorrow, or the expression of fear. It would be patriarchal on our part to interpret the symbol of fire as purifying, which was the rationale used for burning witches. Rather, fire here seems to be an expression of the witch. There is an echo of alchemy in the symbol. Renaissance alchemists were usually men, but each alchemist had a *soror mystica* who carefully and responsibly kept the blaze burning under the alchemical vessel, as long as necessary for the transformational process taking place inside it. Her presence was important, because she brought a trust in the metamorphosis that was supposed to be occurring. Absent such a presence in this film (with the exception of Christophine, who brews a love potion) fire is used in a much more impulsive way, by characters who simply want to destroy the constructions of powerful men.

The ghastly moment when the inflamed parrot crashes to its death from the second story of Nettie's burning mansion sickeningly conveys the failure of the feminine that has sold out to the masculine to contain and transform the tensions. The domesticated bird, with its clipped wings, had been a loyal pet in Nettie's household, a kind of Cassandra, whose echoing words had warned the family of the escalating danger. Parrots, in many stories, especially satiric ones, since the parrot's claim to fame is an amusing ability to imitate others, are symbols of objective self-reflection: the parrot's voice makes his subjects see themselves with a sudden indisputable objectivity, the way a dream sometimes can. That the parrot's demise has occurred in Antoinette's childhood foreshadows the extinguishment of self-reflective instincts within almost every character in this film, the sure background for tragedy. Without the protection of such instincts, the key players are left to their ego defenses, and are driven one by one towards inappropriate actions. The parrot's tragic ending also portends Edward's own future, for he will be blinded by a fire at the end of *Jane Eyre*. The fire therefore brings more than just the collapse of an old collective stance; it ushers in a loss of self-scrutiny, spelling little hope for a thoughtful reconstruction. Indeed, nothing is gained after the first fire, and a great deal is lost. Nettie loses her mind, and her British husband flees the madness of his wife and the island. The problem of standing up to patriarchy that Nettie could not face now becomes Antoinette's.

The Disparate Couple

After the fire, Antoinette becomes a virtual orphan. She is sent to a Catholic girls' boarding school, lodged in a convent, until a marriage can be arranged. Little time is wasted in an attempt to reinstate the old order in this way. Played by the dourly handsome Nathaniel Parker, Edward Rochester is the resolute husband-to-be who faces the first of many challenges when he crosses the sea to meet his bride. In a prophetic scene, indicative of Mother Sea's hearty appetite and Edward's inexperience with her indiscriminately devouring ways, he witnesses the drowning of a sailor.

This fatality imprints itself into Edward's mind, becoming a recurring flashback that haunts him throughout the rest of the film. His fear of the Sargasso Sea is plain, but had he been schooled better in the ways of the Great Mother he would have been better prepared for the capriciousness of her waters, and known how to navigate them. Instead, he is determined to maintain control when he should be flexible in approaching his new life in the Caribbean. With this well-regulated attitude toward the feminine, he encounters the fresh, nubile beauty of his bride and is able to convince himself that the unpleasantness of the Sea, even though it shapes the world around him, was a transient reality, a nightmare from which he will be able to awake. He is naïve. In spite of all his upper class polish, Edward is a novice in this foreign climate of the feminine, totally unprepared to handle the desires and confusion that are about to be aroused within him.

At first, Edward approaches his marriage with Antoinette with an open heart and a liberal, thoughtful spirit. He shows hope for mutual affection with his new bride; he expresses humanitarian concern over slave labor, and he is sensitive to Antoinette's first impressions of him. At this point in the film, we start to feel that something fresh and uniting might possibly emerge from this hastily arranged marriage. An exchange between Antoinette's Aunt Cora and Antoinette's guardian, Richard Mason, brings us back to the harsh reality a young woman faces in such an arrangement. Aunt Cora gives voice to the suspicions that need to be brought forth. She has heard this story before, and she knows how it goes: a man needs land, and finding a wife who has some becomes a means to that end. Mason, she concludes, has brokered a financial arrangement with Edward Rochester's father. The impending marriage is not about love or relationship; it is a business deal—that is the cold, hard truth.

The aunt is right. In the midst of his biography of Jean Rhys, Arnold Davidson puzzles over the historical precedents of such arrangements, in which women have been valued purely on a superficial/fiscal basis. What, he ponders, is:

> the relationship between eros and economics, and, more specifically, how does the capitalization of beauty along with the stereotyped sex roles of western society…impel women to embrace their own "commodityness?"… [W]hat is the essential difference between a prostitute and a princess elevated to her new status by a storybook marriage? (1985, 9).

Women throughout history have asked themselves similar questions with regard to their worth. Though Antoinette's intuition warns her that something is amiss, she can't quite put her finger on the problem. In spite of her attraction to Edward, in a brief moment of clarity, she listens to her fears and decides not to marry him, "I'm afraid of what may happen if I become your wife. You don't know me, and I can't live in the town like an English lady. The way we live is so very different." But, the unsolicited Edward persists. He assures Antoinette that she can live wherever she likes. At that moment, he speaks from what seems like a genuine desire to meet her half way: "We're complete strangers from opposite sides of the world. I will trust you, if you trust me." Edward says he wants a wife and pledges "to honor her until death do us part." In reality he has no comprehension of (meaning no cultural exposure to) what it means to be that kind of partner. In citing these words, he is merely mouthing his primary allegiance to conventional expectations, which in fact are that after the wedding the man will assume full control of the marriage, as evidenced by a perfectly plain letter written behind closed doors soon after he has made his solemn promise to Antoinette:

> Dear Father, the 30,000 pounds has been paid to me without question or condition. I will never be a disgrace to you or to my dear brother, the son that you love. I have property now at the edge of the world.

This commercial dispatch sounds cold to us as we watch the film, but it does not occur to Edward that it calls his love for Antoinette into question. It is just another reminder of the collective complex that divides the couple, and the enormous compromise of the feminine that has resulted. Antoinette has relinquished all of her resources with the simple words "I do." "Eros and economics" have become one and the same. The evil in this is that Antoinette has been led to fully and tragically embrace her "commodityness." (Compare the "honest courtesan" in *Dangerous Beauty*,[6] who works hard to separate "eros and economics," thus showing an alternative way to relate to men that does not sacrifice so much feminine potential.)

To be sure, Antoinette makes an admirable attempt to stand for herself, to present and promote her unique contributions. For a while, she discloses her own discoveries of the feminine to him, reveling in her eccentricities, for instance sleeping under a full moon, which delighted her with the possibility that she might be afflicted with a lunar madness. She plays at being a prankster and a tease. She luxuriates in her self-indulgent, spoiled and frivolous lifestyle. In the honeymoon phase of their relationship (which is also a phase of courtship, since they had not known each other before), Edward is enchanted and intrigued by the impassioned pleasures to which his new bride introduces him. Quite pleased with his find, he wonders "What would my friends in England think of you? They'd think you were a wild creature, untamed, Mrs. Rochester!" She excites and entices him with the possibilities of the feminine, so different from anything he has known in England. But just when Edward's stuffy and stiff demeanor has begun to melt away is when that pesky Daniel, Antoinette's half brother, appears to Edward for the first time. Like a black Iago taunting a white Othello, Daniel encroaches on their lives with his poisonous insinuations of Antoinette's tainted past. And, like Othello, Edward becomes paranoid.

The previous values that have governed Edward's life are reawakened, and he is brought back to his patriarchal senses. Hunger for his father's approval makes Edward more and more suspicious. He grows increasingly judgmental and touchily reactive as he tries to regain the familiar masculine footing that Antoinette had temporarily led him dangerously beyond. The strange island surrounded by the foreboding sea steadily becomes repugnant to Edward. He does not have the wherewithal to befriend this wilderness, and he is rapidly losing faith that anything fruitful could come from such an outlandish land. The re-emergence of his British patriarchal complex isolates him from Antoinette's odd colonial adaptation to this unruly world, and his increasing contempt for her embrace of disorder threatens their conjugal tie.

Edward never refers to his own mother, a fact that makes us guess that, like Antoinette, he was deprived of a parent who could offer a protective feminine presence in his life. That he dreams of being drowned in the ultra-feminine sea makes us see that he really has no survival skills in the feminine realm. Had he been reared by a self-assured woman who could hold her own with his father, he might have been able to let Antoinette guide him in this new territory. As it is, he is unprepared to let a woman influence him so much, and he starts to feel threatened by his wife's increasingly captivating influence. He begins to distance himself from her expressions of love, a rejection which of course is devastating to her. As part of Edward's frantic efforts to regain control of their relationship, an uncharacteristic brutality erupts. He rapes Antoinette, then perplexed by what he has done, wonders where this savagery came from. Like a modern analysand, shocked by what has just come out of his unconscious, he asks: "What am I doing hurting you? I'm sorry, I'm sorry. I don't know what came over me, Antoinette. I feel so ashamed." Although that question is never properly addressed by the character, its answer is plain to the psychologically minded viewer. He is acting out patriarchal conscious-ness, and he has no idea how much that consciousness is driven by an unconscious cultural complex[7] that insists on asserting power.

Ann Ulanov describes the dilemma that ensues for the woman trying to hold her own with a man caught in such a complex:

> Matriarchal consciousness can operate as a regressive undertow against the development of a patriarchal head ego that demands separation from the unconscious and the development of clear and precise discriminations. Regression occurs instead of creation, madness instead of healing, a feeling of senseless drifting instead of contemplation. The moon spirit can show its negative side; it may represent the devouring unconscious in the form of a bloodsucker or eater of human flesh; it may act as a bringer of madness....[This is] a conflict between the patriarchal ego of clarity, force, and assertion as symbolized by the sun, and the matriarchal ego as symbolized by the moon (1971, 180).

Without a sanctioned place in an English marriage for the life-enhancing "moon spirit" that Antoinette wants to bring into their couple, she has come to embody for Edward everything dangerous about women, a feminine energy that must be guarded against.

Ulanov describes the elementary phase of anima development in which Edward is stuck:

> A man at this stage of development remains, however, in passive identification with his anima, carried by its erotic passion but not consciously related to it or having it openly at his disposal. His ego identity, that is, his sense of who he is, his anima, that is, his emotionality, and his eros, his drive to involvement, are all mixed together....[B]ecause eros is undifferentiated from the sexual drive, this urge becomes sexual (1971, 222).

Embarrassed, guilty, and unable to make sense of his behavior, Edward tries to flee from Antoinette's equally baffling world. Attempting to restore some semblance of sanity, he goes to his fellow British people in town. He dances the disembodied dances that reacquaint him with his past. Surprisingly, his return to this past does not work for him anymore because he can no longer deny his fellow expatriates' pretensions. As he eagerly goes back to his bride, we pray that this time the two will learn from their mistakes and be able to see and honor their differences and allow them to commingle.

But it's too late. Antoinette has experienced his departure as a replay of her mother and father's inability to stand by her. The rape was harsh, but it was nothing compared to outright desertion. Her original traumatic wound has now been fully reopened. Antoinette finds the gulf between her world and her husband's as painful as what she witnessed in her own parents' marriage, and she knows she does not deserve this fate. Consumed by hurt and fear, she starts to rely on her mother's defense mechanisms—she drinks with abandon, attacks with impunity, and withdraws helplessly into a senseless oblivion. Her regressive behavior recalls the ex-slaves' ineffective style of antagonism at the time they set the fire to her stepfather's house. Like them, all she accomplishes by her rebellion is a reinstatement of the patriarchal pattern: the "masculine" Edward assumes control as the "feminine" Antoinette predictably disintegrates. Antoinette, of course, continues to long for a mutual relationship, but now she does not have enough sense of herself to help shape one.

Fueled by letters from Daniel describing Antoinette's demented mother and philandering father, Edward's suspicions about Antoinette's character multiply, and these set off her own self-doubts and a number of nightmares. The opposing energies that initially were played out in the film between the blacks and the whites are now firmly ensconced in Antoinette and Edward's marriage. Now the real terms of their engagement, undisclosed to Antoinette until now, are made clear to her, and Edward asserts a patronizing domination over everything that he finds inferior, inept and ignorant about her world. Though the two continue to snipe at each other, Antoinette is clearly losing ground.

Antoinette's vulnerability to Edward's bullying might be explained by present day research into the impact of attachment and its loss (themes highly relevant to the psychology of the feminine). When an individual has been deprived of empathically attuned caregivers, the person's subsequent life is characterized by a difficulty modulating emotions, an inability to care for self and others, a lack of curiosity and adventure, a marked defensiveness, and a series of desperate but unproductive attempts to be loved and protected (Flores 2004, 218-219). We see in the film that no caregiver was consistently available to Antoinette except her nanny Christophine; as a consequence she lacks the emotional foundation to maintain a sober, sane composure in the face of Edward's disregard.

Antoinette's may therefore seem to be an extreme plight of the feminine within a patriarchal system—unfortunate parenting followed by an equally unfortunate marriage, followed by madness. But this is to take her simply as a particular woman. In the film, she is clearly an emblem of the feminine in all of us, which finds patriarchy maddening. To approach this understanding, we need to ask what the feminine is more normally like under patriarchal conditions. Certainly, she is expected to be compliant and cooperative in spite of disparaging treatment. When she falls out of step, then all are shocked and dismayed: "What happened to our sweet little girl?" Whatever abuse she reports, it is presumed that she asked for it; she is just getting her comeuppance. She must be put back in her proper, constrained place. This is how the feminine, in men and women, has been treated, in the nineteenth century and still too often today; yet even therapists, like the people around Antoinette, continue to puzzle over why the feminine in ourselves so often shows up in our dreams and in our feeling states associated with images of incompetence and uncertainty. Absent empathic sponsorship, the feminine's chances of surviving any affiliation with the better-attended-to masculine are simply not very high. In order for a new paradigm to emerge, the feminine potential, not just within women, but also in men, must be reclaimed, mirrored, and respected. For that to happen, we have to be able to recognize the feminine on her own terms and refuse the temptation to "discriminate" her through a patriarchal lens. We have, in other words, to stand up to the Edward within.

Antoinette's ultimate collapse makes clear what a daunting task it can be to stand up to this deep-seated patriarchal system. Like all cultural complexes, precedents that unwittingly get passed from one generation to the next, patriarchal assumptions about the feminine become "internalized to form unconscious 'internal working models' which guide expectations and perceptions, so serving as a template for future relationships" (Knox 2003, 78). As a result, the feminine sides of our natures get, like Antoinette in the film, projected onto them a feeble, distorted caricature of the feminine that leaves them chronically disabled.

At the same time, in addition to the haunting memory of a crazed Antoinette, the image one takes away from this film is of an intense young woman who believes that she brings something special to the marriage and who cautiously opens her heart to a stranger. She is, ironically, someone who never stops expecting to be loved. That initial image is never quite overshadowed by her madness, so that her madness is not just an image of wounded disability, but an aspect of the feminine we have already learned to love in her. Her madness conveys, among other things, the inherent untidiness of relationship. When this is not understood, of course, the less differentiated, more emotive and tender feminine, sides of the relational psyche sink into a hysterical mess or congeal into the bowed spirit of a chronically psychotic persona. Or there may be a turn to demonic power. Particularly, when the feminine is not able to effect an attachment, the result, as Jung so aptly describes, is that "where love is lacking, power fills the vacuum" (1954, par 167, note 4).

Instead of relying on her conscious feminine powers, Antoinette turns to black magic. Here Christophine helps her, but with unintended results, because the nanny does not figure on the extent of the new master's fear of the feminine, or the degree to which Antoinette has already abandoned her feminine self, who before feeling so rejected by Edward might have been able to use a little love magic with a light, playful touch. Instead, Antoinette serves Edward a heavy drink concocted by Christophine, which creates a drugged, dream-filled sleep that takes him back to the dreaded tangled seaweeds where he becomes once again engulfed in the sea's negative embrace. Upon awaking, he strikes back at Antoinette in a gruesomely vengeful manner by accepting the sexual invitations of their light-skinned black house servant Amelie. The exhibition of debauchery between Edward and Amelie, which occurs within earshot of Antoinette, is the coup de grace that breaks Antoinette's spirit. She fades like her mother into an autistic fog, while Edward affects a cold-blooded show of indifference. In a final betrayal of her feeling, he ships Antoinette off to England, a place that never had any appeal for her. Only he knows the degree of denied longing for the feminine that lies behind these acts.

The Unmothered Mother

We have to ask, what was missing in Antoinette's upbringing, and in Edward's, to lead them to create such a disaster. We certainly feel what was missing in Antoinette's early life. Just as there is a dearth of paternal support for healthy animus development, it should also be obvious that very little maternal wisdom is available to Antoinette either. Though numerous unconventional women with unusual attributes populate this film, a healthy, conscious appreciation for their traits never really develops in Antoinette. The best mothering she receives comes from the island itself, and from her "da," Christophine, who was her coffee-colored Martinican nursemaid, and is ethically a cut above every other character in the movie in the way she attempts to care for Antoinette. Antoinette loves Christophine, but she does not seem to be able to integrate any of her wisdom, and Christophine is finally powerless to protect her from patriarchal abuse once the truly sweet honeymoon with Edward is over.

Antoinette's actual mother, Nettie, is much less helpful. Although she is proud of her French Creole heritage and apparently struggles against becoming too identified with the patriarchal structure of the colonizing British, she is convinced that the only way to make ends meet financially is to sell what she has—herself, her land, and her feminine essence—to the first rich man who will marry her. The result, a common theme in films about the feminine, is a bastardized version of marriage. Both proposals that Nettie accepts do not lead to sacred unions in which each partner promises to bring the best that he and she has to the partnership. Rather, eschewing mutuality, Nettie allows herself to rely on men who place little value on her as an individual or on the world in which she has been raised. The men she accepts are ones who tend to find value only in that which serves their needs. As Nettie clutches the last remnants of her own enfeebled autonomy (the status of her animus at this stage is embodied by her inert son Pierre), she treats Antoinette as an annoying afterthought, a nuisance. (Nettie's amalgamation of deluded self-contempt is painful to contemplate, but it is only a mirror of the larger social world in which she lives, where everything is so at odds with itself.)

In a heart-wrenching passage in Jean Rhys's novel, the indifference of Antoinette's mother to the feminine self in the form of her daughter's development is plainly depicted. Recollecting how her mother related to her when she was small, Antoinette tells us:

> She pushed me away, not roughly but calmly, coldly, without a word, as if she had decided once and for all that I was useless to her. She wanted to sit with Pierre or walk where she pleased without being pestered, she wanted peace and quiet. I was old enough to look after myself. 'Oh, let me alone,' she would say, 'let me alone' (1966, 20).

Nettie's essential disavowal of any responsibility for what happens to Antoinette speaks to how shockingly disconnected she is from her own roots. The lack of care about attachment takes us back to the core dilemma of the film—a difficulty asserting feminine values as ends in themselves. To succeed in marriage, a woman needs to be able to come into the relationship as an equal, offering the unique gifts and talents she has cultivated through finding her feminine identity, and with the self-respect that creates the greatest likelihood that she will also be treated with respect. Because Nettie entered matrimony and motherhood as neglected as her daughter, her solution is to simply surrender her identity to the masculine, with the result that the daughter whose name derives from hers, is but one more later sacrifice.

Mother and daughter both show us how vulnerable the feminine is when defined entirely in the context of a woman's ability to submit to a relationship with a man. To be sure, the more demure, relational side of the feminine can acclimatize itself to masculine expectations: that is something the feminine does well. In that sense, the feminine lends itself to patriarchy. But when dominance and mastery rule as values, as is the case under patriarchy, the invitation is open for the forceful masculine spirit to assume control of the man-woman relationship. Such subjugation of the feminine is not always done by a man to a woman, for a woman can use a forceful animus to subjugate the anima of a man or her own feminine self. Wherever the feminine turns out to be poorly equipped to hold her own in the presence of masculine energy, it is because some of her more rugged qualities have long ago been banished, and the guardians defending them emasculated. When the feminine is still in touch with her feisty, intuitive, imaginative, spontaneous instincts and can rely on her "Stygian depths and orgiastic emotionality," she is not so quick to say "I do" to a demand for submission. She makes sure first that there is a chance at an even playing field. And when the masculine does not assume that its purpose is to establish sovereignty, then the feminine retains the autonomy she needs to offer her gifts freely.

Thus empowered, the feminine is a boon to heterosexual relationships, but this happy outcome can only come when women attend to their inner development, for as Jung has shown, they must work in an inner way to contend with masculine energies and learn to collaborate with them. Similarly, men need to work within, on the heroic overdevelopment of the masculine, before they can keep that energy from taking the lead in relationships. One hope of all this personal work in a time of rapid cultural change is that women who are being trained in the outer world to trust their capacity for sharp intellectual prowess, and in other ways to endorse their native masculine potential, will not feel they have to sacrifice the caring side of their natures and give up that part of the integrity of the feminine.

Wide Sargasso Sea, like the novel on which it is based, makes clear that the patriarchal problem is not restricted to men. Antoinette's mother, Nettie, may be proud of her island heritage, but this turns out to be the heritage of colonialism: she enjoys the memory of privilege, but she has not learned from the Sea to honor her feminine soul, and she repudiates her daughter's affections because they are painful reminders of what she has kept herself from expressing. She has chosen rather blatantly to rely on the men with enough money to define and protect her status, since she does not trust that she has the capacity to stand in society apart from them. She is the perfect embodiment of the colonized woman, her spirit entirely a product of masculine occupation. Yet at the same time, like the successfully colonized everywhere, Nettie harbors enormous resentment towards the men that bankroll her.

It is crucial, if we are going to learn anything from this film, that we recognize the splitting in the feminine that results when Nettie chooses the patriarchy over her daughter. Mother and daughter, despite their similar names, are worlds apart. To be sure, Antoinette still longs to be seen by her mother, and even hopes that her mother will one day see herself as a powerful embodiment of Creole identity. But being Creole, for her mother, is only a proud persona: she has forgotten what it means to be true to her feminine self. Nettie even repudiates her daughter's efforts to have one, because what Antoinette strives for painfully represents all that life has taught the older woman to disclaim in order to survive. Antoinette's descent into incurable psychosis, though partly a consequence of this abandonment, would seem to prove her mother right. The pathological splitting in Antoinette's personality is a mirror of the split in the archetype of Mother and Daughter, whose bond (acknowledged explicitly in the Eleusinian mysteries), ideally maintains the integrity of the feminine psyche. For Nettie to acknowledge the yearning of her daughter for feminine wholeness as valid would be to dismantle patriarchal defenses and expose wounds that she has buried deep within her soul, wounds that are still unbearably raw and tender. Yet through the character of Antoinette, the film allows us to see a younger edition of the feminine who continues to plead for an uncompromised mother imago, an unsanitized Demeter who will raise her voice to a level of protest that cannot be silenced. In the face of this hope, the silence of Nettie is devastating to Antoinette.

The Jungian analyst Mary Briner has addressed the nature of this kind of "negative mother complex:"

> The mother is basic in determining the daughter's fundamental attitude toward life. A positive mother image and a good instinctive connection—other things being equal—can give her a belief in life and a will to live. She is thus equipped with an attitude that trusts life, even though it may be wary. On the other hand, the daughter of the negative mother is often lamed by fear of life, a fear of death, and a fear of risking; her instincts are crippled and she is at a loss to know where to risk. Too often when she does risk it turns out badly, because something stands between such

women and their own natures. For when a woman feels negative and rejects her mother, she becomes in her own eyes the rejected child. She then in turn rejects herself as a woman...her own body and her feminine instinct; then the animus comes in to take their place....[Such women then] ignore, deny or abuse their bodies. Instinctive disturbances and illnesses grow from such roots (1990, 114).

In order to get the full implications of the wounding Briner is exposing here, it is worthwhile to expand her characterization of the negative mother so that it is not so bound to specific gender roles (literal female mother and literal female daughter). Moving beyond the realm of personal mothers' effects on their daughters helps us to see the collective impact of a cultural negative mother complex. There is presently a lack of understanding throughout the world that has accepted a cultural value from the West (which would include, for instance, the Westernized Far East of today) that supplants a healthy matriarchal influence. Questioning the value of the maternal potential of the feminine for civilization has become a widespread cultural complex, and has produced a certain distortion of how the archetype of mother is received. What we are left with is a very patriarchal transmission of cultural values. Under these conditions, it is quite likely that all of us (whether our personal experiences of our mothers have been pleasant or not) have inherited a warped image of what *mother* offers and a resultant narrowing of the horizon of what we expect from the feminine. Both sexes suffer from this failure to envision the mother's true value. The only way for individuals to outgrow the stunted view of mother that is so commonly taught to them is to develop a more differentiated image of what a mother can be.

This is not a task that has to wait for a new, feminist millennium. As the Jungian analyst Jean Bolen has recently argued, reviving a strong conscious matriarchal presence is urgently needed now, in the present cultural landscape, to balance the excessively powerful patriarchal initiatives that the West has fostered since the time of the highly militaristic and economically hegemonic Roman Empire and that now threaten world destruction, whether by bomb or by more insidious forms of environmental destruction. If countervailing values do not come to the fore, the needs and resources of this planet's children are in peril.[8] Dramatizing the absent values of relationship, partnership, and empathic nurturing, as consequences of the lack of a strong mother willing to defend these values, is the strategy of *Wide Sargasso Sea*. The film, like the novel, movingly documents Antoinette's doomed efforts to assert these values without any personal or cultural support. The absence of her own mother's protesting voice makes the viewer feel (and be moved to redress) the lack of sound feminine authority. Such authority would have to come from a woman who understands the necessity of having the opposing masculine and feminine sides face one another until they become authentically responsive to the other. The recognition that this is necessary comes from Antoinette's "da" (nanny) Christophine, who finally agrees to ease the path by offering Antoinette a bit of her Caribbean magic. Antoinette, not comprehending the extent of the problem of her marriage, relies on Christophine's love-drug as a quick fix to her current heartbreak. Without a better understanding of the underlying issues, such "medicine" cannot possibly assist in bringing about a cure. This witch wisdom, though worldly, is no match for Edward's father complex. Patriarchy, which finds its representative in his soul, reveals itself as a colonizing attitude that prefers to extinguish rather than hold the tension of opposites, attempting to achieve this goal by domination and suppression of the feminine side of the archetypal clash.

Patriarchal energy often moves to suppress feminine approaches to problem-solving because patriarchy's values are achievement, responsibility, and accuracy, and from the perspective of accomplishment, it is easy to get impatient with the inefficiency of always attending to relationship, a value at the heart of the matriarchal attitude. The patriarchal strategy in dealing with any problem is simply to bypass the tedious steps necessary to integrate feminine and masculine perspectives toward its possible solution because such tactics "muddy the water." Working in the Sargasso Sea of relationship seems to be a job that only a maternal perspective is capable of pulling off. Such a perspective fully understands the emotions that make the water muddy, and knows how to help us navigate them. The ways of the Great Mother, however, are slow and even allow some things to languish. Though her methods work, patriarchal thinking resists trying to appreciate their differences. A further befuddling aspect, part and parcel of matriarchal consciousness, is lack of interest in conquest. The man or woman who honors the cycles and nuances that pertain to the interdependent nature of life rather than life's profitable mastery is living out of a state of mind and heart more in line with matriarchal spirit. Such a consciousness is all but absent in this film. The upsurge of the feminine of which Edward is so clearly afraid is only a potential buried in the unconscious within the guzzling Sargasso Sea, or expressed self-destructively through Antoinette's psychosis, which is understood only as madness. Nevertheless, Edward is run by fear of the feminine, and his paranoia starts to rule him. He becomes an image of the patriarchal masculine that is utterly intolerant of difficult feelings and painful experiences. When emotions erupt, he makes sure his ruling principle of staying in control intervenes and prevails. In his marriage to Antoinette, he undermines her attempts to assert feminine values and erodes any possibility of partnership. Edward does not understand Antoinette's desire to negotiate with him. Like many men who insist, heroically, on mastering their partners, there seems to be in Edward an unconscious "positive" mother complex, which leads him to understand relationship in an infantile way, as being given what he wants. Such a complex supports men's inconsiderate ways and assures them that their privilege is to be given precisely what they want. What Antoinette cannot articulate to Edward is perhaps best put by the Jungian analyst Ann Ulanov, writing with her husband Barry:

> For two to become one, they must remain two. How else should they be able to unite? It is only in their separateness that they can be assured of coming together. The alternative is that external intercourse, the man forever caught within the woman, never to exit and thus never to enter (1994, 84).

What is missing therefore in both Antoinette and Edward is differentiation of their psyches from their different kinds of unconscious mother complex and a mature integration of the values of relatedness and separateness that are hidden in such complexes. Antoinette could have succeeded in getting Edward to accept these values had she herself had more backing in her intuition of them. He could have been more ready to receive them if he had an experience himself of a wise and appropriate mother who had been able to stand up to his own father, on the issue of his inheritance, for instance. Neither of the partners in this unhappy marriage has experienced full-bodied mothering energy in a personal way. Mothers that raise their daughters to stand on their own and raise sons who are comfortable in listening to women, will produce daughters that will command respect from their husbands and sons that will want to respect their wives. In this film, Christophine, Antoinette's nanny from Martinique is her only defender, once she is married, and the only one willing to talk to Edward about what Antoinette needs. As a woman of color, however, Christophine has no real purchase with Edward, and her wisdom, like her witchcraft backfires: her influence wanes drastically in the second half of the film. From that point, the plot is driven (with greatly destructive consequences) by Edward's ideas of what should be done with Antoinette, who moves inexorably toward her fate as the madwoman in the attic.

The Unlikely Helpers

In company with the evident constraints upon Antoinette and Edward's marriage that have led to this bleak outcome, there have along the way been untapped, but amazingly rendered, assets in *Wide Sargasso Sea* that might have helped them chart a healthier course. The three unlikely characters that could have steered the pair in a different direction are Amelie, the Crab, and the discredited Christophine. Even though each of these figures are held by one or the other in the couple in such low esteem that their potential for assistance remains obscure, we can identify their positive characteristics the more we reflect on the film.

The Shameless Maidservant

The insolent, disdainful, flirtatious Amelie would seem to be nothing but trouble, a definite liability to any marriage; yet in the movie she brings a lot of life to the story. Her spunk and sass represent the opportunistic spirit of the dark feminine, and we accept her because it is clear she would potentially set everybody straight if she could. (There are echoes in her character, from the introductory montage, of the Little Colonel's incisive upturn in response to her grandfather's put-down[9] and Celie's sharp retorts in response to her husband's incessant jabs:[10] these are tricksterish aspects of the feminine that must not be discounted.) The scene when Antoinette tentatively allows herself to be invited into the drum circle of the domestic congregants outside her mountain cottage is a particularly powerful one, because with each determined step towards them, Antoinette strips herself of her parents' stilted airs and starts to move from her gut. Antoinette allows herself to be drawn by the pulsing, erotic beat of the native drums, and through the dance starts to reclaim an impudent, embodied stance on a par with Amelie's. She needs this attitude, because it can safeguard her from identifying with Edward's later suspicions and judgments.

There is a moment, as we watch her body dare to respond to a more savage authority, when Antoinette exudes the same bold effrontery as Amelie, and we can see the possibility of a transfer of the servant's defiance into Antoinette. This would be an integration of a clever spirit of disobedience to the patriarchy with the power to save Antoinette's life. At this moment, Antoinette is just a hairbreadth away from incorporating Amelie's "devil may care" attitude. Reflecting on this scene after seeing the film, we think: If only Antoinette had danced long enough with Amelie to become marked with the latter's ruthless self-determination! Amelie is calculating where Antoinette is sincere, and if Antoinette had joined forces with her as with a figure in a dream that needed to be integrated, she might have discovered an ability within herself to elude the destiny constructed for her as a casualty of patriarchy.

This moment of contact with her shadow sister turns out to be a lost opportunity, however. Instead of drawing upon Amelie's feistiness to save her marriage, which might have worked, Antoinette falls back upon her mother's helpless and erratic immaturity and her father's narrow piety, which clearly do not impress Edward.

The King of the Pool

The second of the potential feminine redeemers in this film is the crab, who is featured twice. The first time is during the honeymoon phase of the marriage, where Antoinette and Edward are playing at celebrating each other's differences. Antoinette introduces Edward to the crab, "the king of the pool." Unwilling to conceive a crab's regal status, Edward ventures a cocky trespass and dives down to gape at the freaky creature. He quickly retreats when he sees the crab's sinister pincer claws fulminating against the brash young man's breach of this underwater kingdom. We, like the crab, sense the insolence and arrogance in Edward, and we are amused that he has been put in his place by the crab's potentially castrating swipe.

As a totem animal of the feminine, the crab has a symbolic nature that is worth a bit more scrutiny. He personifies the "terrible male" aspect of the Great Mother;[11] as "king of the pool" he is an aspect of the unconscious that relates to the Mother's moon-centered, tidal authority. A faithful participant in a maternal ritual of death and rebirth, the crab steps periodically out of his protective shell, secure in the knowledge that another outfit will soon take its place. The rest of the time, his crusty garment provides a tough, womb-like shield against his predatory enemies. And, like the parrot, the crab is equipped with an uncanny capacity to anticipate danger, an intuitive aspect of the feminine that is not always recognized as such and seen instead as a mood, a depression or anxiety that shouldn't be there. The crab's instincts, however, have remained sharply honed for millennia, making him a worthy defender of the world of the feminine.[12]

Unfortunately, Edward does not want the feminine to have this kind of defender. Had he lived in our far more psychological age, he might perhaps have realized that this strange, heroically proud animal was a mirror of the paranoid masculine stance that had emerged from his own deeply repressed mother complex. Instead of achieving anything approaching this insight, however, Edward, in a scene of chilling malice, comes back to the pool, finds a large stone and plugs the hole into which the crab has retreated, so that it cannot enter the pool again to trouble him. This repressive act implicates Edward, symbolically, in the development of Antoinette's psychosis, for by denying the crab access to the pool, it is as if he is cutting off her psyche from an all-important natural defense against outside violation.

The Wisdom of Christophine

Edward fancies himself, after his victory over the insolent crab, as having gained the upper hand over Antoinette's chaotic world. There is, however, one truly admirable character in the film that is absolutely impervious to his arrogating conceit. Christophine, Antoinette's "da," is a massively underrated figure who exhibits the needed authority and self-assurance that could restore this dysfunctional world. Her statuesque dignity bespeaks of the prudent and sagacious crone that she proves to be. As she offers up her good sense, rather like a magical juice that has been distilled from the bitterness as well as the sweetness of her lived feminine experience, she is willing to share, but not debate, her wisdom.[13] Additionally, her saucy presence traverses the film like another archetype that is closely aligned with the feminine realm:

> The cat...[who] is the exact opposite of existential fear. A cat walks into the room when hungry and meows and gets milk.... She behaves as though she were conferring an honor on you....When the cat has had enough, she walks out! She neither thanks you nor attaches herself to you (von Franz 1993, 206).

Demonized and ridiculed by the whites, respected and feared by other blacks, and the only source of true comfort for our faltering heroine, Christophine is finally a tough, good-hearted Witch, the embodiment of a dark audacious femininity.

Christophine's job is to teach Antoinette how to handle the requisite tribulations involved in creating a true marriage of opposites. Unlike anyone else in the film, Christophine appreciates that a conscious relationship is hard-won, not a guaranteed "happily ever after" cakewalk, and that successful partnerships require the contrary sides to consider the *other* no matter how ridiculous or baffling or inconsequential their stance appears to be. With her schooling in the art of a West Indian voodoo called *obeah*, Christophine understands the value of bloody sacrifice, including a woman's sacrifice of virginity at the beginning of a first marriage. Most important, Christophine encourages Antoinette to stake claim to her own gifts rather than entrusting them to Edward. She recognizes the urgency of Antoinette's incorporating such an attitude in order to successfully uphold her nuptial vows. Indeed, had Christophine's guidance succeeded in emboldening Antoinette to believe in herself, Edward might not have so easily forgotten how intrigued he initially was with his unique bride. Christophine's precautions were meant to equilibrate the dissimilar couple, and had they been heeded, the couple would have grown increasingly cognizant of the other's exceptional contributions and both become better for it.

Jung describes the symmetry-producing tension that Christophine attempts to promote in conceptual language:

> The irreconcilable opposites...*have* to be held together if the balance of life is to be maintained. This can only be done by holding unswervingly to the centre, where action and suffering balance each other. It is a path 'sharp as the edge of a razor'...where universal opposites clash...at the same time a moment when a wide perspective often opens out into the past and future (1954, par. 608).

While providing sanctuary for Antoinette (who despite holding hereditary title to land is penniless prior to her marriage), Christophine advises her charge time and time again to monitor her emotions and learn to be her own repository for her tears, fears and rage, rather than entrusting them to one as uninformed and inexperienced as Edward. Christophine has a native appreciation for the transforming power of the emotional realm, and she cautions Antoinette to discover that truth for herself, rather than hand the job over to her husband, who is too limited to assume it.

The script of *Wide Sargasso Sea* is sprinkled with Christophine's earnest observations and prudent caution. Here are a few examples:

> Get up and dress yourself girl. A woman must have spunk to live in this world....
> I'll tell you a hard thing; pack up and go. When a man don't love you, more you try, more he hate you. A rich girl like you. Pick up your skirt and walk out. Do it and he come after you....
> He worse than Satan's self!...
> If a man don't love you, I can't make him....
> Obeah is too strong for a white man; it will only cause big trouble....
> People tell your husband stories about you and your mother....Cool him, calm him, but don't cry. Crying's no good with him....
> I do what you ask of me, but only if you talk to him first.

Each of these statements is an education in feminine self-suffiency. Christophine is working to help Antoinette believe in herself and take initiative. She wants Antoinette to persevere in the construction of a life that suits her. She wants her to distinguish between modes of communication that are unproductive and those that truly serve a relationship, as well as allowing the feminine to survive. Christophine wants Antoinette to take the initiative and be responsible for her actions, rather than delegating to others. She does not want Antoinette to identify with her mother's cheapened status. She wants her to use her prerogatives as a free agent. Christophine exemplifies trust in the feminine as a source of agency.

Rather than a sentimental figure, Christophine is a credible example of feminine earth wisdom. She is less a mother to Antoinette than a concerned elder sister, telling the truth without mincing words, seeing evil and malignant behaviors for what they are, understanding and tolerating the complexities of relationship, valuing individuality and interdependence. Remarkably, she has the ability described in T.S. Eliot's phrase, "to care and not to care" (1930, 67).

One of the saddest aspects of *Wide Sargasso Sea* is how little Antoinette manages to avail herself of the wisdom of such a teacher, and how easily Edward dismisses her. Under Christophine's tutelage, both of them do make attempts at patching up their damaged relations, but only half-heartedly. Little digs undermine their efforts: Edward resorts to identifying Antoinette by her long lost mother's name, Nettie, while Antoinette becomes contemptuous of Edward's England. Both hit each other below the belt—and hard, causing their affiliation to deteriorate. Edward's recurring nightmare of being sucked into the sea returns, making him even more aggressively unsympathetic. Antoinette grasps for some of Christophine's conviction but then becomes amnesic, adopting her mother's fatal self-sabotage. "He wouldn't come after me, and I'm not rich. Everything I have belongs to him, that's English law." Antoinette cannot seem to preserve faith in herself as someone who can produce her own desires. Instead, like her mother, she resignedly reduces herself to an impotent daughter of the patriarchy, under his dominion, with no capacity to make a difference.

Antoinette's last ditch effort is careless and reckless, attempting to exploit Christophine's supernatural sensibilities without taking in the natural wisdom in which those sensibilities are contained. Antoinette pleads with Christophine: "You can, you can make people love or hate or die. If he'd come one more time, I'd make him love me." Instead of attending to the relationship, as Christophine has suggested she do,

Antoinette foolishly enacts one of Edward's greatest fears. She tricks him into swallowing the *obeah* potion, which sucks him back into his dreaded devouring unconsciousness, where he has no survival skills. Only Christophine comprehends how misapplied this use of dark feminine magic is when it is used for ensnaring those who are not already properly initiated into respect for the feminine.

With the composure of a high priestess, Christophine gently reproaches Antoinette for wasting her emotions on Edward. He has not yet proven himself worthy of her precious heart. Rather than listening to Christophine's concerns and building the requisite vessel that could support the inevitable turbulence, however, Antoinette, just like her mother, becomes completely consumed by her desires for sudden empowerment.

Aware that Antoinette's spirit has been taken hostage, Christophine, in a final gesture, relies upon Edward's compassion and decency. She beseeches him to "love her again. A little like you can, or they tear her to pieces like they do her mother." His heart has become too hard to hear, his focus purely self-preserving. His obdurate retort is one of primacy and preeminence: "She's my wife, and I intend to look after her for the rest of her life." As if that were a satisfactory answer, Edward turns on Christophine, attempting to subjugate her, just as he did the crab and then his wife. But Christophine flouts such imperial posturing: "No man touches me... No soldiers, no chain gang either, no treadmill. This a free country, and I a free woman." In contrast to Antoinette, Christophine's first commitment is to herself. She carries the self-confidence of the Crone:

> A deep sense of...at-one-ment. Without this essential independence from all roles and bonds, she is a potential victim for servitude. [With it, she is] bound by no relationship (Woodman 1996, 135).

Unfortunately, Antoinette refuses to benefit from her example. Failing to rely on her own feminine ingenuity, as Christophine had suggested she do, Antoinette remains at the mercy of Edward's patriarchal whims. When Antoinette is shipped off to Edward's England, her most sincere guardian and governess, who had offered to teach Antoinette the necessary acumen that could have saved her life, is now permanently out of reach.

The Memory of the Maiden

Antoinette Cosway epitomizes the archetype of the Maiden under present-day cultural conditions—our feminine vulnerability trying to survive when her cultural parents, our present-day father and mother complexes, no longer care about her fate. The audience watching her tragedy unfold occasionally gets a glimpse of the precious potential in this figure of the feminine before she is utterly snatched from her natural world, like Persephone by Hades, by the hellish figure of her unempathic husband. That we do get a glimpse of her enormous potential is perhaps the greatest strength of the film. As visualized in Wide Sargasso Sea, the feminine is a promising feminine soul, impetuous and effervescent, eager to love and to be loved, wildly expressive and profoundly sensitive. She is a part of the psyche that reasons with her heart and understands with her intuitions. At her best, she entertains desires that would delight any of us, if our education would permit. But her fate is an attic room in a cold and unsympathetic England that has long been in the business of holding the feminine at a distance. Yet the memory of her vibrancy, as an archetype of life, will not let Edward go. With the tenacity of a resurrected crab, Antoinette's talents continue to irritate Edward's charred mind just like his most unsettling dreams. Earlier in the movie, Edward spoke of his growing disaffection for Antoinette and her beloved birthplace:

> I hated the beauty of the place and its magic and the secret I'd never know. Above all, I hated her. She left me thirsty, and all my life would be thirst, longing for what I had lost, before I found it.

The viewer can take comfort in knowing that this thirst will eventually unbolt the door to the irrepressible feminine—when Edward Rochester encounters Jane Eyre, a young woman possessed of a feminine force strong enough to survive patriarchy's blunders.

References

Bolen, Jean (2005). *Urgent Message from Mother: Gather the Women, Save the World.* Boston: Conari Press.

Briner, Mary (1990). "Mother and Daughter Relationships." In Harry A. Wilmer (ed.), *Mother/Father.* Wilmette, Illinois: Chiron Publications, 107-128.

Davidson, Arnold E. (1985). *Jean Rhys.* New York: Frederick Ungar Publishing Co.

Eliot, T.S. (1930/1998). *The Waste Land and other poems.* New York: A Signet Classic.

Flores, Philip J. (2004). *Addiction as an Attachment Disorder.* Lanham: Jason Aronson.

Jung, C. G. (1934/1950/1969). "A Study in the Process of Individuation."
In *Collected Works*, vol. 9i.

—. (1954/1969). "Psychological Aspects of the Mother Archetype." In
Collected Works, vol. 9i.

Knox, Jean (2003). *Archetype, Attachment, Analysis: Jungian psychology
and the emergent mind.* Hove, England: Brunner-Routledge.

Leonard, Linda Schierse (1993). *Meeting the Madwoman: An Inner
Challenge for Feminine Spirit.* New York: Bantam Books.

Marcus, Kate (1956). "The Stranger in Women's Dreams." *Paper 7.* Los
Angeles: Analytical Psychology Club of Los Angeles.

Neumann, Erich (1954). *The Origins and History of Consciousness.* New
York: Bollingen Foundation.

Rhys, Jean (1966/1982). *Wide Sargasso Sea.* New York: W. W. Norton &
Company.

Schwartz-Salant, Nathan (1998). *The Mystery of Human Relationship:
Alchemy and the Transformation of the Self.* London: Routledge.

Singer, Thomas and Kimbles, Samuel (eds.) (2004). *The Cultural
Complex.* Hove, England: Brunner-Routledge.

The Herder Symbol Dictionary (1978). Wilmette, IL: Chiron Publications.

Ulanov, Ann Belford (1971). *The Feminine in Jungian Psychology and in
Christian Theology.* Evanston: Northwestern University Press.

Ulanov, Ann and Barry (1994). *Transforming Sexuality: The Archetypal
World of Anima and Animus.* Boston: Shambhala.

von Franz, Marie-Louise (1993). *The Feminine in Fairy Tales.* Boston:
Shambhala.

Whitmont, Edward C. (1997). *Return of the Goddess.* New York:
Continuum.

Woodman, Marion and Dickson, Elinor (1996). *Dancing in the Flames:
The Dark Goddess in the Transformation of Consciousness.* Boston:
Shambhala.

Notes

[1] *Jane Eyre* (1847). Written by Charlotte Bronte.

[2] See http://www.didyouknow.cd/sargasso.htm for a further description of this hellish venue.

[3] See http://www.the-bermuda-triangle.com to gain access to the fantasies that have grown up about this broader part of the Atlantic between Bermuda, Miami, Florida, and San Juan, Puerto Rico.

[4] *Lord of the Rings* (2001). Screenplay by Fran Walsh. Directed by Peter Jackson.

[5] See Marcus (1956).

[6] *Dangerous Beauty* (1998). Screenplay by Jeanine Dominy. Directed by Marshall Herskovitz. This film is discussed in Chapter Six of this book.

[7] See Singer and Kimbles (2004).

[8] See Bolen (2005).

[9] *The Little Colonel* (1935). Screenplay by William M. Conselman. Directed by David Butler.

[10] *The Color Purple* (1985). Screenplay by Menno Meyjes. Directed by Steven Spielberg.

[11] Neumann says that "he is the destructive instrument of the matriarchate, as its henchman; he is its authority, as the maternal uncle" (1954, 186).

[12] The crab is a creature that caught Jung's attention as a psychologist. He describes in one of his essays how the symbol of the crab connects to feminine authority in Greek mythology, where Hera rewards the crab clan with the auspicious zodiacal constellation, Cancer, because of its loyal patronage to her. Jung, further, explains that this very astrological sign comes at just the time when the sunny days have peaked out, linking crab's accomplishments to "the death of the solar hero" (1954, par. 604-5).

[13] The Jungian analyst Jean Bolen has referred to such wise older women as "juicy crones," but Christophine is more like a crone with juice.

CHAPTER FOUR

THE PRESENCE OF AN ABSENCE

JOHN BEEBE

Brokeback Mountain
(2005). Directed by Ang Lee.
Screenplay by Larry McMurtry and Diana Ossana.

The narrative risks that *Brokeback Mountain* takes are so extreme as to break the back of a mountain of Hollywood precedent. Perhaps the least hazardous was to develop a major motion picture out of a story about a love affair between a ranch hand and a rodeo cowboy and to cast as the two male leads young stars with heterosexual reputations to look after. Much chancier is that in the screenplay that emerged little happens to the young men until they suddenly get sexual with each other, and relatively little happens after. The most intense scenes in the film are really flashbacks, colored by fantasies about the fearsome consequences of male coupling in Wyoming and Texas. In the scenes that are more trustworthy—the ones we are allowed to see for ourselves in real time—there are social consequences to the men's inadequately concealed romance, but these amount to a series of flat denials by others that theirs is a love, and no harsher reprisal is needed. Even the end of the affair, anticipated by the script from the beginning, is presented as a kind of afterthought. Happily, a process of reflection ensues and rescues the movie, inviting the viewer to feel what was only between the lines of the scenario up to that point. I found a hole in my heart that kept on aching a whole day after I saw *Brokeback Mountain*: what Steven Joseph once described (in an essay about Lacan published in *The San Francisco Jung Institute Library Journal*) as the "presence of an absence."[1]

What then, is the absence that *Brokeback Mountain* records? Throughout most of the movie, its personification is Ennis Del Mar (Heath Ledger). "The truth is," Jack Twist (Jake Gyllenhaal) says to Ennis, "sometimes I miss you so much I can hardly stand it." Ennis withholds himself from Jack because he doesn't believe two men can live openly together in Wyoming, and he lacks the adaptability to join Jack in conceiving of moving to a place where they might. In the course of the film, Ennis barely travels at all, even through time: decades that would age another man leave him almost untouched; a daughter of Ennis's born not long after the movie begins is ready to get married by the last scene. Twenty-five-year-old Heath Ledger, with his tight lips, blond, laconic body and strangled down-under accent, did well with the part of a man who cannot age because he was born old and has no interest in growing any more. The actor intuited an archetype that the literary scholar Ernst Robert Curtius was the first to identify—the *puer senex*, the "old youth" who shadows not just Ennis's image, familiar from photographs of the actual men of the American West, but Western sensibility in general, with its habit of making a virtue of resisting decline.[2] Roman artists were familiar with this gestalt of masculinity. There is something of its vacant sadness in the numerous sculptures of Hadrian's favorite, Antinous—an eternal youthfulness that simultaneously contains a suddenly old emperor's memory of lost possibilities.

Ennis is handsome in the same kind of sealed-off, godlike way as Antinous, and he is similarly unavailable to very much human contact: he comes alive erotically for the audience only when he is remembering Jack. For instance, when the two men reunite, four years after their brief idyll in the midst of a summer working hard-up on Brokeback Mountain as shepherds (Ang Lee, who also directed a version of Jane Austen's *Sense and Sensibility*, here makes the most of a homoerotic trope that informed the eighteenth century English artist Gainsborough), Ennis is a lot more ardent than he had been on the mountain itself. As he showers the returning Jack with kisses, he is spooning the memory of a passion he never expressed so evidently earlier.

Jack, on the other hand, is never at a loss to express his want for Ennis. In the course of the movie, much is made of the way he has to deal with the introversion of his beloved, and their romance carries the charm of a courtship of introverted by extraverted feeling. If Ennis comes across as a somber, manly puer, Jack compensates him by being a soulfully androgynous trickster, one just feminine enough—especially in his large, darkly receptive eyes—to receive the projection of a man who has no other way of connecting with the anima.

The women in the film, all the more real for not being anima figures to the men, handle the men's inattention in ways that are varied, fascinating, and poignant. We particularly notice the wives of the protagonists (neither young man can resist the cultural demand to marry), but there are also daughters and a mother, as well as a deeply disappointed would-be new girlfriend after one of the men divorces, and each in her turn briefly commands the screen. The women serve, throughout the film, as a kind of chorus observing the central action—the men's hopeless love story—from afar, occasionally commenting on it in ways that mostly reveal their lack of comprehension of what these men may be throwing away.

What the movie gets its audience to realize, with tragic force, is not just the stalled lives of a homophobic culture. And although many would like to have it so and are filling *Brokeback Mountain*'s internet website with the stories of their own outcast loves, I don't think the movie is, more broadly, about the suffering that attends a love that lacks a social context. Those themes draw us into the picture, and even start off its meditation, but the basic idea of *Brokeback Mountain*, depicted with appealing baldness through the scaled-down simplicity of its scenario, is the inexplicable unadaptedness of men in relationships. "You know, I ain't queer," says Ennis; "Me neither," says Jack—after their first sex has required that they (and the audience) contemplate the unexpected strength of their interest in each other. And they aren't, exactly, queer, in the sense that they were afraid of in 1963: the strangeness of their relationship does not reside in its socially inconvenient sexual orientation but rather in the fact that it enables them to articulate to each other the disorientation which relationship itself can bring to men.

The New Yorker story from which the script for *Brokeback Mountain* was developed was written by a woman, E. Annie Proulx, and has the advantage of a distance from the male experience she is trying to record.[3] Her guess is that that experience, even at its most passionate, will be as vacant and inarticulate as it seems from outside; in fact, that it is that very vacancy that fuels the passion which men can sometimes bring to each other. It's a brilliant deduction, one that director Ang Lee, holding the similar advantage of distance as a Taiwanese-born man looking at the affective world created by a white Wyoming culture, chooses not to quarrel with for most of the film. His movie really comes alive, though, when the last woman character, Ennis's grown-up daughter, has departed its frame to prepare for her hopefully happy marriage, a move that leaves Lee free, finally, to open up his sparse *mise-en-scéne* and reveal the emotional capability hidden within the apparent barrenness of the cowboys' unfurnished lives. It is the long moment that ensues, during which Heath Ledger grants his auteur one of those culminating star turns that have made the American cinema canonical, that left me feeling not just the enormous sadness of Jack's and Ennis's truncated love, but the hole in my own heart. With Ang Lee, as a contemporary man I experience

that hole as a potential space, open to further development—perhaps a
birthright of maleness itself.

References

Curtius, Ernst Robert (1953/1990). *European Literature and the Latin
    Middle Ages* (Willard Trask, trans.). Princeton: Princeton University
    Press.
Joseph, Steven M. (1987). "Fetish, Sign and Symbol through the Looking-
    Glass: A Jungian Critique of Jacques Lacan's *Écrits*," *The San
    Francisco Jung Institute Library Journal.*
Proulx, E. Annie (2005). *Brokeback Mountain.* New York: Scribner.

Notes

---

[1] Joseph (1987, 16).
[2] Curtius (1953/1990, 98–101).
[3] The story that lends its title to the film appeared in *The New Yorker*, October 13,
1997, and has been reprinted in Proulx (2005).

FIGHTING BACK

CHAPTER FIVE

FEMALE PUER

JOHN BEEBE

Crouching Tiger, Hidden Dragon
(2000). Directed by Ang Lee.
Screenplay by Wang Hui Ling, James Schamus, and Tsai Kuo Jung,
from the novel by Wang Du Lu.

In Ang Lee's films, a couple's happy evolution is often impeded by a conflicting previous engagement. In *The Wedding Banquet*, the groom's impending marriage to a woman his Chinese family thinks suitable is complicated by his long-standing liaison with a male lover. Through most of *Sense and Sensibility*, Hugh Grant's character, Edward, isn't even on screen with Emma Thompson's Elinor because he has previously betrothed himself to another woman and can't go back on his word. *Crouching Tiger, Hidden Dragon* opens with a man and a woman, both martial artists in classical China, who have to deny their love for each other out of respect for the woman's earlier engagement to the man's deceased brother-by-oath. The survival of passion in the face of honor is not a particularly grateful cinematic subject, but Ang Lee is a filmmaker who knows how to make it pay off. With *Crouching Tiger, Hidden Dragon*, the director's fidelity to his theme is rewarded by the story he gets to tell, which is how the Tao of events conspires to transcend Confucian duty.

Lee uses his righteous pair Yu Shu Lien (Michelle Yeoh) and Li Mu Bai (Chow Yun Fat), whose wistful glances toward each other have become a ritual, to epitomize that aspect of the Chinese character that some in the West have called "impassiveness." It might be better, following the logic of this film, to view this as the patience that contains the Chinese soul. The comradely Yu is an escort to merchant caravans across the Empire; her security assures that the goods arrive safely. Yu and Li are supremely disciplined, and there seems little chance that the reserve that defines their relationship will ever be broken.

Into this static universe set on upholding "friendship, trust, and integrity" comes a thief, who steals Li's sword and subverts Yu's security. This thief, a bold girl they come to know as Jen, represents everything they would like to repress, yet they idealize her. She enters the film by night, and the gracious Mandarin pace gives way to a moonlit explosion of kinetic energy. The blue shadowed courtyards open up to long, balletic sequences of rooftop chases interrupted by kung-fu combat. As the characters engage this new possibility for interaction, their normal capacities to find vulnerable pressure points and exercise subtle feats of leverage extend into the ability to scale walls and leap over distances as if gravity itself were only relatively hindering them. The actors transcend the limits of cinematic space to become avatars of the transcendent function itself, [1] moving through air, earth, and water alike with a larky buoyancy.

In his very helpful essay in the book *Crouching Tiger, Hidden Dragon: A Portrait of the Ang Lee Film*, which includes the complete screenplay, David Bordwell summarizes the history of the *wuxia pian*, or film of the roaming, chivalric outlaw hero gifted in martial arts (Bordwell 2000). This is a genre that has been part of Chinese filmmaking since the 1920s, although suppressed on the mainland after Mao took power in 1949 and continued since mainly in Taiwan and Hong Kong. In this cycle of movies, which built on conventions already established in Peking Opera to bring Shanghai pulp *wuxia* novels involving the magical exploits of vagabond warriors to the screen, flying fighters were standard; later, influences from Japanese samurai films were added. In the past twenty years, the *wuxia* movies, which emphasized swordplay with a range of sophisticated blades, have given way to the kung-fu movies that have helped to shape the New Hong Kong Cinema. Throughout the canon, which originates in tales that became popular in China after the ninth century AD, the *wuxia* knight errant might be either male or female, but was always "an outlaw who could deliver vengeance in a society where law held no sway" (ibid., 15).

Lee draws upon this rich tradition to combine elements of the newer kung-fu classics into a much-streamlined kind of *wuxia* film, which conveys to an international audience a sense of Chinese fantasy beyond anything I have previously seen at the movies. The film has fared well both among the critics at Cannes and in general release: the mass audience reacts with delighted attention to the well-printed English subtitles that support the dazzling visual storytelling, exactly as it might to reading a terrific comic book magically projected on the screen. In pop guise, *Crouching Tiger, Hidden Dragon* encodes layers of Chinese cultural history, not only in its carefully-crafted script developed by a Westerner, James Schamus, with a team of Chinese experts from a portion of a *wuxia* novel but also in its several generations of Asian stars. Cheng Pei Pei, who plays the bandit witch Jade Fox, was in the 1960s the "Queen of *wuxia pian*." Here she brings a mythic majesty to her role as the *wuxia* Lilith who first models what might be called yang-femininity to Jen (Haddon 1987, 133–141).

Guided by the choreography of martial arts master Yuen Wo Ping, the characters wrestle, kickbox, fence, chase, and otherwise fight over deserts, forests, townscapes, and canyons, yet no action is divorced from its dramatic context or fails to advance the psychological fact that humans flourish by clarifying their relationships to each other. *Crouching Tiger, Hidden Dragon* depends for its overall effect upon its ability to surprise the viewer with torrents of beautiful and unexpected human movement and then to stun us with heartbreaking moments when the movement stops.

Despite the sometimes violent assumptions of the sometime girl thief Jen, who is appealingly played by a newcomer to movies, the extraordinary 19-year-old Zhang Ziyi, *Crouching Tiger, Hidden Dragon* is about limitation, not transcendence. There is no way, so long as her father's culture has a will as relentless as hers, for Jen to represent more than the possibility of freedom. The most passionate sequence occurs when she leaves the moonlit midnight world of the thieves' Peking behind for the far sun-drenched Gobi Desert. This time the poaching amateur finds herself in hot pursuit of a real bandit who has stolen her jade comb. The comb becomes the emblem of the hardness that she would gladly surrender to him if only she could. It is the feminine counterpart to the Green Destiny sword that Li cannot quite rid himself of, another glimpse at what the genders might be free to exchange in a world that permitted them options. The poignancy is underscored by Tan Dun's music, which emphasizes native instruments like the *erhu* and is flooded with plaintive cello solos from Yo Yo Ma.

Jen, however, is not a victim. She survives all the weapons the martial warriors for the status quo can throw at her to force her to submit as they have done, and she survives the envy of her mentor, Jade Fox, at her superior ability to put one over on patriarchy. Jen's secret lies in her instinctive selfhood, which is beyond the need for any initiation into a more chastened adulthood. Moving against the flow (and the gravity) of an atmosphere that Jungian analyst Gareth Hill has described as the "static masculine"[2] (the cinematographer Peter Pau's painterly opening shot is like Vermeer's *View of Delft*), Jen proudly arrogates to herself the energy of the feminine, its natural capacity for autonomy, initiative, and agency, and she animates the landscape of the film. This "dynamic feminine,"[3] to use Hill's phrase, is for Ang Lee the Tao, the "crouching tiger and hidden dragon" of the movie's title and his own solution to the cultural problem he has identified, and not just for the Chinese psyche, of restrictive premature commitments based on gendered assumptions. Jen, in a word, can really choose what kind of a person she wants to be, and she chooses to stay poised on the threshold of life's possibilities. There, she finds a place in the Chinese imagination once occupied only by a male hero of legend. She floats in the moviegoer's mind as an immortal image of the female *puer*[4]—perhaps it would be better to say, of the invincible vulnerability of yang-femininity.[5]

References

Bordwell, David (2000). *Crouching Tiger, Hidden Dragon: A Portrait of the Ang Lee Film.* New York: Newmarket Press.

Haddon, Genia Pauli (1987). "Delivering Yang-Femininity." *Spring: An Annual of Archetypal Psychology and Jungian Thought*, 133-141.

Hill, Gareth S. (1992). *Masculine and Feminine: The Natural Flow of Opposites in the Psyche.* Boston & London: Shambhala.

von Franz, Marie-Louise (1970). *The Problem of the Puer Aeternus.* New York: Spring Publications.

Notes

[1] See this book, Chapter Two, 19.

[2] See Hill (1992, 13-16).

[3] Ibid., 17-22.

[4] The term *puer*, Latin for boy, is shorthand in Jungian discourse for *puer aeternus*, the mythologem of the eternal boy. See von Franz (1970) and this book, page 207, for a further discussion of this archetypal figure, who is often literally or metaphorically in flight (e.g., Peter Pan). Often the term *puella aeterna* is used for the corresponding archetype in a woman's psyche. Both the *puer* and the *puella* live, as it were, off the ground. In this movie, however, it feels to me as if we are seeing not a slightly androgynous puella joining a man in a stratospheric flight (an archetype so memorably rendered in the movies by Audrey Hepburn in *Roman Holiday* that her short boyish haircut in that film was shortly after adopted in *A Star is Born* by Judy Garland) but a somewhat rarer phenomenon, the female puer, because the female martial artist really transcends the limitation of her own gender identification to enter a realm defined by her culture as male, and needs to draw upon archetypal energy that is also male to do so.

[5] See Genia Pauli Haddon (1987).

CHAPTER SIX

ON HER OWN BEHALF

VIRGINIA APPERSON

Dangerous Beauty
(1998). Directed by Marshall Herskovitz.
Screenplay by Jeannine Dominy.

"Dangerous to whom?" we are tempted to ask, when the title comes up on the screen. Aesthetic perfection, which so draws us all, is surely not bound, at its secret depths, to be an annihilating force, is it? That it might be is an uneasy, but not entirely unsuspected intuition!

Beauty, we know, can be dangerous to the one who embodies it, marking her or him as a jewel ruthlessly to be possessed. And of course loveliness may seduce and beguile. But at the movies, we can usually trust the visual image. In film, if it looks truly beautiful, as opposed to merely sexy or disarming, it is normally *not* dangerous. Beauty is a virtue on the screen, its grace a reassurance that a measure of perceivable harmony is possible in life. Feminine beauty, as a cinema archetype, inoculates against the ugliness of life.

Dangerous Beauty, from Margaret Rosenthal's more plainly titled book, *The Honest Courtesan,* features the lovely English actress, Catherine McCormack, whose perfect face is as open as it is ravishing. It is surprising that McCormack has not gone on to be a star since she is far more attractive than most of the Hollywood actresses who might have landed such a role. Her appealing presence on the screen is what attracts us into the story of Veronica Franco, the courtesan who created an uproar in sixteenth century Venice by standing up to a church-led uprising against her and succeeding. Franco's life is well documented; she seems to have been a remarkable woman, not just because she was on sexual call to selected statesman, admirals and members of the clergy, but really more importantly because she was possessed of intelligence, autonomy, and integrity that commanded respect wherever she went.

Born in 1546 in Venice, which was then at the height of its power as a
seagoing empire, Franco grew up in what at that time was perhaps the
most culturally liberal city in the world, a city-state whose waterways
snaked through all its social subdivisions. Veronica's archetypal role as a
kind of prostitute makes her an envoy from the feminine realm to the
masculine, and the way that she spreads her favors evenly among the elite
positions her to breach splits of power even as she brings pleasure to the
power-brokers.

Her curative approach is simply to be true to herself, and it is through
her incorruptible character that some of the best of the feminine virtues are
portrayed. Watching Veronica, a realized woman with a strong sense of
self, enables the viewer to discover a more complete picture of what the
feminine has to offer than we usually see on the screen, where women are
most often asked to play roles that can be more narrowly defined in terms
of particular archetypes (e.g. the heroine, mother, oppositional, witch,
puella, anima, and demonic roles that Beebe has identified in his
typological analysis of film story[1]). As might be expected, her easy
assertion of self creates a hullabaloo among her fellow Venetians, and
eventually she has to stand up in the Doge's court for her right to live her
life as she chooses. Although Venice's patriarchal establishment seems to
enjoy her sensibility and has come to treasure the private pleasures that
she provides, the Renaissance Italian city-state, for all its liberality, is no
less limited in its comprehension of the virtues of the feminine than the
conservative, British-dominated 19th century Caribbean island culture that
we have already visited in *Wide Sargasso Sea*. Both 16th century Venice
and the 19th century Caribbean have watery settings that naturally suit
them to be havens for the feminine, but as governed by landed colonial
gentry they could only occasionally grant a natural, fluid expression to the
feminine. Unlike Antoinette Cosway, who succumbs to the patriarchal
tyranny inflicted onto her Jamaica, Veronica, in many respects, thrives in
masculine-dominated Venice. She refuses to compromise her core values,
and she never gives up her lucid sanity. Rather, her wit enables her to call
the city fathers to task for their misogynistic defenses under stress.
Unwilling to be their victim, though a few of them try hard to make her
take up that role, she manages to make them take a hard look at
themselves and to reconsider the plague-panicked, puritanical mindset that
threatens not only her life and reputation, but to cloud everything Venice
stands for. The attempt to brand her a witch whose beauty is a grave
danger to the realm loses in court after she testifies on her own behalf.[2]

Veronica's story works on screen as a parable of feminine
vulnerability. We are reminded, watching Veronica's struggle, that

present-day consciousness is no less ambivalent about feminine autonomy than in Venice in the 16th century. We may no longer have an out-of-control Inquisition, but Veronica's arguments, that are really much more on behalf of the value of love and relationship and desire than defending her profession, still manage to challenge our cultural biases around what is respectable.

The powerful men of Venice are not the only ones resistant to privileging Veronica's development of a fully-embodied feminine agency. The city's women also engage in directing negative projections her way, passing between them attitudes toward the feminine that force them to be at odds with one another and lead to further disempowerment, rather than female solidarity. In her foreword to *The Honest Courtesan,* Catharine Stimpson has described the imbalance that permeated Venice in Veronica's time as the "common Western polarity in the representation of women." A young woman living in Venice in the 16th century found herself forced into a system of representations that, as Margaret Rosenthal has put it, placed her

> ... between angel and witch, virgin and whore, Virgin Mary and Eve, or, in Venice's self-presentation, between an immaculate, pure, virtuous city and a luxury loving, bejeweled, voluptuous one. In part to ensure the purity of its women, especially the wives and daughters of the elite, Venice regulated them strenuously. Their space was to be private, not public. Because 'good women' were so restricted, 'bad women' had this social role of playmate and source of sexual release.

As Rosenthal notes,

> the courtesan, like the Japanese geisha, was expected to provide cultivated company and good conversation as well. However, during periods of grave social and economic danger, such as mid-1570s when the plague infected Venice, the courtesan and prostitute were conveniently available as symbols of disorder and vileness (Rosenthal 1992, vii-viii).

Under less stressful times in the life of the city, Venetian courtesans were lauded "for their talents as highly sophisticated conversationalists and cunning rhetoricians and for their dexterity at navigating their way through a loosely organized maze of social structures and class hierarchies" (ibid., 2). Meanwhile, dutiful wives (locked in their ivory towers) protected their exalted but dull status. If they were resentful and jealous of their infamous sisters' freedom, they could be consoled by their own standing in society. Such extreme role divisions between women only serve to weaken the authority of the feminine as a whole, thrusting them, once again, in the service of archetypes. When one group of women is ruled, as it were, by Hera, Hestia, and Demeter and the other by Aphrodite, each of the camps loses out on the talents of the other.[3] Despite the fact that such disharmony enables women to succeed within a patriarchal system, it destroys the vibrancy and vigor of the woman's ability to access in herself a multi-faceted feminine team of archetypal roles and perspectives, and this puts her ego at risk of being narrow and brittle. I have already tracked the sexism in the world of *Wide Sargasso Sea*, where the demure bearer of feminine charm is idealized and any more openly lusty lady is considered suspect. In *Dangerous Beauty* we also find that when patriarchy tries to seize control of the feminine, polarizing initiatives supplant unity between the complementary sides.

The pedigreed wives' response to the courtesans is simply disdain: their husbands can allow "the ladies of the night" to flaunt their charms without reproof, as long as the men keep them apart from their families. The protection of the men, however, cannot be counted on, particularly when her intellectual gifts are as enviable as her sexual charms. For example, Veronica is a very accomplished poet, a fact that becomes a problem early in the film because, though Venice enjoys a reputation as progressive and open-minded, many still cling to the belief system that "women's speech [leads] to sexual temptation" and "that eloquence [is] tantamount to promiscuity" (Rosenthal 1992, 6). What underlies this judgment, applied equally in respected households as well as a courtesan's chambers, is the attempt to hold any woman's voice that acquires star power suspect, lest her different perspective start to interfere with the (patriarchal) order of the day. Though enjoyed, women are to be treated as objects, not subjects, of desire: it is expected that their individual impact as persons can (and should) be turned off and on, according to men's caprice. In Venice, two extreme reactions appear in the personae of women (silent good girl/precocious bad girl). The psychological question that the viewer is asked to contemplate is how to heal the rift that is exposed, a rift within the feminine itself?

The way *Dangerous Beauty* addresses this dilemma is interesting, and to understand that, it is necessary to underscore Veronica's occupation, which is very much front-and-center in both the book and the film. The life of a woman who sells herself sexually and stays in control doing so is not a new subject for movies. For the trope to work requires considerable care on the part of actress, director and cinematographer, and when such a collaboration gels we get great screen performances, for example: Jane Fonda's Bree Daniels,[4] Liza Minnelli's Sally Bowles,[5] and Julia Roberts' Vivian Ward.[6] The sacrifices made for the courtesan lifestyle and the constraints endured are painstakingly revealed in the films that effect these characterizations. *Dangerous Beauty* shows us, in particular, that despite the fact that a Venetian courtesan enjoyed freedom and status that many properly married Renaissance women were denied, trading in one's own sexual allure is inevitably low in status: its glory short-lived and ultimately vulgarizing of the feminine spirit. (A woman whose face has been cut by a jealous lover and now must work as a poor street prostitute makes the case for how transitory such a living can be.) Although Veronica's own mother advances the argument that a courtesan's level of autonomy is a step in the right direction because it guarantees her economic and even creative freedom, we gradually sense, watching this film, that the actual costs of prostituting oneself are colossal, no matter how classy one is in the role.

To make sense of Veronica Franco's life, the psychological viewer would be advised to use corrective symbolic lenses, to see Veronica, for instance, less as an historical woman, and more as a heroine in a cultural fairytale (like, say, the successful third wife in the variants of "Bluebeard"[7] for example, in the tales collected by the Grimm Brothers, "The Robber Bridegroom" or "Fitcher's Bird"[8])—in other words, as a role model for women and as an instructor to men. By withholding judgment on her chosen profession, we can allow the ambivalence of her role to speak for itself. Observing Veronica's skill at negotiating the disjointed Venetian culture, which bears such a strong resemblance to the contradictory attitudes towards women's freedom in our present world, can help us to examine the fissures that still exist within the psyches of modern women and men. Veronica's story is told as a series of debates, and in verse, and the repartee is replete with contradictions that women and men have to face up to when asserting their competing claims within patriarchal culture. The movie shows what we are all up against when we try to claim a life of our own. Money over love, duty over passion, propriety over courage; these are the age-old tensions Veronica has to deal with (and she is not alone). What makes her refreshing is the undimmed force of her belief in her own character in the face of apparently irrefutable evidence that her life is scandalously unconventional. In my previous chapter, "Mad," (on the film *Wide Sargasso Sea*) I explained how easy it is for an increasingly constricted feminine potential to spin out of control; whereas *Dangerous Beauty* shows the capacity of feminine character to expand its range under challenge. In dramatic contrast to Antoinette Cosway's rapid decline, Veronica Franco rises to the occasion of being accused by her persecutors, displaying a mettle that ultimately bests her naysayers and shows the receptive contemporary audience a confidence that is a refreshing approach to the self-defense of the feminine. Veronica carves out a niche in Venice, not only for herself, but for the transformative possibility of a dynamic feminine power. In the process, she opens up a new cast of characters—the allies of the feminine.

A Shrewd Madam

Veronica's father, like Antoinette's in *Wide Sargasso Sea*, drank away the family resources (a motif that suggests that the masculine has become intoxicated with its own power and gone rancid). Not infrequently, a defeat for the masculine can cause the feminine to retreat as well, because now she has no protector. In contrast, however, to Mother Cosway's pathetic renunciation of her own resourcefulness, Veronica's mother reacts to the plight of pennilessness with cunning calculation: Signora Franco implements an unusual and controversial career plan for her daughter. Rather than further bankrupting the family by becoming identified with her husband's shameful ways, she turns the fact that they are already shamed to account by proceeding in a somewhat ruthless and single-minded manner. Signora Franco (beautifully played by the still-lovely Jacqueline Bisset) had been a courtesan in her youth; so it is not that hard for her, when the rug is pulled out from under the family, to return to that role, or to teach her skills to her daughter, so that she will have them at her disposal now that it is her turn to earn a fortune. This maternal role model offers a drastic revision of the stereotypical older woman in films from before women's liberation, who is so lost in her own disappointments that she has little to offer her daughter. Paola Franco has wrapped her heart in the steely resolve of someone who is desperate to make ends meet, and she sets the stage for a radically different path for her daughter.

Veronica Franco, as played by Catherine McCormack, is on the other hand a welcome throwback to the great beauties of the 1940s (like characters played by Maureen O'Hara or Geraldine Fitzgerald at a time when some women actually looked like that); her unsullied, confident femininity creates an interesting anxiety in the viewer of the film: can she retain this inner freshness in the face of the pressures upon her to become simply an anima figure to powerful men, the kind of woman that will simply be discarded when her youthful bloom fades? This feminist update of the problem faced by Leslie Caron in *Gigi*[9]—how to learn to be a courtesan without losing her own identity (and future) as a woman—recovers a face of the feminine for us we thought we had lost somewhere around 1950, the kind of beauty whose integrity is her most haunting and valuable feature. Because Veronica's mother has taught her to face a hard truth about matrimony ("Marriage is a contract, Veronica, not a perpetual tryst"), Veronica's sense of self, unlike Gigi's, does not depend upon marrying another. (Minnelli's 1958 film made its peace with the idea that women would not be able to live well outside of marriage.) Mother Franco, on the other hand, cautions her daughter to make herself a priority and thereby a financial success: "Whichever devil you choose," she tells her daughter, "you'll look him in the eye first, which is more than my mother ever gave me."

With such original counsel, it is not surprising that Veronica has so much more individuality than Leslie Caron's delicious dewy-eyed Gigi. Nor will Veronica be able to hide behind the kind of ignorance of what men are capable of in marriage that Antoinette Rochester had inherited from her mother. Paola's alternative maternal voice in *Dangerous Beauty* insists upon a conscious participation in life, admonishing Veronica that whatever its unkind inequities may be, these are to be faced head on. She lays on the table her daughter's meager options: loveless marriage, scullery maid, nun, or courtesan, and asks her daughter, which is it going to be? Signora Franco's firm authority in these matters provides an antidote to the cluelessness we kept encountering in *Wide Sargasso Sea.* Where the native nanny Christophine, with little success, attempted, too late, to teach the right kind of self-assertion to Antoinette Rochester, Signora Franco is adamant early that her daughter accept her lot in life and make something of it. Offering the needed initiation, she enlists Veronica into an unorthodox boot camp of her own devising, where the issued uniform is sumptuous silks and very high heels, and the rigorous basic training focuses on poetry and tête-à-têtes.

One of Signora Franco's first lessons concerns desire: "Desire begins in the mind . . . it's wanting that keeps us alive." This is important: rather than squelching or taming or rebuking the longings of the heart, Veronica is encouraged to open her heart and to take her passion seriously. She is just not to be stupid in doing so. To honor one's own and others' desires is, according to her mother, one of the most honorable and life-giving talents that a person can possibly develop. Today's psychologists would agree: desires form the heart of agency, though few of us are deeply schooled in the matters of the heart.

As a progressive mother, Signora Franco is at times almost too ideal. One wonders how in reality it would work to have a parent committed to fostering her daughter's gumption, when most of us have had to develop that through at least some struggle with our forebears. And most of us would find it odd to learn from our mothers to separate the act of loving from the object of love, as when she says, "Love, love, but do not love the man or you will be in his power." But how can we deny that this is a

necessary corrective to traditional Judeo-Christian education, with its
counsel to women to be "helpmeets" to their men, subordinating their own
ambitions to what their husband is planning. Taking this a bit deeper,
when the feminine is too busy adjusting herself itself to a masculine
criterion that dictates what is important (such as postponing one's own
desires in deference to one's husband's or one's animus's louder demands),
then the woman has nothing within to guide her as to what is crucial for
the survival of femininity. She has ceased to care, and becomes gradually
possessed by the kind of animus that can bring more certainty so long as
she accepts that her role is to serve and to please. If a woman loses her
ability to discriminate what is important for herself and becomes identified
solely as the manager of the man's household, then the masculine has
gotten the better of the feminine within her own psyche as well. The loss
will not only be of power, it will be of identity, and the opportunity to
nurture a feminine consciousness.

Signora Franco is a figure representing the other possibility: the
feminine supporting the woman's ego, as an emancipated mother teaching
her daughter to stay grounded in her own potential. At the level that she is
a human figure, rather than a signifier of an unconflicted feminine
authority, Signora Franco is a woman that has learned the hard way the
necessity of protecting her turf. What is quietly conveyed by Jacqueline
Bisset's understated performance in this role is: if you don't take care of
yourself, nobody else will.

Her way to do this—loving love and not the object of love—is
radically simple. Without a principle guiding her to privilege what she, not
anyone else, is feeling, a woman's traditional emphasis on relationship can
play false, resulting in an enmeshed, convoluted merger—ever the recipe
for mutual loathing. In loving love, the woman gains a steady anchor that
keeps her from getting unmoored during the stormy and volatile tides of
intimacy. She is protected from her own predilection for adolescent
romance, as well as from her partner's tendency to override her or flee
when matters get too complicated. Signora Franco's advice offers a way to
maintain a balance of powers between men and women, between the
masculine and the feminine, making the rules of engagement clear from
the start, so that who loves most and best, not who is the most lovable, in
the end actually has a chance to prevail.

Because of her own wounds, however, Signora Franco has an
unsympathetic, defensive edge, and it is this that leads to what for many
viewers will remain the elephant in the room, mother's habit of treating the
art of loving solely as a business venture. Under her mother's stern
direction, Veronica does learn how to run a business, but Veronica knows

that a thoroughly insulated heart will eventually result in emotional isolation. Once she has digested the best of what her mother has to offer, her next step is to risk a love in which she cannot be altogether sure of protecting herself. Veronica is able to successfully navigate this pass, too, and handle the impact of loving another because her feminine side is differentiated enough. That is no doubt, in no little measure, a consequence of following her mother's advice about keeping her own desires in mind, but the release from cynicism is something Veronica has forged for herself.

On her deathbed, Paola Franco seems to understand that she has gone too far in teaching her daughter to avoid commitment and live only for self-interest, and she asks her daughter's forgiveness. Veronica is compassionate and understands the choice her mother had had to face, between abandoning her daughter to a safe life of "perpetual inconsequence" and urging her to follow her own notorious example in order to become a self-sufficient woman. This is the differentiating step that too often is neglected in women's education and that puts feminine agency in peril time and again. Veronica is grateful: she understands that having learned to trust in her own resourcefulness has given her the fortitude to testify through life on her own behalf, without having to sacrifice her erotic *raison d'être*, her life lived for love.

Ann Ulanov, confronting the situation that masculine priorities are often excessively developed by members of both sexes at the expense of the feminine, has said such privileging of the masculine other may be what is at the root of war, since war is always based on human self-assertion at the expense of others. Ulanov argues:

> The true war is love's war—to fight for love and to reconcile the opposites, not to fight to kill others and to obliterate their civilization (1971, 261).

By contrast, Signora Franco's scope with regards to matters of the heart was too narrow to understand love's reconciling potential. Nonetheless, the tough, unusually feminine matriarch managed to instill in her daughter a love for herself that has served to immunize Veronica against being too eager to please, which in her profession soon would have destroyed her. As the movie makes clear, we could all use such a mother, bidding that we keep an eye on our own desire, and, for women particularly, that precept has the power to keep us from prematurely capitulating to love's call in the wrong way, before we have developed what might be called female authority.[10]

The "Good Women" of Venice

Playing by the rules, kowtowing, no questions asked, mindless, eager
to please, and upon occasion maliciously spiteful, the wives of the male
power-brokers in *Dangerous Beauty* are caricatures of the feminine
"principle" of eros[11], sad parodies of devotion, men's minions. Rather than
standing solidly behind their own talents, they have long since become
"bent in the direction of the masculine" (Jung 1952, par. 627). These
gloomy figures try to interfere with Veronica's attempt to hold onto her
vibrancy. Julia, the wife of Veronica's chief love interest in the film,
Marco, is one such dismal bride. As Marco appeals to his wife's interests,
all that he meets is dead-air space:

> Marco: Tell me a secret?
> Julia: I have no secrets....
> Marco: Tell me a desire, deep desire?
> Julia: I hope to give you strong sons....
> Marco: For you, just for you?
> Julia: To be a good wife to you is my only desire.

A cardboard, antiseptic puppet with all semblance of initiative squeezed
out of her, Julia's character is a pathetic image of the woman who has
given herself over to patriarchy. Research in our own time has shown that
something very like what is imaged in Julia starts to develop as early as
nine or ten years of age, when little girls discern that it is not cool to know
the answers, to speak up and out because it just is not ladylike. Girls at that
age begin to be taught that pliability brings favors, while expressions of
intellect and passion are censured (see Debold, Wilson & Malave). This is
the analogue of the way little boys are treated when they expose
vulnerabilities and shed tears, to be respectable little men is to be
emotionless and invincible. Both methods create one-dimensional children
who grow up to be only a fraction of their full potential.

The wives of Venice are the evident result of this familiar "good girl"
education that is inherently sexist. They have adapted to become smug,
persnickety daughters ruled by their father complexes and (true to type)
shockingly intolerant of what Jung calls the innate "chaos of the maternal
womb" (1954, par. 184). Jung further elaborates that such a woman, who
has complied with patriarchy's demands, is:

> ...unpleasant, exacting, and anything but satisfactory partner...she rebels
> in every fibre of her being against everything that springs from natural
> soil... [E]ven at her best she will remain hostile to all that is dark, unclear,

and ambiguous, and will cultivate and emphasize everything certain and clear and reasonable (ibid., par. 184).

Jung's words reach back centuries. No wonder the Venetian men in *Dangerous Beauty,* who have unconsciously participated in encouraging the development of such women, exercise their "husband's rights" by shamelessly fleeing the bedrooms in which these wives present themselves for the more alluring boudoirs of courtesans like Veronica. The attraction, as portrayed in the film, has very little to do with sex. The real draw seems to be the discovery of women who are genuine and confident because they are connected to themselves, not to someone else's privilege. The wives' success in conforming themselves to the patriarchal ideology of woman as principled eros has betrayed and lamed the very essence of their femininity, so that they are ironically no longer interesting to their husbands.

Veronica is the unapologetic heroine who provides the refreshing contrast of vitality that shows her to be aligned with her truest self. Even in her bleakest moments, she never loses her astonishing outer beauty. But what is far more captivating about Veronica is her exquisite capacity to express herself. From her literary endeavors, including "duels" in which men and women trade insulting verses, to her final showdown with her Inquisitors, she savors (and skewers) her male companions' endowments without compunction. Her trademark is the flair that she typically brings with her, often flaunting it to the point of being brazen, for example, when she "instructs" the wives in how to relish the Great Mother's bounty by eating a banana all the way down in one long swallow. She has the good sense, too, of when to keep quiet. Recognizing the limited scope and narrow existence from which the wives operate, she wastes little time responding to the wives' weak verbal reprisals. Veronica is even able to forgive them, because she is familiar with her own over-accommodating, conciliatory, dependent side, which she characterizes as "the self-destructiveness of her own selflessness" (Rosenthal 1992, 236). Such sympathetic insight about her own vulnerabilities helps her understand why women are often so quick to sell out:

So as not to spoil the world...a woman keeps silent and submits to a villainous and tyrannical man, who is then so very pleased at ruling over everything....[M]en honor women so highly because they (women) relinquished power to them and always preserved it for them (ibid., 239)

From Veronica's perspective, being this kind of wife is little more than a form of detention, and she is not moved by the promise of respectability to try to become one of them. For this reason, Veronica is able to withstand the wives' demeaning projections, which she knows only serve to perpetuate a split within the feminine world. She can resist their initiative towards a catfight because she is backed by a belief in herself.

Though "the good wives" did not appreciate what their "sister" Veronica had to contribute, our present collective can take heart from Veronica's verve (a number of films in the past two decades show the possibility of women standing up to patriarchal oppression—films like *Norma Rae*,[12] *Erin Brockovich*[13] and *North Country*[14] have helped their stars win Academy Awards or nominations). Of all the films in which women stand up for what they believe, *Dangerous Beauty* is one of the most satisfying, because its heroine is unwavering in her firm belief in herself.

Masculine Buffoonery

What, however, is the impact on the men of Venice of having such a female presence in their midst who is so transgressive of the system by which men define women? The most vehement response comes from Maffio, who is particularly well-played by Oliver Platt, a petty, small-minded courtier turned insinuating fundamentalist. Like Iago, he is a foul derivative of a male-dominated culture, which condemns his sister courtesans with virulent attacks while at the same time prostituting himself to the will to power. As a poet, he would look, one would think, for support from one of the muses, perhaps Clio, Erato or Polyhymnia, but instead his tongue is backed by the Titans. In offering up paeans to patriarchy expressing worn out, hero-driven values, he merely reveals that he is caught in the clutches of a hierarchical regime and has become its bitter pawn. Utterly unrelated to the feminine in any real way, his own, badly neglected anima gives him a sorry look: he has become moody, unstable and envious. Rather than tending to his own unresolved issues, he sees them only in Veronica—a common projection by the man who has denied his own feminine influence.

Unlike Iago, though, Maffio has a motive. Maffio's desire to hang onto what prestige mighty men have offered him is what fuels his desperate need to squash anything, like Veronica Franco, that threatens his rhetorical ascendancy. Yet when she offers her own quatrains in the public poetic duels with him, his poems begin to sound like infantile narcissistic rants. Veronica is even lauded by Maffio's own benefactors. Her success and his patrons' betrayal awaken a cutthroat, bloodthirsty resolve in Maffio to bring Veronica to her knees. A fresh outbreak of plague gives him his opportunity. In the midst of the predictable Catholic anxiety (in this age before germ theory) that the city is being punished by God for its licentiousness, Maffio metaphorically points to Veronica and trumpets:

> She is the woman who is at war with good health. A sea swarming with illness. The woman who came into this world with the crow. The woman who makes our present century blind and contaminates it. The woman against whom no prescription can prevail (Rosenthal 1992, 166).

> Veronica, veritably unique whore. Franca…foxy, flight, flimsy, flabby, smelly, scrawny, scrimpy, and the biggest scoundrel besides, who lives between Castillo, Ghetto, and the Customs. A woman reduced to a monster made of human flesh: plaster, chalk, cardboard, leather, and wooden board, a grisly spook, a scabby {poxy} ogre, a crocodile, a hippogriff, an ostrich, a knock-kneed mare. To sing of all that is wrong with you, your flaws, your faults, would take a hundred concepts, thousands of pens and inkwells, and countless poets, the prospect of bridges and hospitals (ibid., 188-189).

To the analytical psychologist, the Veronica Maffio is complaining about here is easily recognized as a projective identification of his own stunted anima, but for a time he is able to make others see the woman he wants them to see. She is arrested and brought to trial.

Maffio's squealing indictments of Veronica in the Doge's courtroom reek of a disproportionate need to regulate the feminine. Fortunately, in the end, this simply will not fly in Venice. Over and over, the quick-witted Veronica disarms Maffio by refusing to entertain his propositions, to identify with his judgments, and to retaliate with similar puerile recriminations. Her plucky spirit simply dismantles his accusations.

An Unproven Suitor

A more problematic aspect of the film is how to feel about Veronica's suitor, Marco, a young married man who is smitten with Veronica. (He is played by the lingeringly boyish Rufus Sewell as a somewhat hapless though handsome twenty-something looking for a safe berth to park his extramarital passion, but the actor succeeds in making Marco sympathetic even as he conveys his weaknesses.) As dashing and endearing as Marco is, he is so bound by his need to fulfill patriarchal expectations that he cannot decide who and how to disappoint. Marco displays the kind of extraverted feeling that supports the family system that has arranged his stale marriage, a system that affords him privilege and power, but precludes more than a discreet affair with Veronica. Marco's upper class lifestyle affords him every opportunity in the world, except the right to choose a conscious loving relationship.

Marco proposes an exclusive partnership time and again; each time Veronica bluntly reminds him that he asks of her what he is not willing to give. Though equally desirous of uniting with Marco, Veronica understands the implications of such a compromised union. He has sold his soul to patriarchal convention; she is not willing to sell hers and forfeit her own freedom in the bargain. Each time Marco pleads for Veronica's trust, she candidly exposes his double standard. Without Veronica's equilibrating influence, Marco could forever swing between his flawless façade and a chronically unfulfilled craving for connection:

> [A] typically masculine, ideal state…is threatened with an enantiodromia…. No path leads beyond perfection into the future—there is only a turning back, a collapse of the ideal, which could easily have been avoided by paying attention to the feminine ideal of completeness (Jung 1952, par. 627).

Veronica's moral fiber slowly cracks Marco's archaic ethical structure. As he begins the protracted process of extricating himself from his inherited confines, Veronica's capacity to be true to her feminine values further serves to re-animate Marco. Having allowed Veronica's syncretizing ways into his purview, he finally questions the underlying ancestral dictum: "What God and greed have joined together, let no love put asunder."

A Chivalric Rejoinder

By the time the film reaches its final section, the Plague has claimed 56,000 Venetian lives. The sea-empire capital's notorious opulence has been called into question by the fathers of the church, inflamed by Maffio's rhetoric, which speaks of lascivious profligacy. Panicked, the Venetians are ready to accept a superficial analysis and to punish anyone they consider blameworthy. The courtesans become the targets. Veronica, called before the Inquisition, is accused of witchcraft. It is said that the leading men of the city are her pawns, victims under her spell. The simplistic aim of the men is to "get rid of everything doubtful, ambiguous, vague, and muddled by projecting it upon some charming example of feminine innocence" (Jung 1954, par. 169). She must confess her crimes if Venice is to be saved (the fact that she has already saved it from the French king, by giving him the gentle chastisement that he secretly craves, is now forgotten.) It does not take much to see that there is nothing inquisitive about this Inquisition that already has all the answers.

Veronica, refusing to submit to the unintelligent slander that Venice's troubles are all her fault, cleverly and often quite poignantly rebuts the allegations. When asked by Maffio, who serves the court as her interrogator, if she knows why "Venice, ever a noble republic, home of learning, art, commerce has been brought low by war and plague," she replies:

Veronica: I am not that wise....I enchanted no one....I never feigned love.
Maffio: Then for what did they pay you?
Veronica: For the dream of love, as it cannot exist in this world that you've created.
Maffio: You say this. You who fill your home with feasting and dancing while Venice suffers, who creates a sumptuous world of flesh and depravity, of orgiastic rites invoking the devil....I was bewitched by this woman. In my weakness, I fell under her spell to pathetic ruin. It is only by the grace of God that I stand here today.
Veronica: I did not seek your love....I loved another....I did what was necessary to live....What other profession will you allow me? How shall I survive if I cannot marry?...You are determined to damn me, whatever I say.
Maffio: Look at her. Feel her wrath, her power. She, who lures the noble fathers of Venice from their wives, their children, their very ability to lead the republic. It is she and her kind who have turned God's hands against us. Your Grace...we must do our duty.

While waiting in her cell for her final sentence, the very accommodating Marco pleads with Veronica to play along with the Inquisition:

Marco: You must save yourself....Confess whatever foolishness they put before you....There is no honor with fools like these....
Veronica: If I give them my lie, I give them my soul. I'll lose everything I ever was. My love, my words, my heart.
Marco: Yes, but you would live.
Veronica: As someone else....There is no choice.

Veronica once more refuses the fraudulent plan that Marco proffers. She returns to court:

Inquisitor: Veronica Franco, you have been denounced a sorceress. Either confess and plead mercy or stand to receive my judgment.
Veronica: I will confess, Your Grace....I confess that as a young girl I loved a man who would not marry me for want of a dowry. I confess I had a mother who taught me a different way of life. One I resisted at first but learned to embrace. I confess I became a courtesan. Traded yearning for

power, welcomed many rather than be owned by one....I confess I
embraced a whore's freedom over a wife's obedience....I must confess my
evil as the church instructs. These are my sins....I confess I find more
ecstasy in passion than in prayer. Such passion is prayer....If this had not
been mine, if I had lived another way, a child to a husband's whim, my
soul hardened from lack of touch and lack of love, I confess such endless
days and nights would be punishment far greater than any you could mete
out....You, all of you, you who hunger for what I give but cannot bear to
see such power in a woman, you call God's greatest gift—ourselves, our
yearning, our need to love—you call it filth and sin and heresy....I repent
there was no other way open to me. I do not repent my life.

It is apparent at last that Veronica's eloquence is deeply rooted in fidelity
to the feminine. She stays true to what she learned from her mother: to
cherish her innate capacity to love herself and others, to venerate her
emotions, and to tolerate life's precarious ambiguities. And, as sometimes
happens in life, her consciousness is contagious.[15] The pure fire of her
spirit finally kindles a dormant cinder within Marco and his sister
Beatrice. No longer willing to collude with the inquiry through their
silence, they put themselves on trial alongside Veronica.

Marco: I demand the same rights of confession....I confess, I am her
accomplice. If she is a witch, then I am damned with her. Damn me....I
will not live without her....Arrest me too...Arrest the Senator of Venice for
witchcraft....
Beatrice: If she is a witch, then so is every woman in Venice.

Marco and Beatrice are emboldened not just by Veronica's own
forthrightness, but even more by the integrity that guides her life. They
know she is right not to yield. By refusing to sacrifice her fundamental
nature, Veronica revives the memory for all in the court of a markedly
different way to live in this world—where compassion, companionship
and compatibility inform the law—a loving spirit that, it turns out, still lies
deep in the heart of Venice. Now fully engaged, Marco makes a shocking
proposal to his countrymen:

Marco: I am not alone in loving this woman though I love her far, far more
than they. We accomplices were many and proud. If we do not speak now,
if Venice does not stand up now and acknowledge who she is, then we are
all damned not before this court, before eternity....Stand! Stand! Stand!
Declare your sins! Stand up with me as we stood against our enemies at
sea.

For an interminable time, no one budges.

Marco: Then I stand alone for Venice and this woman.

Then one at a time, Veronica's clients stand up. The male elite, uncharacteristically hesitant and awkward, but finally ruled by their conscience—civil servants and soldiers, the decrepit and the brawny, the intellectual and the landed—each one stands on Veronica's behalf. It seems that even the clerics are implicated, and the Doge himself is moved. In this sweet finale, the privileged males take the risk of exposing a relational side in men that is too often overlooked by women who imagine they have a corner on the feminine, and by men who focus only on maintaining a stalwart persona. Accepting Marco's challenge, each man has finally stepped out of the closet to expose his gratitude to Veronica. At last, Veronica no longer stands alone.

A Beauty's Distinct Mark

Though faced with considerable opposition, Veronica prevails, and we have to ask why. The answer the film gives is the entirety of her life, and her willingness, and the willingness of her many friends in Venice, to speak up for feminine principles. But what got her started on this provocative path? I believe it is that she listened to her mother, who right up until her death never stopped encouraging her daughter to shape her life according to her innate interests. Born during the feminine's sojourn under patriarchy, and bound by patriarchy's constricting stipulations, Signora Franco somehow managed to pass on to Veronica an unconventional legacy. Fortunately, of all that she anticipated for her daughter, Signora Franco's pragmatism is what Veronica integrated. Veronica took her mother's pragmatism and went on to make it her own, allowing herself to be propelled towards a life that her mother never dreamed could be viable. Because Veronica was such a quick study, she was able to surpass her mother's expectations and to transcend all the blinkered minds that tried to jeer her out of her way of meeting the world. In Veronica's final speech, spoken with her characteristic discrimination and feeling, we get to see how dangerous this beauty really is: having lived her life authentically for eros, and we realize that she has motivated those around her to embrace that kind of relatedness as well—wielding a mortal blow to the status quo.

References

Beebe, John (2000). "The Wizard of Oz: A Vision of Development in the American Political Psyche." In Singer, Thomas (ed.), *The Vision Thing*. London: Routledge.

—. (2002). "An Archetypal Model of the Self in Dialogue." In *Theory & Psychology*, vol. 12(2): 267-280.

Debold, Elizabeth, Wilson, Marie, and Malave, Idelisse (1993). *Mother Daughter Revolution: From Betrayal to Power*. Reading, MA: Addison-Wesley Publishing Company.

Friedrich, Paul (1979). *The Meaning of Aphrodite*. Chicago: The University of Chicago Press.

Grimm, Jacob & Wilhelm (1884). Margaret Hunt, trans. Online at: http://www.surlalunefairytales.com/authors/grimms.html

Jung, C. G. (1952/1969). *Answer to Job. Collected Works,* vol. 11.

—. (1954/1969). "Psychological Aspects of the Mother Archetype." In *Collected Works*, vol. 9i, 90-98.

Perrault, Charles (1697). "Bluebeard." In *Histoires ou Contes du temps passé*. Eng. trans. in Andrew Lang (ed.) (1965). *The Blue Fairy Book*, New York: Dover. (online at: http://www.surlalunefairytales.com/authors/perrault/bluebeard.html).

Rosenthal, Margaret F. (1992). *The Honest Courtesan: Veronica Franco, Citizen and Writer in Sixteenth Century Venice*. Chicago: The University of Chicago Press.

—. (2003). "Franco, Veronica (1546-1591) Venetian Courtesan Poet." http://www.lib.uchicago.edu/efts/IWW/BIOS/A0017.html (online, Italian Women Writers website of the University of Chicago).

Ulanov, Ann Belford (1971). *The Feminine in Jungian Psychology and in Christian Theology*. Evanston: Northwestern University Press.

Young-Eisendrath, Polly and Wiedemann, Florence (1987). *Female Authority: Empowering Women through Psychotherapy*. New York: Guilford Press.

Notes

[1] See Beebe (2000, 2002).

[2] To be sure, the film has made Veronica Franco's social victory seem more secure than it was. She did not get out of the trial unscathed. As Rosenthal (2003, 2) has written, "Her own defense, the help of Domenico Venier, and the predisposition of the Inquisitor freed her from the charges. But this began a downward spiral as her reputation was irreparably damaged. She was also severely impoverished by the plague years of 1575-77 in which she lost many of her valuable possessions through theft, and her faithful patron and friend of many years, Domenico Venier, died in 1582. Her tax declaration of 1582 stated that she was living in a section of the city where many destitute prostitutes ended their lives. Her death at forty-five ended a life that had included a decade of sumptuous wealth but also many difficulties, dangers, and losses."

[3] This discordance between the two feminine camps is deeply embedded in the mythology of the feminine in the patriarchal era, dating as far back as ancient Greece (see Friedrich's *The Meaning of Aphrodite* [1979], which traces the structural split between the goddesses in Indo-European civilization).

[4] *Klute* (1971). Screenplay by Andy Lewis and Dave Lewis. Directed by Alan J. Pakula.

[5] *Cabaret* (1972). Screenplay by John Van Druten. Directed by Bob Fosse.

[6] *Pretty Woman* (1990). Screenplay by J.F.Lawton. Directed by Garry Marshall.

[7] See Perrault (1697).

[8] See Grimm, Jacob & Wilhelm (1884).

[9] *Gigi* (1958). Screenplay by Alan Jay Lerner. Directed by Vincente Minnelli.

[10] See Young-Eisendrath and Wiedemann (1987) for an understanding of the implications of this term within Jungian psychotherapy.

[11] In Jungian psychology, eros is often described as "the feminine principle," but Ulanov points out that a "serious problem arises from the inevitable association of eros as psychic relatedness with Eros the masculine god of love. If the feminine principle is linked mythologically with a male god, then one is almost bound to conclude that the determining principle of the feminine is masculine….To associate the feminine exclusively with eros (relatedness and value reached through feeling) and to associate the masculine exclusively with logos (spirit and truth reached through objectivity) is to introduce a split in the sensibilities of woman." (Ulanov 1971, 336-37)

[12] *Norma Rae* (1979). Written by Harriet Frank Jr. and Irving Ravetch. Directed by Martin Ritt.

[13] *Erin Brockovich* (2000). Written by Susannah Grant. Directed by Steven Soderbergh.

[14] *North Country* (2005). Screenplay by Michael Seitzman. Directed by Niki Caro.

[15] This was a phrase the late Edward Edinger liked to use.

CHAPTER SEVEN

FEMININE HERO

JANE ALEXANDER STEWART

The Silence of the Lambs
(1991). Directed by Jonathan Demme.
Screenplay by Ted Tally, from the novel by Thomas Harris.

She emerges almost as if out of the earth and pulls herself up a steep incline, out of the abyss of a dark morning fog. As she reaches the top of the hill, she hesitates for a moment to get her bearings. The wings of a bird shudder and flutter. She starts to run. Alone in the woods, her footfalls echo in dead leaves crackling over hard ground. She picks up momentum, running slowly at first and then more rapidly, speeding through the deserted forest. Her eyes dart from side to side and she pushes herself to run faster with the resolve of a woman being chased, as if she fears some shadowy pursuer. Her breathing gets heavier. She scales a webbed fence three times her height and falls to the ground on the other side. Is there a sound of someone pushing his way through the bushes behind her? She breathes so loudly now that she would fail to hear the approach of any intruder and if he's there, she certainly doesn't see him. A man steps out behind her and calls out: "Starling!" She breaks from the obstacle course and, by the look in her eye, it's clear she works to be strong enough to compete with any man, that she won't be defeated by her size, her vulnerability, her sex. "Jack Crawford wants to see you in his office" (Tally 1989).[1]

In this very first scene, Jonathan Demme's terror-filled film *The Silence of the Lambs* from Ted Tally's Oscar winning screenplay sets the audience in position to identify with a new heroic journey of the feminine. When Jodie Foster makes her appearance, an FBI agent-in-training alone in the forest, we feel the context of danger that is the familiar hallmark of a woman's life. "She's not safe," the red light flashes in our brains. Any woman alone, anywhere, puts us on signal alert. Watching *Lambs* terrifies us because we, especially we as women, know the danger so well. We know a woman isn't safe living alone in her own apartment; and she tempts the fates when she chooses to run by herself through a park. Though classical mythology likens the female spirit to a nymph, at one with nature, invisible killers haunt the contemporary American landscape and women live with the fear that attack can come from out of nowhere. Not only do they fear men's attacks on their bodies but also they face denigrating social systems that reinforce a second-class status and devalue what it means to live through a feminine point of view.

The character of Clarice Starling represents an emerging model of a new female heroine. She embarks on a journey of confrontation with this hidden and pervasive annihilating force against the feminine in American society. Instead of following the precedent of most action/adventure films starring women, *The Silence of the Lambs* does not focus on the way in which a woman has to function from her masculine side in order to do a job that would conventionally have gone to a man. In Clarice, we see an action/adventure character who is full of feelings from beginning to end, one who never doubts that feelings are an asset, a source of power. We watch her balance her intuitive clarity with a skillful maneuvering of frank and intimate conversation. She has an uncanny ease with emotionally piercing scrutiny by her male bosses, peers and even the male killers. Close examination of her most private thoughts does not rattle her. If anything, she becomes more focused. She is responsive, not passive, in the face of male betrayals and holds a mirror for the transgressors to look at themselves. And, against all warnings, she continues to place importance on establishing real interpersonal trust with Hannibal "the Cannibal" Lecter.

Clarice begins her story where classic stories of the heroine's journey end; at the return to ordinary life after the descent. Whether or not the filmmakers are aware, the first image of *Lambs* shows Starling pulling herself up from a metaphorical feminine center like Inanna (the Sumerian goddess),[2] a vision that suggests a heroine making her return from the deep process of self-examination and affirmation. She lifts herself out of the abyss, stands at the top of the hill ready to go forward, to forge a career for herself guided by the strength she discovered on the inner journey. When Clarice Starling succeeds, she succeeds as a heroine who carries a set of feminine ethics. She goes beyond self-growth or professional accomplishment. She manages to achieve a far greater victory: she establishes the strength of the feminine up against unmitigated evil and creates hope for the safety of a feminine presence in our society. Clarice is a larger-than-life heroine, one who leads us on a newly unfolding quest to transform *fear* of the feminine and for the feminine into a *triumph* of the feminine.

To imagine that a woman is safe—safer—because she adheres to her feminine values sharply contradicts our usual thinking. Conventional male-oriented rules for survival are symbolized in *The Silence of the Lambs* by the FBI training that Clarice Starling receives: be strong, handle a gun properly, cover your back. By inference, this schooling suggests she must suppress her feminine qualities, qualities that are regarded both as provocation for attack and as explanation for women's helplessness. Even if the intention behind such training is coming from a desire to help women, schooling women to perform like men in order to achieve safety shows a refusal to trust or rely upon what the feminine has to offer.

The terror of *The Silence of the Lambs* is built upon our subliminal acceptance that a woman is, by her very nature, an invitation to irrational aggression from men. Before she receives her assignment, Starling has a moment alone in Crawford's office where she reacts to the pictures of serial killer Buffalo Bill's victims posted on Crawford's office walls. We know from the tensing in Jodie Foster's face that this photographic vision of mutilation of the feminine affects Clarice in a more personal way than it ever could affect one of her male colleagues. Here is the first of many examples of this theme: women experience things differently from men.

At this early point in the film, we simply feel the fear behind that difference. We imagine the worst: unlike male trainees, Clarice could become a victim of an attack like this herself. We feel doubly frightened when we see the emotional way in which photos of the victims of Buffalo Bill affect Clarice because we *expect* those feelings to render her a helpless victim. We anticipate that, because she reacts emotionally, she will be unable to shield herself from that terrible, lurking violent force we have all come to accept as a part of the fabric of our daily lives.

Because we in the audience have worked so hard to numb ourselves in our own lives, our judgment of Clarice is unconsciously guided by the expectations of societally-learned prejudices against the feminine. We hope that Agent Starling will submerge her natural inclinations to be emotional, that she will inhibit her true self; that if she insists on trying to become an FBI agent, she will at least be smart enough to realize that this is man's work and must be approached as if she were a man, performing the job the same way he would. We hope that she will emulate the male role model. And that hope is our Achilles heel. We are afraid to identify with Starling, to choose her inclusion of emotionality as a path of honor and nobility. Her lack of regard for the rules heightens our fear even further as she ignores what we have been taught makes a woman safe.

"Do you spook easily?" Crawford asks Clarice just after he enters the office. On the surface, Jack Crawford appears to be the perfect father-figure and mentor, tough but interested in helping Starling's advancement within the FBI. He evaluates her outstanding record as if she were any of one his trainees, and our inclination is to interpret his treating her without special attention to gender as proof of his open-minded professionalism. But, this indifference speaks to a subliminal prejudice. Pretending to ignore Clarice's sexuality reinforces the belief system that says we should discourage the feminine approach in this arena where crimes must be solved and killers brought to justice. This is the Department of Behavioral Science, a world where agents must be trained to deal with serial killers who skin their victims. And Clarice is about to encounter a man who eats people alive, so terrifying that he can't even be trusted behind normal lock and key. An almost morbid curiosity is set in the minds of the audience: if men fear Hannibal Lecter so greatly, what spectacle will we observe when a woman encounters him?

We hesitate embracing Clarice Starling as an authentic hero for this story. The majority of stories told in our culture feature boys or men as protagonists and present human dilemmas through the masculine ethic. Using Joseph Campbell's outline[3] of the hero's journey, it begins with the "call to adventure." The assignment—such as Luke Skywalker accepting the challenge to rescue Princess Leia—will be of the highest order and promises to put the hero to the ultimate test, helping him to learn what unique gifts he has to offer the world. The key to any heroic adventure is in the central character recognizing himself as in some way unique and outstanding. The mentor, Obi Wan Kenobe, teaches Luke that the Force is within him, that he must discover his inner power.

The stories of our culture, in the film arts as well as in literature, support a man's adventure to discover his outstanding qualities but inner feminine principles are not viewed as heroic. "'Cries very easily',," writes Susan Brownmiller in the chapter "Emotion" from her book entitled *Femininity*, "was rated by a group of professional psychologists as a highly feminine trait" (1984, 207). The goal of the study, she goes on to remind us, is to elucidate the way in which "stereotypic femininity was a grossly negative assessment of the female sex and, furthermore, that many so-called feminine traits ran counter to clinical descriptions of maturity and mental health." In a letter to the *Los Angeles Times*, a female probation officer took offense to Jodie Foster's Academy-Award-night acceptance speech in which she called her character in *The Silence of the Lambs* a feminist hero. "The only way," this woman wrote, that Clarice Starling "got any pertinent information from Hannibal was to use her femininity (read 'vulnerability'), not through any superior analytical investigative skills." In other words, the only method of heroic behavior many women in positions of power know how to embrace is that which can be identified with the masculine: find out the facts, crash down the door, shove the gun out in front, throw the perpetrator on the floor, force his arms behind him and clap on the handcuffs.

Suspense builds as Starling makes herself an exception to these masculine rules of survival. She acts in a spontaneous and natural manner, following a compelling instinct to establish a relationship with Lecter. In her book *Psychotherapy Grounded in the Feminine Principle*, Barbara Stevens Sullivan writes the following:

> Masculine consciousness depends on splitting the world into opposites, on separating elements from their union with each other....Masculine consciousness separates the individual from his dark inner labyrinth: instead, the individual reaches in and pulls something out to be examined in the clear light of day, in the process of differentiation....The central value of the dynamic feminine principle is Eros: the connections between individuals, the relationships that encircle our lives....We call this feminine consciousness "wisdom." It is the intelligence of the heart, even of the stomach, it is the wisdom of feeling (1989, 17-27).

In what might be described as the metaphorical inner labyrinth of our country's soul, Clarice makes a connection with what the masculine-oriented world hides away and dismisses as an enemy. Throughout the film, Clarice reaches out to intermingle with the "opposite," regarding the darkest areas of human nature as something she can learn from instead of categorizing them as monstrous and abhorrent. Her success lies in her wisdom of feeling. Through the power of her relationship with Lecter, she is able to draw him out and gain critical insights.

"Just do your job," Crawford commands Clarice. His advice is clear: feelings will work to her disadvantage. In a man's story, the strong and rational Crawford would be an appropriate mentor. In Clarice's story, he fails to see the force within her: "You're to tell him nothing personal, Starling....And never forget what he is." True to the cultural prejudice against women, Crawford's message to Clarice says she must learn to be someone other than who *she* is. Her inner forces (for example trusting in intuition, in revealing herself and interacting on the level of intimacy) are seen as her worst enemies, perhaps greater enemies than even the outer threat of an adversary like Hannibal Lecter.

This figure who in a classic hero's story would prove to be a mentor turns out to be a symbol of patriarchal disregard for the feminine in

Lambs' heroine's story. In a hero's story, Jack Crawford would send his trainee to see Lecter as if he were going off to slay his dragon. In giving Clarice her assignment, Crawford downplays its importance (he calls it more of an "interesting errand" than a true assignment and assures her he expects little or no results). A few scenes into *The Silence of the Lambs* and it has already been established that agent Starling has to depend on skills her FBI training does not provide. Crawford's half-hearted deception/offer hardly resembles a hero's call to action but something in his presentation arouses the heroine's attention. "What's the urgency?" Clarice wants to know. Intuition tells Clarice that she is onto something important. She senses Crawford's dishonesty. She refuses Crawford's attempt to gain obedience by frightening her with his simplistic description of evil. She shifts from intuition to another feminine trait we see her use often, the depth-searching question. "What is [Lecter] *exactly*?" Clarice wants to know.

"He's a monster," the chief psychologist Dr. Chilton answers in an elliptical film-cut to the maximum security asylum. "Crawford's very clever, isn't he, using...a pretty young woman to turn [Lecter] on." Now we learn that Crawford deliberately misled her, hoping her innocence would be disarming to a menacing killer he knows might have information regarding the Buffalo Bill case. Crawford dismissed her ability to be effective if she knew the seriousness of her task. Crawford not only fails to acknowledge Starling's value, he feigns a protective attitude as a cover to exploit her femininity, as a lure to engage her cooperation without revealing his motive.

Where Crawford veiled his sexism, Dr. Chilton can't seem to contain a leering misogyny: "We get a lot of detectives here but I must say I can't ever remember one quite as attractive," he says upon meeting Starling. From the moment she leaves the training ground, in the very first encounter of her very first case, Clarice endures an open verbal assault on her sexuality. Chilton alternately insults her and then flirts with her, refusing to accept her lack of interest and professional manner. She holds her ground as Chilton reveals he has no respect for Starling, not because she is a trainee, but because she is a woman; he amplifies his disdain when she refuses his advances. Again, the experience of the heroic journey changes because Agent Starling is a woman. She can't rely on the patriarchal system to nurture or respect her talents.

As they travel down into the cellars of the building, below the ground, towards the gallows where the state keeps its most demonic criminals, Dr. Chilton coldly briefs her on the rules regarding conversations with Hannibal Lecter. His prelude would frighten even the strong at heart.

Clarice surprises us. She stops and asks to proceed alone. While Clarice's request might be interpreted as an effort to take control and assume a certain masculine bravado, her agenda remains hidden: she wants to approach Lecter on her own terms. She knows everyone has failed in trying to gain cooperation from Lecter and maneuvers an opportunity to be alone with him, using feminine wiles for the first time in order to gain advantage. She finesses her rejection of Chilton by flattering him as someone with a power that Lecter reviles. Going alone to the interview with Lecter, Clarice will be able to test and challenge herself, to plumb the depths of her personal strength. Like a true heroine, she furthers her own spiritual search as she pursues the information necessary to solving the Buffalo Bill case.

If the opening scene of the movie hinted at the way in which we fear for a woman's ability to protect herself, Clarice's slow approach to Hannibal Lecter's cell vividly reminds us that locks and keys are not adequate reassurance. Even the following written description of this scene from Ted Tally's screenplay sends chills:

INTERIOR. DR. LECTER'S CORRIDOR.

MOVING SHOT—with Clarice, as her footsteps echo. High to her right, surveillance cameras. On her left, cells. Some are padded, with narrow observation slits, others are normal, barred....Shadowy occupants pacing, muttering. Suddenly, a dark figure in the next-to-last cell hurtles towards her, his face mashing grotesquely against the bars as he hisses: "I can smell your cunt!" (1989, 8-9).

Clarice's dress surely does not project an invitation to seduction in this scene but nevertheless she draws out sexual advances from hidden places by her sheer physical presence. The whispered obscenity of Lecter's cellmate, Miggs, burns like a hot coal reminding us of Clarice's inherent vulnerability. She has entered into America's underground, the place we hide away the worst imaginable sociopaths, the physical representations of our greatest fears; and the object of their aggression is female sexuality. This symbolic underbelly of society holds a dark male secret, a lust for and hatred against the mysterious power of the feminine. From emotional fragility all the way through to the flash of a leg out of a slit-backed skirt, woman is seen as target in our culture. And because Clarice goes alone, we as the audience get our first view of what sustains the female heroine and helps her hold steadfast while being tested and degraded.

The confrontations between Agent Starling and Hannibal Lecter take us into new territory where we can begin to see the advantage of a woman at work with the demonic. Her method is receptive and responsive from the outset: she avoids a power struggle with the supernaturally charismatic doctor and instead defers to his authority. "I'm here to learn from you," she offers, reaching out to Lecter with an odd respect. He tests her sincerity immediately, asking what Miggs said to her, wanting to see how capable she is of emotional honesty; and she meets his challenge without reservation. Everything Clarice has been taught and told, from the most subliminal messages of systemic sexism to the direct warnings she's received from Crawford and Chilton, urges her not to allow Lecter even the most minimal insight into her feelings. Still, within moments of their first interaction, this heroine appears almost reckless in her willingness to engage Lecter.

That orientation towards personal connection affects Lecter more than even he might suspect. Where Crawford approached Clarice's gender with indifference, and everyone from the respected psychiatrists of the world (Chilton) to the deranged deviants (Miggs) respond to her sexuality with varying degrees of uninvited arousal, Hannibal Lecter acknowledges Clarice as unique. He finds himself fascinated, not titillated, by her character. In their first meeting, Jack Crawford read Starling's resume. Lecter reads her soul: who are you, where do you come from, what have you run from, and where do you want to go?

Her individuality intrigues him. She reveals herself and makes it clear that she is more than an FBI agent. She is a person, and, even more important, a woman. Later in the film, when the mother of the latest Buffalo Bill captive makes a televised plea for her child's life, Clarice remarks on how smart it is to make the killer aware of the girl as a feeling human being. "If he sees her as a person," Clarice says, "it's harder to tear her up." By giving Lecter a sense of who she is, Clarice has affected his desire to destroy her.

In their first meeting, Lecter does dismiss Clarice in an angry fit over her bold assertion that he use his high-powered perception to evaluate himself, but when, on her retreat from Lecter's cell, Miggs defiles Clarice by flinging his animal-semen at her face, Lecter is highly agitated. Witnessing this degrading attack on Clarice's sexuality spurs Lecter into a frenzy, and he offers her a proper call to adventure. He calls Clarice back and awards her with information directly related to the Buffalo Bill case.

Though the audience audibly gasps each time Clarice violates the rules and ignores the warning to remain impersonal, the underground demon surfaces now as Clarice's mentor. The true call to heroine action, the call to rise above ego, comes from the dark side. "Go deep within yourself," Lecter says echoing Obi Wan Kenobe, and he gives her a real life and death assignment that will lead to her finding Buffalo Bill. Her interpersonal treatment of Lecter elicits his feelings of empathy for her and prompts him to give her what she wants most: "advancement."

There is no doubt that on the surface he means to say he offers her advancement within the FBI system. However, the advancement he offers holds symbolic meaning as well and refers to her heroine's journey. Starling's "job" involves more than just catching a criminal. This story focuses on a woman who, while in training to develop her masculine side, discovers her exceptional nature lies in her ability to utilize feminine powers. She confronts an almost mythic demon who demands an emotional exchange whereby she must yield her softest innards in order to gain his cooperation. She opens herself up to Lecter and trusts—not in him—but in her own feminine capabilities as weapons in her fight for life and safety.

In translating Thomas Harris' novel into screenplay form, the filmmakers changed the name of the storage facility from "Split City Mini-Storage" to "Yourself Storage," heightening the metaphor of the heroine's journey, sending Starling literally deep within herself. And why did Demme photograph the scene to feel as though it were underwater? Here is a quotation excerpted from *The Woman's Encyclopedia of Myths and Secrets*:

> Students in mythology find that when the feminine principle is subjected to sustained attack, it often quietly submerges. Under the water (where organic life began) it swims through the subconscious of the dominant male society, occasionally bobbing to the surface to offer a glimpse of the rejected harmony (Walker 1983, 1066).

In fact, the filmmakers continually photographed Clarice's voyage to feel as though it occurs in the underwater and the underground, the arenas of feminine exploration, emphasizing the closeness to the ebb and flow of nature and darkness that a woman experiences. She then resurfaces to resume her FBI training where her methods contrast against and test masculine rules for success.

"I don't know how to *feel* about this, sir," Clarice says when Crawford tells her that Lecter induced Miggs' suicide, presumably on her behalf. "You don't have to feel anyway about it," he responds. This is a key scene regarding the delineation between the masculine and the feminine principle. Crawford thinks answers lie in the facts of what Lecter says while Clarice searches for meaning from the way his actions make her feel. Again from Sullivan's book:

Masculine knowing seeks laser-like clarity that fosters perfection,
analyzing life from a rational perspective, breaking it down into
component parts, examining each piece, judging it in a directed,
disciplined logical way....Feminine knowing orients toward a state of
wholeness that includes imperfection and that blurs edges and
differentiations, a consciousness which exists within close proximity to the
unconscious (Sullivan 1989, 17-27).

The masculine approach disregards feelings and exalts factual
information. The heroine works through feelings in order to make sense of
factual information. Clarice has a "feeling" that Lecter was speaking
metaphorically when he gave her the assignment to check out his former
patient Hester Mofet. Clarice evaluated the message in context of Lecter's
character and decided he couldn't have been sincere about telling her to
"look deep within yourself," that there must be some hidden message
behind the phrase. Nothing in the facts of what we have seen would lead
us to deduce, logically, that Hester Mofet was an anagram or that Lecter
wanted Clarice to discover a "Yourself Storage Facility." She uncovers
those details through some unexplained intuitive understanding of Lecter's
mind and, because of that ability, finds herself pulling back the American
flag, deep within "Yourself," from the coffin-like hearse that holds the
first clue connecting Lecter to the Buffalo Bill case.

This American flag Clarice pulls back is the first in a long list of
references *Lambs* makes to American society. A close viewing reveals that
when Clarice finally kills Buffalo Bill, a stray bullet breaks open a
window and a small, tattered flag finally sees the light of day. The
American flag also hovers above Buffalo Bill's sewing machine and he
abducts his Wonder Bread-fed size fourteen girl-next-door victims from
the very heartland of the country. When we meet the U.S. Senator's frizzy-
haired blonde daughter, Katherine, just before she becomes Buffalo Bill's
next captive, she's belting out this Tom Petty lyric, singing along with her
car radio:

After all it was a great big world
With lots of places to run to
And if she had to die tryin'
She had one little promise she was gonna keep...

O yeah, all right
Take it easy, baby
Make it last all night
She was an American girl (Petty 1979)

* * *

The filmmakers clearly wanted *The Silence of the Lambs* to be more than a horror film; this is intended to be a culturally meaningful story about the patterns of our society that lead to this unacceptable victimization of women. What dynamics of the feminine do killers exploit? What societally suppressed powers of the feminine need to be re-emphasized in order to change the cycle of brutality? How is it that our mothers, sisters, and girlfriends find themselves cowering in the back of a van, trapped by a serial killer?

Haven't all women, at one time or another, walked from their cars, maybe even carrying groceries, and found some stranger or neighbor in need of a hand? The threat of danger usually overrides the natural inclination to offer assistance to someone in need; but every now and then, hasn't everyone just decided to put those groceries down and help push that car up the driveway or grab the end of that heavy couch? In her book *In a Different Voice*, Carol Gilligan writes:

> The moral imperative that emerges repeatedly in interviews with women is an injunction to care, a responsibility to discern and alleviate "the real and recognizable trouble" of the world. For men, the moral imperative appears rather as an injunction to respect the rights of others and thus to protect from interference the rights to life and self-fulfillment (Gilligan 1982, 100).

Women like to help. It's part of their desire to make connections, open up possibilities, to give and receive from each other. The violent serial killer, like Buffalo Bill, appeals to that desire and then exploits it. He draws upon a woman's generosity and then attacks her; and (the male-oriented) society turns the event around, blaming the woman for engaging in the interaction in the first place.

Blaming the victim distorts and undercuts a woman's ability to protect herself. American culture socializes women away from their natural means of defense. The character Katherine hesitates when the stranger asks her to step into his van and carry the couch all the way back where she'll be unable to escape if he is indeed Buffalo Bill. Her intuition tells her she should switch off her helping mode and stay out of the van, but she does as she's told and steps into danger anyway. She doesn't back away, retreat. Why? Like Katherine, American girls are taught from childhood to be the "good girl," to be agreeable and compliant, to promote an amiable emotional environment, to nurture even when it goes against innermost

intuitive feelings of danger. In 1848, pioneer feminist Elizabeth Cady
Stanton, made the following, capitalized declaration to reporters:

SELF-DEVELOPMENT   IS   A   HIGHER   DUTY   THAN   SELF-
SACRIFICE (Gilligan 1982, 129).

By contrast, whether its message is directed toward a woman who follows
the traditional goal to "stand by her man" or toward one, like Clarice,
whose professional training suggests the importance of *being* like a man,
patriarchal society teaches women to serve its goals at the expense of their
own, less-linear, values.

The breakthrough aspect of *Lambs* is that the closer Clarice comes to
accepting her true feminine self, the closer she gets to solving the crime;
and the closer she gets to solving the crime, the more she has to grapple
with who she is as a person. In their first meeting, Lecter chides Clarice
for trying to cover up her hinterland roots. She surfaces from their tense
confrontation in tears and has a comforting vision, from her provincial
childhood, of her father returning home. Contrary to the negative
assessment of what it means to cry easily, here we see a woman's inner,
private life appearing to nurture her and help her work through the fear she
has just been courageous enough to confront. When Crawford pulls her
out of class and steps up her participation in the Buffalo Bill case, Clarice
ironically has to go back to Virginia, the unsophisticated "state" from
where she came. Both *Lambs* and Clarice Starling take Elizabeth Cady
Stanton's advice by taking the next step. Clarice's self-development
overcomes her fears of inadequacy and leads her to an even higher duty of
asserting her feminine presence in the world. Self-acceptance leads to self-
expression.

With her penchant for matter of fact confrontation of authority figures
and her reliance on feeling, Clarice exhibits a growing confidence in her
feminine complexity after she returns from her mission into the "self-
storage" facility to meet with Lecter for the second time. Anything but the
good girl, Clarice sits on the floor, wet from her submersion into the
unconscious state of exploration and discovery, and she thoughtfully
exposes her exhilaration at finding the beheaded former client of Dr.
Lecter. As her emotional bravery becomes more visible, we are impressed
and tentatively begin to look for Clarice Starling to be the one who will
find the killer through her privileged conversations with this demon. We
begin to trust in what initially we feared the most and are prepared to
follow her on the heroine's journey that could transform our constrictive
beliefs about the feminine.

Our first inclinations lead us to fear that Lecter has the upper hand, that he feeds Starling information in a way that will further endanger her. Because she reveals herself, maybe she isn't "watching her back," and ultimately Lecter will make his offer of collusion in an effort to do her in. Somewhere, somehow, he has a master plan to get out and kill everyone; and Clarice must be playing directly into his hands. Though resistance toward taking the path of heroism through feminine principles is difficult to overcome, the audience enters wholeheartedly into this heroine's quest; we want Starling to succeed in her unorthodox method not just for her but for ourselves as well. We begin to trust Clarice not because she is capable and resilient but because she has exceptional talents suited to this particular battle.

Clarice's ability to set the boundaries between revealing herself and allowing exploitation defines both the level and the complexity of her heroic interactive skills: it puts her on par with Lecter's analytic prowess. Though she tacitly gives Lecter permission to probe her with personal questions, when he uses that privilege to focus on Jack Crawford's sexual interest in her, she stops him cold, refusing to dignify his verbal fantasy of Crawford's special interest in her with an answer. "Frankly, doctor, that doesn't interest me," she asserts, "It's the kind of thing Miggs would say." That emotional sophistication protects her both from her fear of Lecter and from our own subliminally-accepted sexism out in the audience. The ability to differentiate emotional rapport from exploitation is one of the distinctive, heroic capacities of feminine instinct. Acting upon it enhances Clarice's status and establishes a boundary with Lecter: Lecter cannot take her as a fool. From this point on, Clarice's subtle, unspoken pride in her inner power must be honored. This is not to suggest that Lecter stops testing her or that he divulges his secrets to agent Starling easily. As always, the demon/mentor has more in mind than helping Clarice solve the Buffalo Bill case. Clarice has established for herself a relationship that parallels the Obi Wan Kenobe/Luke Skywalker model: as she presses for answers that will help her complete her outer pursuit, Lecter holds out in order to teach her about her inner quest.

"All good things to those who wait," is Lecter's tutelary snake-like response to Clarice's demand to know who killed his former patient. This epithet, especially suited to the heroine's journey, speaks to the importance of the feminine ideal of immersion and contemplation, to let one's growth process "happen," so as to avoid blocking a discovery that is trying to surface in its own way.

Throughout this testing of her patience, Clarice is learning to accept and rely upon her unique self, now, in *all* its facets. Confronted by the grisly reality and heinous condition of the killer's latest victim in an autopsy scene, she drops any countenance of urbanity. Now, both her gender and her provenance work in her favor. Her understanding of the specificities of the habits of a "girl from the city" (versus one from the town) leads her to uncover things about the victim (the way her nails are painted means she is more likely to come from a particular area) that no other examiner can see. She is coming to a fuller awareness of the significance of self-respect or, in other words, she is learning the importance of cherishing and not disqualifying for any reason one's personal background experiences as valuable and relevant to the task at hand.

More important, we see Clarice consistently return to her inner gifts in order to further her double goal in the outer world which is to solve the case while gaining recognition for feminine principles. This dual agenda emerged in an earlier scene, when Crawford had resorted to a sexist ploy to win over the local sheriff. The FBI is being met with a cold reception for intruding into the community grief at the funeral of a hometown girl. Under the pretense of protecting Starling's delicate ears from hearing the description of the condition of the skinned girl, Crawford seeks—and obtains—a private conversation with the sheriff. Far from shielding Clarice, the exclusion draws attention to her sex from a roomful of male deputies, all of whom are already hostile to the FBI's intrusion into their investigation. Crawford leaves her standing alone to withstand the probing social gaze of these local policemen whose attention he has focused on her alleged inadequacy. Once again, we got a chance to see this action/adventure heroine plunge down inward. Without an ally to protect her from the invasive stares, she withdraws from a scene as uncomfortable as any of the film's more graphically malevolent moments by entering into the room of mourners and recalling a fantasy memory of her father's funeral.

Clarice's recurrent retreats into childhood memory imply that feeling images, even sad ones, have restorative power. Clarice's feminine strength helps her gain control of her emotions. She "resurfaces" from this immersion into self and handles the deputies with a heroic feminine gesture. Choosing not to assert her authority as an FBI agent to dismiss the deputies' participation from the autopsy, Clarice speaks up and assures the men she understands their concerns. She asserts her control by taking their feelings seriously, deftly circumventing the power struggle in an unexpected way. Later, in the car, Crawford acknowledges his mistreatment of her. He tries to seek her approval, and she holds her ground to make what appears to be a small point, illuminating the higher value of the act. "Cops look at you to see how to act. It matters," she reprimands. Her point is taken: as a man in a position of authority, his devaluing of her leads to a greater acceptance of sexism. This is a subtle representation of what is the larger and most important issue that the film addresses. It is not sufficient to make a place for a woman on the job: what is needed is a place for the feminine to be expressed. Those men who hold positions of authority must break old habits of sexism and interact with the values and perspective of the women close to them.

The feminine hero wants male respect both for her ability to hold down a traditionally male job and to assert her own way of being in that job. She wants to enter and wield power in traditionally male institutions but with her feminine intact, perhaps even doubly committed to feminine values. She may lack development in the male skills, be symbolically "in-training" like Clarice, but she is also making demands on her colleagues and superiors to accept the intrinsic value of a feminine orientation, one that has developed as a consequence of experiencing life as a female. Just as Clarice's goal involves more than finding the killer, the new heroine's goal reaches beyond any desire to overthrow the patriarchy: it strives instead for a transformation of what has become heartless in patriarchy, seeking above all, a societal rebalancing.

"What did you mean by transformation, doctor?" Clarice asks Lecter after she has revealed her worst memory of childhood and earned her turn to question him. Quid pro quo—a fair exchange: that is the ethic of Clarice and Lecter's confrontations with each other. The startling realization that these two could share an ethic suggests a symbolic basis for healing the imbalance in masculine and feminine principles that creates such frightening aggression in our culture. "Billy wasn't born a criminal, Clarice. He was made one through years of systematic abuse," answers Lecter. "Billy hates his own identity, you see, and thinks that makes him a transsexual. But his pathology is a thousand times more savage, more terrifying."

Buffalo Bill's character suffers from a severe detachment from his feminine, a theme that touches on us all, regardless of gender. This is a killer so out of touch with what it means to be feminine that he thinks he can achieve womanhood through stitching together a costume made from the hide of the outermost definition of what it means to be feminine. This is a sinister aggressive new strategy by the masculine to take an unmerciful hold on the feminine by appropriating its persona. Risking a homophobic interpretation, Demme presents the psychological disarray of Buffalo Bill (a character who disappointed many viewers, in contrast to the texture found in Starling and Lecter) as a masculine dementia driven to the point of pathological persecution and destruction of the female in the outer world. It is noteworthy that the pathological behavior of coveting what is coveted (in this case, a woman's appearance—her outer skin) finds credence as a desperate attempt on the part of a male killer for some remnant of self-esteem. This is an even darker thread of the evil wrought by the schism between masculine and feminine: a man trying to reverse self-hatred by killing and then clothing himself in a superficial representation of what he lacks within.

Resistance to using a feminine orientation as an inner authority is particularly intense because claiming authority as Clarice does means confronting that which male authority often fears the most: its unknown territory, its darkness. Masculine-oriented storytelling builds the hope that we can dominate life, that we can exclude darkness. Stories in which the good-hearted hero defeats the evil villain carry on the fiction of possibility that we can live happily ever. This masculine ethic of transcendence through domination reinforces an escapist interpretation of institutionalized aggressive behavior. The familiar result, socially, is to live in a false state of security, a world run by the masculine principle of protection from harm where killers lurk behind every tree. In such a world, women aren't safe to offer the counterbalance that includes respect for the dark side, an embracing of the side of humanity where solutions are not clear and problems of the shadow persist to the point that evil is a fact of life that must be continually confronted.

While Clarice does manage to fulfill the audience's expectations for heroic action by killing Buffalo Bill, the rescue sequence in the murderer's house is a parade of the heroine's powerlessness against controlling the evil underworld rather than the usual heralding of an FBI agent's ability to save the day. It is hard to recall a film in which the triumphing hero seemed more vulnerable. As in her submersion into "Yourself Storage", or her descent to visit Lecter's gallows, Clarice almost swims through the depths of Buffalo Bill's sub-aqueous maze while he toys with his power to reach out and touch her in the darkness. What would in the usual detective film be the hero's victory in battle against the antagonist feels instead like a narrow escape from victimization; only in a flash of frightened intuition does agent Starling manage to fire her gun in the right direction and save herself from the very fate of the kind of girl she has set out to liberate. This thin victory leaves the audience feeling unsettled because the threat of victimization continues: we don't feel secure about the defeat of the villain.

The masculine journey, to which we have become so inured, resolves through conquering and winning, (Lucas made it work by locking into the joy of his boy-hero in Star Wars) but this feminine journey fails to wrap itself up so neatly. When in a masculine hero's journey, our knight slays the dragon, the new equilibrium is one of safety and the townspeople shower gifts upon their savior. Solving the Buffalo Bill case, on the other hand, gives Starling little more than an official commendation, and leaves the largest relationship of *The Silence of the Lambs* unresolved: we know that Lecter escaped and remains at large. Even as she graduates with honors, with the always reticent Crawford adding his supposedly supreme compliments, a dry assurance that her father would be proud, Clarice gets a phone call from Hannibal Lecter. Crawford's awkward and indirect praise is contrasted with Lecter's presumptuously easy style and pointed congratulations, which imply that he hasn't forgotten their negotiation for a fair exchange. We respond to his insinuation uneasily: does she still owe him something? Even though we allow that their connection is strong and Clarice has proven herself a worthy adversary, we slip back into identifying with a woman who has violated all the rules, revealed herself and told too much. It's clearly not over. "I'll not be coming after you." Lecter's words are so unexpected that they ring out even as he speaks them in soft tones. "The world's a more interesting place with you in it." he explains. What has moved Lecter, the symbol of pure evil, to set this boundary of safety for Clarice? Why does the demon choose to let the heroine live? Is it possible that vulnerability has developed a safe passage instead of invited disaster? Could empathy and intimacy have protective power? We are left with questions.

Symbolically, this is Clarice's greatest triumph: she has achieved a new state of equilibrium on the darkest level where feminine values can not only withstand but *co-exist* with the hidden and terrifying consequences of an extreme masculine emphasis on control of objectionable elements. When Lecter asks Starling for reciprocity, for his liberty from her pursuit, she defines her power through empathetic language, "You know I can't do that,"—and here again she appeals, with confidence, to the connection between them. She doesn't say *I* can't do that, as if she were now separate and apart from him. She does not abandon the feminine orientation but keeps it as a basis for action. Her honesty is part of the balance, part of the give and take that is key to the bargain that the *Lambs* characters have established as a precedent for collaboration. Above all other imposed responsibilities, codes of honor or magnanimous pacts of exchange, it is Clarice Starling's prerogative to affect the world through asserting her principles and she takes it as her duty to do so. On a literal level, she can't let Lecter go because he is a criminal and she is an FBI agent; more profoundly, she can't let aggression that breeds on detachment live freely without offering the opposition of intimacy as a balance. In symbolic terms, the masculine and feminine opposites are not independent of each other: one force simply cannot prevail without influence from the other. *The Silence of the Lambs* ultimately suggests that the feminine hero's goal lies not in destroying the demon that masculinity has become under patriarchy but by creating a relationship with him, to affirm feminine value in a hostile world that has forgotten how desperately it needs her.

The Silence of the Lambs is an unusual story of a woman who, even in the face of all the pressure to behave like a man in order to remain safe and achieve success, confronts her fear, and in turn challenges our fear that to be feminine means you are a vulnerable target and a deserving victim. A symbol of the modern woman who no longer finds herself in the role of looking solely for personal approval or acceptance in a professional position, Clarice is neither demanding nor rebellious. She asserts her values with a self-possessed presence and a matter of fact manner of expression. She is able to gain crucial information from the most renowned serial killer alive as well as to learn from him. She succeeds where men have failed. By the time the movie ends, the hero has done the usual. She has saved the girl, destroyed the bad guy and graduated with honors; but something does not feel usual, ordinary. This hero won the day not by being an expert, male-identified FBI agent, but by breaking away and asserting herself as a woman who could rely on her feminine self to provide her with the special or "super" strength she needed. In this breakthrough film, as Jodie Foster recognized, the filmmakers vaunt a new type of heroine, one whose *feminine* capabilities make her exceptional.

References

Brownmiller, Susan (1984). *Femininity.* New York: Fawcett Columbine.
Campbell, Joseph (1949/1968). *The Hero with a Thousand Faces.* Princeton: Princeton University Press.
Demme, Jonathan (dir.) (1991). *The Silence of the Lambs.* Videocassette. Orion Home Video.
Gilligan, Carol (1982). *In a Different Voice.* Cambridge: Harvard University Press.
Perera, Sylvia Brinton (1981). *Descent to the Goddess.* Toronto: Inner City Books.
Petty, Tom (1979). "American Girl." Almo Music Corp. (ASCAP) All rights administered by Almo Music Corp. (ASCAP) For the World. All rights reserved. *International © Secured.*

Tally, Ted (1989). *The Silence of the Lambs*. Unpublished version of the screenplay based on the novel by Thomas Harris, with notes, 28 July 1989.

Sullivan, Barbara Stevens (1989). *Psychotherapy Grounded in the Feminine Principle*. Wilmette, Illinois: Chiron Publications.

Walker, Barbara G. (1983). *The Woman's Encyclopedia of Myths and Secrets*. San Francisco: Harper and Row.

Notes

[1] This speech and those following were transcribed by the author from the video of *The Silence of the Lambs* (Demme 1991).

[2] See Perera for the extraordinary relevance of this Sumerian goddess to the psychology of contemporary women (1981).

[3] See Campbell (1949/1968, 36-37).

OPPOSING PERSONALITY AND TRICKSTER

CHAPTER EIGHT

HITCHCOCK'S OPPOSING PERSONALITY

JOHN BEEBE

Marnie

(1964). Directed by Alfred Hitchcock.
Screenplay by Jay Presson Allen, based on the novel by Winston Graham.

With its compelling but strangely mismatched stars, Tippi Hedren and Sean Connery, and its gothic psychoanalytic plot, Hitchcock's *Marnie* draws the viewer into an emotional field that is uncanny and archetypal. It does this primarily through the director's dialogue with his central image, which is the character Marnie herself.

Hitchcock's famous interviews with François Truffaut were conducted in 1962, just as he was planning *Marnie*. At just this time, Andy Warhol was making the silk screens of celebrity images that launched Pop Art. Images we had taken for granted began to be seen in a new way, inaugurating an interrogation of the image, which has since exploded into everything we now know as postmodernism. To the French New Wave director Hitchcock confided, "One of the reasons most films aren't sufficiently rigorous is that so few people in the industry know anything about imagery" (Truffaut 1967, 201).

It is easy to forget that we are looking at images on the screen and not flesh-and-blood human beings. I became aware of the difference when I was filmed for Stephen Segaller's 1990 documentary about analytical psychology, *The Wisdom of the Dream*. There was an interesting person up there on the screen, but I couldn't identify him as me; he was my lunar twin saved on the silver screen. It is said that Garbo, in New York, used to go to the Museum of Modern Art for private showings of her own movies. As she watched, she would say things like, "Watch her now! She's going to ask for money. Then she'll go outdoors and smoke a cigarette. Oh my, look at the way she's done her hair" (Bainbridge 1971, 4). The star in retirement knew she was not the same as her screen image, and I suppose that saved her life.

It is important that we recognize these personality manifestations as images, if we are going to talk about them psychologically. If one reifies them too much into men and women, one loses some of the movement that takes place in the mind when one is able to stand back and contemplate the image. Of course we do not just contemplate these images, we also identify with them. All of film watching involves a balance, a teeter-totter between contemplation of the image and identification with it. Hitchcock is quite aware of that balance in the psychology of viewing, and he spends a lot of time playing with it. Consider the film's opening sequence:

> After the titles, we see "a yellow handbag, a deserted platform, a woman with her back to us" (Bellour 2000, 219.) We hear Mr. Strutt, the head of an accounting office, bark, "Robbed! Cleaned out! Nine thousand nine hundred and sixty seven dollars! Precisely as I told you over the telephone. That girl did it. Marion Holland, that's the girl, Marion Holland." Mark Rutland (Sean Connery) appears in the doorway while Mr. Strutt is giving his evidence to the police. The camera shifts to Marnie (Tippi Hedren) arriving in her hotel room, briefly observed by Hitchcock himself. She rinses black dye out of her hair, which we had assumed was a wig, and reveals herself, full-face, to be a beautiful honey blonde. She puts on different clothes and assumes a new identity. The clothes belonging to her old identity she locks in a bus station locker, dropping the key into a grate in the floor.

In his book, *The Analysis of Film*, the great French critic Raymond Bellour remarks of *Marnie*: "The credits have barely begun and already a body has been snatched." He is referring to this unusually redundant pair of titles: "Alfred Hitchcock's *Marnie*/Directed by Alfred Hitchcock." The effect of the *auteur*'s anticipatory possessive is to seize Marnie's identity away not only from Winston Graham, who wrote the novel, but also from Tippi Hedren, who plays Marnie, and even from the character herself.

In the published gossip that surrounds the making of *Marnie* (Spoto 1984, 495-505), it is recorded that Hitchcock, after decades of impeccable behavior with leading actresses, gave himself over to active sexual harassment of his star, Tippi Hedren. She turned him down. He is reported to have said to someone else that she "did what no one is permitted to do—she referred to my weight" (Burgess 1999), and from that point they were not on speaking terms. I have never been certain if Hitchcock really fell victim to the anima problem that seems so evident in his films, or whether the great trickster was slyly trying to get his actress into character. All I know is that he managed to evoke in Tippi Hedren just the right resistance to being possessed by a man, and that is very much in the foreground of this film.[1]

Once we actually get into the movie, the opening image of the handbag is (like the tunnel at the end of *North by Northwest*) to most eyes blatantly Freudian. With Hitchcock you never quite know. One critic has said that the bag is shaped like an eye, so that as we are looking at the film, the film is looking back at us, which is one of the quintessential Hitchcock effects. As a Jungian analyst, I would comment on the yellowness of the bag. In my view, it is not a particularly good yellow, but a rather cold, almost jaundiced color. This film has much alchemical imagery in it, for instance the rinsing of the hair. We can give the yellow an alchemical reading, in accord with the notion that the work of transformation proceeds through a series of color changes. The *nigredo* (the black hair of Marnie's false self) is giving way, not to the *albedo*, which would be white, but to the peculiar yellow of that handbag. I would associate the yellow with the later, *citrinitas* stage of the alchemical opus, which Hillman (1991) has called "The Yellowing of the Work." It is the moment at which everything one has been working on begins to be seen with a jaundiced eye. This is a jaundiced film with a jaundiced view of the man-woman relationship.

The way the woman walks away from the camera, her image receding into a virtual vanishing point along the platform, is intensely significant to me. The image, although tracked by the camera, quickly takes on a life of its own, in a passive-aggressive fashion. By having its back turned to the camera and moving away, it announces its own independence and autonomy.

Then we cut to the delightful sound sequence with Mr. Strutt, who has just been robbed. We realize that it is his money that is stuffing Marnie's handbag. As his name implies, Mr. Strutt is invested in his pride, in the values of the persona. So, when he recalls the image of Marnie, Mr. Strutt speaks entirely in terms of its surface characteristics. The erotics of that for him are perfectly obvious to everyone. Strutt seems to me, in the way he speaks, an extraverted thinking type. (One way to look at a cinematic character is to see it as one of the part-personalities that make up the total personality of the film. The character is thus one voice in a polyphony of psychological types—according to the eight-type model of attitudes and functions Jung outlines at the end of his book *Psychological Types*—that combine to define the type profile of the film.) Strutt's collective description of the absconding employee, his absolute belief in the reality of the name given—Marion Holland—and his certainty that by invoking this name he has regained some kind of control, distinguish him as extraverted thinking. Just after he insists on this name, we see that the woman's identity, like the identities of many women, is quite interchangeable. Marnie simply goes into her purse, looks behind the mirror, and pulls out several cards of identity, any one of which she can choose. Identities are just a set of outfits.

Marnie, then, is some kind of ongoing masquerade. I associate that strategy of psyche to a particular defensive figure, aligned against the heroic ego, that I call the "opposing personality" (Sandner and Beebe 1995, 324-327). In a woman's psyche, this figure, though often hard and contrasexual in a false-masculine way (one hears this, later, in Marnie's voice) is also a great female impersonator. The idea of womanliness itself as a kind of masquerade is one that Joan Rivière put forth in a pioneering essay (1986), and I think the figure of Marnie conveys what she means. When we finally see her face, Marnie, with her feminine mask now restored, has a rather defiant gaze. As in the gesture of walking away from the camera after she has robbed Mr. Strutt of some of his authority, the triumphant way she asserts her new identity has a decidedly oppositional quality. Cinematically, she defines an image that opposes itself to the director's camera following and tracking her.

Hitchcock makes this explicit by the intrusion of his own image into his text. Opening a door into the hotel hallway in which Marnie is smoothly heading for her room, he looks at us looking at her before he goes on looking at her.

In the dialogue that precedes this odd little bit, we have heard the comment from Sean Connery's Mark that Marnie had "improved the looks of the place" she went on to rob. Looks, or what feminist film critics call 'gazes,' are very important all through this particular film. Who looks at whom and when, and what gets to be seen under what circumstances form a politics of the film, as more than one critic has observed (Bellour 2000, 221-222; Columpar 1999; McElhaney 1999; Piso 1986). There is quite a power struggle around that in *Marnie*.

We first meet Mark when he appears in the doorway of Strutt's office, his raincoat slung over his shoulder. His is a very hermetic figure. Hermes is always found in the doorway, and this god defines a certain ironic, tricksterish viewpoint that is a dominant perspective of the film. This is one of those films that I would call a trickster work of art (Beebe 1981a); you cannot get to the bottom of it. Like *Hamlet*, it puts you in a double bind and never lets you free. You cannot be certain whether this is a feminist text or a misogynist one—whether Hitchcock is anti-patriarchy or anti-woman. Is he toying with Marnie or is the movie deeply compassionate?

Our hero, Sean Connery, casts an ironic and closely watchful eye, personifying the peculiar tone of the movie. Typologically, I would call him introverted sensation, and I see Hitchcock also, and the eye of

Hitchcock's camera, as having an introverted sensation perspective. I should take a moment here to point out the difference between introverted and extraverted sensation. Extraverted sensation delights in the surfaces of things, the textures. Introverted sensation notices these things but has a cool contemplative distance and takes its sensory observations into the inner world, comparing them in some way against an archetypal standard of "is this real?" or "is this not real?"

Marnie, within and beyond her masquerade, seems very interested in the textures and the fabrics. She seems to enjoy touching her own hair, doing herself up, and the clothes with which she gets her effects. She is narcissistically involved in the surface. When she looks into the mirror, she takes defiant pleasure in her blondeness, the perfectly recreated persona that she has been able to achieve. Already in this first sequence we have a developing dialectic between what can be described typologically as Sean Connery's ironic, detached introverted-sensation perspective and Marnie's opposed extraverted sensation. Personified before us in this way is the director's dialogue with the image.

Hitchcock has taken this image of the avoidant, oppositional, shadowy, passive-aggressive, false-feminine part-personality that he calls Marnie[2] (and that I call the "opposing personality"[3]) and presented it to himself and to us as something to be inquired into more deeply. That is his psychological "work" in this film. He engages us from the beginning in wanting to look beneath the surface of the oppositional image to find out "Who is Marnie really?" Marnie, as autonomous image, defiantly asserts her right to keep her secret, to get rid of the key to the *citrinitas* state of mind that Hitchcock would like to explore. The key (which is yellow) may linger for a moment, but she defiantly kicks it down the drain, meaning that the oppositional affect-image is going to defeat the effort of the director to get to know it.

The drama is perversely satisfying. We have the fantastically superficial Hedren resisting the inquisitive Hitchcock. Probe as he may, his engagement with his character/star can never be achieved through a surface description of her image, such as Strutt provides. That is a dead end, both cinematically and dramatically. Marnie is going to get away with the theft back of herself, but we do not know what will happen once Mark is on to her game.

Now let's go to a scene much later in the film. By this point in the story, Mark has hired Marnie, recognizing her as the same woman who had robbed Mr. Strutt, and, predictably, Marnie has started to steal from him. Mark catches her in the very act of stealing and uses the discovery to blackmail her into marrying him. The problem with this new arrangement is that Marnie won't have sex with Mark. It turns out that she has an absolute, phobic aversion to male touch, even though she is presented in the film as a heterosexual woman with some degree of initial interest in Mark. (That Mark is played by Sean Connery, who looks in this film like a Hindu love god, adds to our sense of the perversity of the defense that leads Marnie to resist him.) He decides to try to figure out what is wrong with his wife, and that leads to this scene:

> Observed by Mark's former sister-in-law, Lil, Marnie is in the process of awaking from a nightmare. Mark, determined to get to the root of her neurosis, with its twin symptoms of hostile avoidance of men and compulsive stealing from them, invites her to read Jung's *The Undiscovered Self*, and then engages in a sort of association experiment as he offers a set of loaded stimulus words involving elemental and color symbolism. The sequence ends with Marnie, in the grip of a complex response to the word 'red', crying out to Mark, "Help me!"

Played by the dark-haired Diane Baker, Lil, the sister of Mark's former wife, makes a much better visual match to Sean Connery than Tippi Hedren does. Lil and Mark seem to rhyme visually. Her function in the film—and I must say, she is not a terribly well drawn character—is that of extraverted intuition, the inferior function of both Mark and Hitchcock's film standpoint. Mark and Lil, who, in their different ways, share a suspicion of Marnie, define an axis between introverted sensation and extraverted intuition. There is a natural typological kinship between them, and Marnie, who is visually quite different from Mark, is outside that axis. Mark's and Marnie's is the repellent magnetism of opposition. While he batters against her defenses, she is in defiance of him.

The difference between Lil and Marnie in relation to Mark is an example of something I have come to emphasize in analyzing the fantasy material of men, that there are two primary female figures in the male psyche. One of these is the compatible anima, carrying the inferior function in a way that complements the man's heroic superior function. The other is the opposing personality, which competes with the man's superior ego function (thinking, feeling, intuition or sensation) by manifesting that same function with the opposite attitude (extraverted or introverted) from that with which the man typically deploys it. In this scenario Mark's marked preference for introverted sensation is opposed by Marnie's insistence upon extraverted sensation, and the drama concerns his efforts to redeem her opposing personality and bring it in line with his own will. There is virtually no attention on his part to rescuing or redeeming or even relating to the anima (Lil).

Jung tells us that when we are struggling with an emotion we do not understand, it is helpful to get an image of that emotion so that the process of active imagination can begin. I think I was the first analyst to say, for a seminar I conducted in 1981, that, in its way of engaging the unconscious, film is analogous not to dreams but to active imagination. At that time I noted that in the work of auteur filmmakers, one can see the visionary artist engaged in imaginal dialogue with the materials of collective film—the genres, the stars, and the formula stories (Beebe 1981b). Out of these collective materials, in an alchemical way, often a central image is distilled, which the director proceeds to interrogate throughout the course of the film. I see Marnie as such an image.

In Jung's 1916 essay "The Transcendent Function" where he first describes active imagination (*CW* 8, 84-86), he argues that the dialogue with the image can take two paths, which I will call the analytic and the aesthetic. Although Jung's own terminology does not quite admit this, both are forms of understanding. One is concerned with psychological meaning, the other with affective significance. For Hitchcock, the elaboration of the image, its clear formulation in aesthetic terms to expose its exact affective impact, is his primary interest. Whereas the patient in analysis is stuck with the emotion and wants the image—Hitchcock appears to be stuck on the image and wants the emotion to flow from it. If we read his film this way, we would have to say that the image of Marnie has presented itself to his creative psyche, and he is trying to find out from the emotion he can get out of Tippi Hedren what it consists of.

From watching this film, I have learned how ruthless the artist's interrogation of an image can be. As the image begins to deconstruct under the pressure of Mark's relentless inquiry, Marnie starts to look different from that 'together' Marnie we saw in the mirror in the first scene. Yet as this scene shows, the image seems secretly to respect the integrity of the work on it. She rises to the occasion with a form of defiant compliance and, at a certain point, even begins to ask for Mark's help.

Meanwhile, Mark is much too curious about the cause of Marnie's repression to rely solely on questioning her. He does some detective work on the side and uncovers the fact that Marnie has a mother. In fact, Marnie has been stealing to take care of her mother, a bitter, crippled woman who is played with perverse appeal by Louise Latham. In the film's last scene, the image's story is finally told.

You can see even at the beginning of this sequence, when Marnie and Mark are in the car, that Tippi Hedren again looks different than she did in the previous sequence. It is this deconstructed image that is able to undergo a healing regression to recover an archetypal memory. This was a point that *Marnie*'s critics have largely missed. If we understand the regression only psychoanalytically, then we have the cliché of reductive analysis to the buried traumatic memory, and the sentimentality of the assumption that that alone can produce a cure. It is clear to me that Hitchcock did not intend for us to accept this pat mechanism. One clue to his attitude is that he uses a rather crudely painted backdrop of a ship at the end of the street in Baltimore on which Marnie's mother lives. If you watch the movie to the end, after he and Marnie leave, that painted backdrop ripples just a bit, and looks very phony. In this sequence, at the end of the film:

> We see Mark, determined to get to the bottom of Marnie's neurosis, driving her to her mother's house. Mark confronts Marnie's mother with the fact that she was working as a prostitute when the events occurred that caused Marnie to be traumatized without knowing why. Mark and Marnie's mother start to raise their voices, as a thunderstorm rages outside. The overstimulation causes Marnie to regress, and in a child's voice she recalls what happened the night of her mother's accident. A sailor "client" [Bruce Dern] had come to spend the night with her mother, and in the midst of a thunderstorm came out to comfort six-year-old Marnie, who had begun to cry. Marnie's mother, fearing that his coarse, drunken gestures of comfort will turn into abuse of her daughter, starts to struggle with him. Marnie joins in and the sailor dies. When Marnie's recollection is complete, her mother comments that she always thought that Marnie's forgetting what happened had been a sign of the Lord's mercy.

A lovely book called *Hitchcock and Art* (Paini and Cogeval (eds.) 2001, 340) reproduces a 1928 surrealist painting by Raphael Delorme, *Untitled (Woman and Steamship)* that shows a naked woman going past a steamship that is very like the hokey-looking ship in *Marnie*. Hitchcock knew the visual vocabulary of the surreal well, and he used it to subvert the notion that the personal psyche is all there is. That Hitchcock would undercut the plausibility of his apparent story with that phony backdrop was a sign of his artistic integrity, but it caused many critics to assume that he was simply in decline.

The text itself tells us that the catharsis is by no means a cure. After Marnie leaves her mother's house, some children playing on the street are heard chanting: "Mother, mother, I feel worse. Send for the doctor, send for the nurse, send for the lady in the alligator purse!" In this way, the movie itself asks for Marnie's original image back, so deconstructing any notion that Marnie is grateful to have her false-self persona dissolved.

When the image is tortured, deconstructs, and regresses, however, the point of the cruel work of this passive-aggressive film is revealed.

Marnie's image gives over to something even more primal than itself, something more fundamentally archetypal and upsetting, and that is story. Jung writes that the archetype is, finally, not an image but rather a typical situation, a whole, just-so story. What I admire about the ending of *Marnie* is how successfully Hitchcock creates an archetypal story for us.

It is not an archetypal story that at first glance we already recognize as classical myth. Rather, it seems to belong to the myth that Americans have been living by in the last four decades, since the publication of *The Feminine Mystique* (Friedan 1963). Within this myth, another image than Marnie's is opened up for us, and that is the image of the wounded mother. This mother has become a monster. With a strangely deformed voice and face, she is a truly grotesque woman. The mother is an image of what Julia Kristeva in her long essay *Powers of Horror* (1982) calls the "abject." The state of abjection that she amplifies in that essay is that state of mind in which one cannot get away from one's horrible mother. The question Kristeva raises, which a viewing of *Marnie* makes us revisit, is: what is the horror associated with the mother? What is it about mother that makes us abject contemplating her?

As Kristeva's analysis makes clear, the idea that mother is the Medusa because she does not have a penis is much too simple-minded. Something else has happened to mother to render her abject. The achievement of *Marnie* is to give us a little mythic story that actually shows the wounding of the mother. Hitchcock seems to understand that unless that is visualized for us, we cannot get to the heart of this enormous problem that we have with mother as some kind of intolerable image.

The sailor, played by Bruce Dern, is to me a rather marvelous character. If I were to type him, I would assign him extraverted feeling, but I would say that like the feeling of the film itself, his is a tricksterish extraverted feeling. Although he comes across as loving, consoling, and concerned with the feelings of the little girl, there is no question in my mind that Marnie's mother is right: he is on the verge of abusing her daughter. It is a sexual kiss that he starts to give to little Marnie, and the mother is justified in defending Marnie against him. Diane Johnson (2001) has observed that this is a Demeter-Persephone scenario, in which the Bruce Dern character becomes a kind of Hades who is threatening to rape Persephone. But the emphasis here shifts to what happens to Demeter. What we get a rare glimpse of is Demeter's transformation into something abject, something perverted and monstrous, the sickening, vertiginous twisting of the mother's leg suggesting the warping of the archetype.[4]

It is this warping of the mother archetype that produces the monstrous mother of contemporary fantasy. Barbara Creed in her essay, "Horror and the Monstrous-Feminine," (1999, 252) says that Kristeva, in talking about abjection in the mother-child relationship, enables us to see that

> . . . definitions of the monstrous as constructed in the modern horror text are grounded in ancient religious and historical notions of abjection— particularly in relation to the following religious 'abominations': sexual immorality and perversion; corporeal alteration, decay and death; human sacrifice; murder; the corpse; bodily wastes; the feminine body and incest.

All of these elements are in the final sequence of *Marnie*. We are in what Kristeva would call "the absolute space of the abject."

Within analytical psychology, Marie-Louise von Franz (1985) has argued that alchemy emerged to solve certain problems that Christianity could not. These were the problems of the feminine, the problem of the body, and the problem of opposites, and they are all present within *Marnie*'s scenario.

Mark and his sister-in-law, Lil, together define a psychological axis of inquiry oriented toward the story Marnie and her mother would prefer to conceal. Though Mark's type is introverted sensation, he more and more takes up the extraverted intuitive project of shaking down the image and getting it to say what on earth it contains. Mark and Lil together remind us of the ruthlessness that the artist, in his integrity of purpose, brings to the interrogation of the image until the image reveals its story.

Marnie and her mother form an axis in opposition to this attitude. They resist the inquiry as far as possible. Mother says, "Forget, Marnie!" She does not want Marnie to remember. With her religious interest, the mother seems to me to be an introverted intuitive, the inverse of Marnie's extraverted sensation. Theirs is the axis of the resistant unconscious within the active imaginal dialogue. But when the resistant unconscious is held with integrity, the demonized mother[5]—the monstrous abject—disgorges her story, and out of that, for those in the audience that are not diverted from contemplating the horror on the screen by the script's glib promise of cure through the recovered memory, comes an authentic revelation that has the quality of a spiritual infusion. We don't get a cure, but we do receive an epiphany at the end of *Marnie* that significantly lifts a cultural repression. We get to see what has happened to the goddess in our time.

References

Bainbridge, John (1971). *Garbo*. New York: Holt, Rinehart and Winston.
Beebe, John (1981a). "The Trickster in the Arts." *The San Francisco Jung Institute Library Journal* 2-2, 22-54.

—. (1981b). "Film as Active Imagination" (audiotape). Seminar presented at the C. G. Jung Institute of San Francisco, October 10-11.

__. (2004). "Understanding Consciousness through the Theory of Psychological Types," in Cambray, Joseph and Carter, Linda (Eds.), *Analytical Psychology: Contemporary Perspectives in Jungian Analysis.* Hove and New York: Brunner-Routledge, 83-115.

Bellour, Raymond (2000). *The Analysis of Film.* Bloomington: Indiana University Press.

Brody, Richard (2005). "Get Hitched" (review of Alfred *Hitchcock: The Masterpiece Collection,* Universal Studios), *The New Yorker,* Oct. 10, http://www.newyorker.com/archive/2005/10/10/051010gomo_GOAT_movies1 (online).

Burgess, Steve (1999). "Master of imperfection." *Arts & Entertainment,* August 13, http://www.salon.com (online).

Columpar, Corinn (1999). "*Marnie*: a site/sight for the convergence of gazes." *Hitchcock Annual 1999-2000,* 51-73.

Creed, Barbara (1999). "Horror and the Monstrous-feminine." In Sue Thornham (ed.), *Feminist Film Theory.* Edinburgh: Edinburgh University Press, 251-266.

Friedan, Betty (1963). *The Feminine Mystique.* New York: Dell.

Graham, Winston (1961). *Marnie.* New York: Carroll & Graf.

Hillman, James (1991). "The Yellowing of the Work." In Mary Ann Mattoon (ed.), *Personal and Archetypal Dynamics in the Analytical Relationship.* Einsiedeln, Switzerland: Daimon Verlag, 77-96.

Johnson, Diane (2001). Personal Communication.

Jung, C. G. (1916/1958/1960) "The Transcendent Function." In *Collected Works,* vol. 8, 67-91.

—. (1957/1970). *The Undiscovered Self.* In *Collected Works,* vol. 10, 245-305.

Kaplan, E. Ann (1990). "Motherhood and Representation from Postwar Freudian Figurations to Postmodernism." In E. Ann Kaplan (ed.), *Psychoanalysis & Cinema.* New York and London: Routledge, 128-142.

Kristeva, Julia (1982). *Powers of Horror: An Essay on Abjection.* New York: Columbia University Press.

McElhaney, Joe (1999). "Touching the Surface: *Marnie*, Melodrama, Modernism." In Richard Allen and S. Ishii-Gonzalès (eds.), *Alfred Hitchcock: Centenary Essays.* London: British Film Institute, 87-105.

Paini, Dominique and Cogeval, Guy (eds.) (2001). *Hitchcock and Art.* Montreal Museum of Fine Arts.

Piso, Michele (1986). "Mark's Marnie." In Marshall Deutelbaum and
Leland Poague (eds.), *A Hitchcock Reader*. Ames: Iowa State
University Press, 288-303.
Rivière, Joan (1986). "Womanliness as Masquerade." In Victor Burgin,
James Donald, and Cora Kaplan (eds.), *Formations of Fantasy*.
London and New York: Routledge, 35-44. (Original work published
1929.)
Sandner, Donald and Beebe, John (1995). "Psychopathology and
Analysis." In Murray Stein (ed.), *Jungian Analysis*, second edition. La
Salle, IL: Open Court, 297-348.
Smith, Allan Lloyd (2001). *Marnie, the Phantom and the Dead Mother*,
http://www.scope.nottingham.ac.uik/phprint.php (online).
Spoto, Donald (1994). *The Dark Side of Genius*. New York: Ballantine.
Truffaut, François (1967). *Hitchcock*. New York: Simon and Schuster.
von Franz, Marie-Louise (1985). Interview in *Matter of Heart* Film.

Notes

[1] Richard Brody (2005) notes that "Hedren, who is not an accomplished actress, is nonetheless an astonishing presence: she stares into the camera with a cold, defiant glare that seems to have brought the spurned Hitchcock a masochistic pleasure."

[2] Marnie's last name is Edgar, so her initials are "M. E."—as Tania Modleski (1988, 93) has noted, the same as those of "Madeleine Elster," the "person with no identity" in *Vertigo*. Hitchcock's reference to Jung's *The Undiscovered Self* in *Marnie* further suggests that he is indicating the unknown woman is also "me."

[3] See Beebe (2004, 106-108).

[4] Brody (op. cit.) notes "The film's resolution does nothing to dispel an uncanny chill that suggests, more than in any other film by Hitchcock, a world out of joint."

[5] What makes Marnie's mother not only demonized but demonic, that is absolutely undermining to Marnie's psychological development, has been best explained at a personal level by Allan Lloyd Smith (2001), drawing upon psychoanalytic conceptions that emerged a generation after Hitchcock's film was released: the mother is a "dead mother," in the sense of being no longer affectively alive to her daughter, to whose unconscious she has passed on a "phantomatic" secret that haunts Marnie in such a damaging way precisely because it has been kept from her. All that Marnie is permitted to experience is a neurotic terror that "has to do with her fear of losing her mother—either through sex with a man, through her being hurt by a man, or through not being lovable herself" (Kaplan, 1990, 137).

CHAPTER NINE

BITTERSWEET

VIRGINIA APPERSON

Chocolat
(2000). Directed by Lasse Hallström.
Screenplay by Robert Nelson Jacobs,
from the novel by Joanne Harris.

Films about the feminine tend to present us with paradoxes, and so it is not surprising that they often are given names containing pairings of ideas that would seem to work against each other (like *Monsoon Wedding*, implying a dissolving resolution, or *Dangerous Beauty*, suggesting the undermining quality of feminine loveliness). Such antithetical combinations of words defy the Law of the Father to be clear, to the point of seeming to be malapropisms, misnomers for what the films really mean to convey, but they do better than masculine logic would at getting at the way the feminine tends to intrigue and to frustrate us at the same time. (John Beebe has suggested that Hecht and Hitchcock may have had this intention in mind when they came up with the haunting but slightly confusing title, *Notorious,* which implies a greater degree of celebrity than Ingrid Bergman's deliberately low-profile character actually had in the film, but that very title teases us perennially with the thought that this film will expose a shadow problem we really ought to know more about, which it does: the devaluation of the feminine in our time.) *Chocolat* is a title like this, suggestive of something rich, ambrosial, and maybe just a tad sinful, with the capacity to transform us in a secret way. Like *Notorious*, *Chocolat* is a film about a wayward woman, Vianne Rocher, who comes to a small village in France to set up a chocolate shop where she turns dark potions into medicinal candies. Although eventually she becomes a welcomed interloper, whose lusciously provocative treats provide just the right remedy for the plain bread and butter folk of the village, initially she and her delectable wares are considered a threat to the community's sense of order. The cherry on the top outcome of this chocolate sundae of a film is the way the village gives back to the woman who has given them so much. Vianne, who has never intended to stick around for good, gets unexpected recompense from the townspeople, who offer her a chance to experience a constancy and fidelity that she never allowed herself even to want.

This is a not unfamiliar twist to a stranger-comes-to-town confection, but the title lets us know that the film is not an ordinary piece of movie candy. For an English-speaker slowly to say *chocolat*, even if he or she is one of the worst bumblers of the French language, is a delicious experience that makes use of the entire mouth. With every syllable, one's appetite is whetted by visions of soft, molten, curvaceous morsels of pleasure, beautifully suited to being consumed in the lovely French setting that provides the tableau for this appealing movie. The film title trades shamelessly on the culinary and erotic associations the world has to France—a country that is distinguished for its wine, its bread, and its kisses. And a hope springs, as we mouth *chocolat*, that the gustatory payoff from the film will be as deeply satisfying.

Before, however, getting lost in the heavenly promise of a chocolate movie binge, it is best to realize that this film, like *Notorious*, has a fairy tale structure, and to remember that fairy tales are rarely just about *joie de vivre*. These tales also carry a cultural responsibility to reveal unsavory sides of the shadow and other arcane elements in the psyche with which collective consciousness has not yet come to terms. In preparation for entering *Chocolat's* demesne, the viewer should be fully aware that swallowing the film's particular delicacies does not merely satiate, but also dishes up sticky situations and can cause psychological bellyaches. With its essentially bittersweet nature and malleable texture, its murky color tones, its deep organic roots in countries from the Southern Hemisphere whose people sometimes pride themselves on self-indulgence, and its thickly varied presentations from chip to syrup to truffle or fudge, chocolate evokes some of the feminine's ability to counter the patriarchal assumptions of the dominant Northern Hemisphere.

Chocolat, in other words, has numerous qualities that are ideally suited to the elucidation of the feminine's ability to subvert established order. Like other films that John and I discuss in this book, its fairy-tale-like quality enables it to operate insidiously to address serious imbalances in our persistently patriarchal culture, particularly how the feminine is assigned to the shadow role. According to Marie-Louise von Franz, the doyenne of Jungian fairy tale interpretation, there are many ways that fairy tales can be spun, but they all:

[E]ndeavor to describe one and the same psychic fact, but a fact so complex and far-reaching and so difficult for us to realize in all its different aspects that hundreds of tales and thousands of repetitions with a musician's variations are needed until this unknown fact is delivered into consciousness; and even then the theme is not exhausted. This unknown fact is what Jung calls the Self, which is the psychic totality of an individual and also, paradoxically, the regulating center of the collective unconscious.... Different fairy tales give average pictures of different phases of this experience (1970, 1-2).

According to the classical Jungian tradition, out of which von Franz's work emerges, the phases of the experience of the collective unconscious, made evident in a tale's series of encounters with fascinating characters, can be divided up as the phase of the shadow (involving figures of the same sex as the person undergoing this exposure to the unconscious), the phase of the anima/animus (emphasizing contrasexual figures), and the phase of the Self (often involving figures of the same sex who seem to represent a greater personality). As each phase is experienced and integrated, there is a growth of consciousness and a greater unification of personality (individuation).

Some tales focus on content specific to only one of these phases of individuation, such as anima development or integration of the shadow, whereas others focus on the individuation process as a whole. In a psychologically complete fairy tale, each phase is present, and it is not hard to notice as well an overarching image of the feminine in the background casting her spell over the whole tale (the way Glinda the Good seems to oversee Dorothy's trip to Oz until she feels Dorothy is ready to return herself to Kansas).[1] *Chocolat*, like *The Wizard of Oz*, is one of the more comprehensive tales, and like Dorothy's story casts the stranger who has come to an unfamiliar place as an appealing young woman with unusual charisma. Challenged by the dares of life, Vianne gives her best and comes out better for it. Like any good fairy tale, this one covers much ground on how to tap into one's potential, using chocolate as a brilliant metaphor for the dark, transformative feminine that serves to fuel the expedition. Bearing witness to Vianne's capacity to persevere in spite of her detractors turns out to be a fulfilling and healing one for all who partake in her bold enterprise.

As the fairy tale's heroine, Juliette Binoche's Vianne Rocher provides just the right perplexing personality; she is the one who gives the film the problem it must work through. On the one hand, she is unflappable and self-possessed, as autonomous and filled with self-determination as a modern female audience could wish, and on the other she betrays a kind of rueful smile that suggests a fate-haunted life that has left her fearful of any dependence on others. Her most admirable quality is her utter confidence in her own gifts, and it is this confidence (born of experiences which would have made plenty of other women merely hard) that enables her to survive the suspicion she initially meets within the stolid little village where she and her daughter Anouk open *La Chocolaterie Maya*. Slowly, but obscurely, as she melts her chocolate, Vianne does not just melt the confines around the villagers' hearts, but also the ones that have kept her own heart cloistered, but this alchemy does not occur without enormous resistance from all. As a way of amplifying what makes Vianne such a telling image of the feminine, I will occasionally return to some of the film clips from the introductory montage of this book (Chapter One). Hopefully, this will remind us how the feminine has typically been rendered in films as a problematic person capable of making a difference by opposing the status quo.

For instance, the warning voiced by Bette Davis's Margo Channing in *All About Eve*, to expect a "bumpy ride" in a movie that promises to tell us all about the feminine, is appropriate to what we need to bring to our contemplation of Vianne's tampering ways. Vianne's assignment, as emissary of the feminine in a very patriarchal town, is simply to get the locals to accept pleasure, but because this is such a foreign notion to the villagers, her *chocolaterie* cannot help but be a place even more scandalous than a chocolate factory. Her apron and ladle plainly disguise her true identity as an itinerant matchmaker whose stealth tactics are simple enough: combining the seditious ingredients, cocoa, cayenne and cream, inviting others to stir the pot, and then patiently waiting for her handiwork to congeal. Once her shop is presentable, she wastes no time liberally doling out scrumptious tricks-and-treats to all who walk (they more often actually sneak) through the doors of her establishment.

Her tactics are ingenious; her weapons are her wares. Inhaling the fragrances that begin to emanate daily from her shop makes the boring fare to which the townspeople have grown accustomed start to wear thin. They are confused by their reaction to Vianne's charity because they have been instructed by the town mayor, the sanctimonious Comte de Reynaud, to be highly suspicious of fun and flavor. The locals are so well-versed in the provincial religion of reserve that they feel torn between following the creed they have been told they should live by and accepting the new shopkeeper's generosity. (They are not unlike the dutiful Austrian nuns in *The Sound of Music,* who are suspicious of Maria's spark.) The Count's retaliatory response to Vianne's open-handedness is fueled by a determination to cast the apparently irredeemable chocolate-maker out, once and for all, before everyone is under her loving spell. His campaign intensifies each time someone enters her den of iniquity and follows every precious indulgence that she proffers.

Vianne responds to this predictable counterattack from the patriarchal establishment with impetuosity reminiscent of Shirley Temple's Little Colonel in our collage: Vianne meets the Count's every malicious punch (just as Shirley's character countered her elder Colonel) with a new just dessert. The imperial spirit that Shirley Temple radiates in her first films seems to come from the fact that she had not outgrown her childhood spunk; part of the appeal of her character is that this child has clearly not yet learned to check the expression of what she thinks and feels. What supports Vianne's older, but still sassy spine is less clear. She comes by her unedited self just as naturally as Shirley Temple did, but her prerogatives are informed by experiences unknown to the viewer that seem to have grounded her in a very definite sense of purpose and conviction. What we do know is that she inherited from her parents a radical spirit that unceasingly supports her unconventional ambitions. She was born of a gypsy mother who refused to answer to anyone but herself and a mysterious father who dabbled in alchemy and looked well beyond any typical patriarchal Christian tradition. Above all else, Vianne was taught by these parents to pursue her fancy. With this background, she has no compunctions about pointing her confectioner's arrow at uncalled-for pride and piety, and her aim is pretty good.

Count Reynaud then becomes as much her primary target as she is his. Her intent in teasing him with tasty creations is only to break down his steely persona, not to wound the better man that lives inside. Since it never occurs to this Count Mayor that Vianne might contribute to the townspeople's morale or that her morsels might feed their souls, and even his own, he reacts to her presence by further tightening up his straight laces. He is determined to treat her as an intrusive pariah until she cries "uncle." Icily played by Alfred Molina, Count Reynaud has a bit of the arrogance of Professor Henry Higgins, but he is much worse in his depreciation of the feminine. Not only does he want to shape Vianne into one of his own, but with his authoritarian methods, he wants to permanently break the *esprit de corps* that she brings. She is everything he has been raised to ridicule—relational, self-exhibiting, and impertinent. Prior to her arrival, he had successfully managed his and everyone else's lives in the town, with the exception of his wife who is on an extended vacation in Venice (still, as in honest courtesan Veronica Franco's time, a haven of the feminine). For Vianne, there is no escape from the mayor's ire. It is her job to play not just his nemesis, but also the sculpture to his Pygmalion, and she has to enter this role before she can subvert it.

In her imperviousness to the many slights the Count engineers, Vianne carries herself not unlike Mary Poppins, that other skirted and inappropriate nomad, who was also a purveyor of sugary delights that contained a power to fertilize the feminine. Like Mary Poppins, Vianne lends her support to people in the town who are weird and wacky, impoverished and peripheral, creative and contrary. In spite of the fact that the ragtag teams they form sometimes get in the way of their own progress (their uncouth ways justify the naysayer's invectives), Vianne, serving the feminine value of inclusiveness, perseveres in holding a space in the town where everyone is welcome.

Some of these riffraff characters in *Chocolat* (as in *Mary Poppins*) turn out to be heroes. A common fairy tale motif is for the dubious figure to be the one who saves the day. In *Mary Poppins*, this figure was the chimney sweep; in *Chocolat*, it is a river rat. Where Dick van Dyke played the chimney-sweeper as a first-rate mercurial fellow who has everybody's number, handily putting everyone into his own service because he knows how to step above their mundane concerns, in *Chocolat* Johnny Depp offers an equally charismatic outsider in the form of the rogue gypsy Roux. Roux appreciates Vianne's odd, funny temperament because he is cut out of a similar, pliable cloth. Like van Dyke's Bert, he is a Hermetic figure, with an even more Dionysian subtext. He is a welcome change from the Saturnine leading men of most movies, who like the frowning models in men's magazines represents the male standard of our times. Depp's promise of sexual renewal plays well against the teasing sensuality of Juliette Binoche.

Vianne's moralistic, Catholic opponent, the Count, presumes he will win victory in short order, since her decadent desserts, consoling drinks, and unseemly admirers seem to provide little in the way of defensible virtue. But the delectable lava boiling inside her struggling little *chocolaterie* is also on the march: it taps into a concealed discontent among the villagers that has been masked far too long by propriety. Vianne's ability to rally her marginality into a successful challenge to the status quo calls to mind the audacity of Celie in *The Color Purple* when she finally speaks up ("I'm poor, black; I may even be ugly, but dear God, I'm here!") in an irrefutable display of the feminine's right to be. The script of *Chocolat* does not grant its central character a line that is so telegraphic, but Binoche makes it clear that Vianne has a similarly insubordinate decree emblazoned upon her heart. Her triumph comes when her extravagant, insidious goods surreptitiously awaken the hidden promise that is buried deep within the villagers.

A final parallel to Vianne from the opening montage of characters in this book is Audrey Hepburn's Holly Golightly in *Breakfast at Tiffany's*. At first glance, Hepburn's Park Avenue hillbilly has little in common with Vianne's hard-working French parvenu struggling to make it in Flavigny-sur-Ozerain, and Holly's schemes to find the next rich boyfriend in Manhattan bear no resemblance to Vianne's determination to support herself in Burgundy. Vianne does not want a sugar daddy; she is led only by the North Wind, a force traditionally characterized by fury, darkness and chaos (Tresidder 1998, 37). Yet Vianne and Holly are both played by transcendentally radiant anima-women, and both are emblems of the archetype of the *puella aeterna* in that archetype's most culturally creative aspect. Their reliance upon the scrappy devices of the eternal girl has helped them to deal with living in a patriarchal world that would strip them of any confidence to create a life where they could matter to another. And indeed their time in the world has made them somewhat cynical. As mid-life nears for these disillusioned puellas, their *plots du jour* are no longer bringing them the easy sense of victory they once did. Like Holly, Vianne is seriously in need of an experience that can restore her confidence as a free woman with an undimmed spirit.

In *Tiffany's*, Holly's revitalizing move is to find her cat, which the film develops as a representative of an independent feminine instinct that knows how to determinedly establish and maintain its own turf—and yet must be cared for. Reuniting with her own feline essence, by refusing, finally, to abandon her cat, resuscitates her authentic feminine self. The gesture of rescuing the cat from her own indifference enables her both to stand on her own in making an ethical choice and to be available at last to face the man that not only loves her, but that she at long last realizes she loves. The denouement is not quite so simple in *Chocolat*, though it is no less satisfying.

A more mature character than the still-adolescent Holly, Vianne's puella nature is also a bit more complex, and dark: despite her stubborn idealism, she has been hardened by a life of anti-bourgeois activism. Her psychological vocation has been to tend to the discarded and disruptive, and she has learned to do it almost too arrogantly and too well. Living a practically homeless existence has not only toughened her beyond Audrey Hepburn's character's range, but has also helped her to understand that the chaos that comes from one's vulnerabilities and imperfections offers valuable seasoning to one's life. As Veronica Goodchild in her book *Eros and Chaos* has written:

[C]haos can be viewed as guardian and intimate companion of divine and chthonic love, not the matrix out of which order is created. When we make order out of chaos, we kill eros as part of the divine creation, and annihilate our love affair with the world.... [A] heritage based on order...is bound more with our power needs to control, and...ignores the soul's desire for the chaos of creativity and feeling (2001, 4).

In keeping with this view, Vianne sees mayhem is the prerequisite for genuine affection, which of course is an alien philosophy to the staid Burgundians, who, like *petits bourgeois* everywhere, have been taught that correctness in social dealings should take precedence over the vagaries of relationship. Sadly, allegiance to this convention has left the town without a single viable friendship, and the townspeople have not even known what they have been missing. Fortunately, they have good taste, and so their collective witch-hunt led by the Count eventually loses steam, because behind these townspeople's need to maintain the status quo lies an inordinate appetite for just what Vianne has to offer—disruptive, delicious concoctions that conjugate their senses. By the time the film comes to a close, the notorious aromas have won out, and the proof is in the number of people who begin to pair off. The chocolate's alchemy has generated the alchemical operation of *coniunctio*[2] en masse.

Vianne's good work on behalf of the feminine value of relatedness is not complete, however, until she herself practices what she has been preaching. She knows how to be the kind of woman who mixes and meddles and fosters mating. But like all catalysts, she remains alone, strangely outside the chemistry she fosters in others. The tale's individuating job would not be done if it left her in such a one-dimensional role as agent provocateur. Fortunately for the film, she recognizes at the end that it is her turn to risk entering into a relationship. Vianne's prod comes from her daughter, Anouk, who with the kind of brutal honesty that only a child can get away with mocks her mother towards her final task. Anouk demands that Vianne cut the umbilical cord that ties her to the North Wind (in the film this animus symbol is clearly a kind of demon lover) and make an effort to rejoin the human race. Now Vianne must relinquish her defenses and accept her destined match, the one man who totally appreciates her intrepid spirit. This of course is the rakish Roux. Though we are not told, we are led to assume that, because of Vianne's anarchical success, she and Roux actually might live ever after in the village that now accepts her. This is well beyond *Mary Poppins*, and suggests a real integration, rather than a demonstration, of feminine power.

References

Edinger, Edward (1985). *Anatomy of the Psyche: Alchemical Symbolism in Psychotherapy*. La Salle, IN: Open Court.

Goodchild, Veronica (2001). *Eros and Chaos: The Sacred Mysteries and Dark Shadows of Love*. York Beach, Maine: Nicolas-Hayes, Inc.

Tressider, Jack (1998). *Dictionary of Symbols: An Illustrated Guide to Traditional Images, Icons, and Emblems*. San Francisco: Chronicle Books.

von Franz, Marie-Louise (1970). *An Introduction to the Interpretation of Fairy Tales*. Dallas, Texas: Spring Publications, Inc.

Notes

[1] *The Wizard of Oz* (1939). Screenplay by Noel Langley, Florence Ryerson, and Edgar Allan Woolf. Directed by Victor Fleming.

[2] The *coniunctio*, Latin for conjunction, was the alchemist's approach to visualizing the mystery of chemical combination, "in which two substances come together to create a third substance with different properties." (Edinger 1985, 211). The alchemists imagined they could see a male and female couple copulating in the alchemical vessel in which the transformation of substance was taking place.

CHAPTER TEN

DOUBLE BIND

JOHN BEEBE

Mother
(1996). Directed by Albert Brooks.
Screenplay by Albert Brooks and Monica Johnson.

As the uncanny central image of *Mother*, Debbie Reynolds resembles a figure in a dream, her still-youthful face presiding like a mask of frozen intelligence over the stooped and scurrying body that has locked her into the refrigerator of her character's life-history. Reynolds's Mrs. Henderson, a precise evocation of a creative woman's entrapment in a middle-class role, has refined into an art passive-aggressiveness toward the sons that refuse to outgrow her. The more affirmative of the two (Rob Morrow) is a successful Los Angeles sports agent with a family of his own: she dodges his daily calls, refusing to learn to use the videophone he has sent her by sliding her face out of reach of his own importuning image. The one who harbors the negative side of the mother complex (Albert Brooks) calls her bluff by moving back up to her Sausalito home after his second marriage ends in divorce: he wants to see where his problems with women have come from. As played by Brooks, John's feeling is a mixture of not knowing when to stop, insistence on being loved, and a dogged determination to get to the root of the matter. He brings this double bind to the one placed on him by his mother's more ladylike way of digging at his misunderstandings of value. Brooks develops the near-impossibility of his sweet–and–sour face getting a rise out of Reynolds's deadpan into an irony that unfolds the sadness and anger in the situation itself, which has at its core the woman's stored-away self-esteem. This muted dark comedy is a great son-lover movie, and an unusually hopeful one, because the return to the mother actually leads to a rescue of lost initiative in both characters, who bring us close indeed to the archetype that limits, links, and eventually liberates them. The cast stone elephants in the Sausalito Plaza foreground are more than ironic homage to Memory; the face-off recorded in this film is one few adults will be likely to fail to recall.

CHAPTER ELEVEN

MAE WEST IN RETROSPECT

JOHN BEEBE

Among the great archetypal figures that emerged with the triumph of American popular entertainment in the twentieth century, Mae West held a special position. She was a woman, and she joked about sex. Not even Groucho Marx tested cultural limits to her extreme.

At her death in 1980, *Time* said she was "probably the most original aphorist since Benjamin Franklin,"[1] and one likes to think of those two trading repartee in Elysium. But of her mortal career, my favorite moment is not a wisecrack, but a silent bit she did in *Belle of the Nineties*. Standing in one of her famous gowns at the entrance to a New Orleans gambling parlor, she decides to light a cigarette. She is in a world where a woman still may not smoke alone, and she looks around her to see if anyone is watching. Sure that she is unobserved, except by her movie audience, she strikes her match across the lower front of a marble Venus that is in front of her, the audacious sulphur making a crackling sound over the rougher part of the marble.

Her enormous nineteen-thirties movie audience laughed hard enough, but one may wonder if any of them realized then the real target of the irreverence they were gasping at. This great comedienne, ever the arrogant, overweight woman from the wrong side of the tracks, winningly trying to pass herself off as a great courtesan, was the first person to get "modern" people to laugh at their outsize preoccupation with the rediscovery of sex, which, decades after Victoria, had lingered on, like Mae's own span as a supposed Love Goddess.

When the World War II life jacket was named the "Mae West," she cracked, "I've been in Who's Who, and I know what's what, but it's the first time I ever made the dictionary." Taking on the dictionary, she made the word a servant of her incessant sexual puns, and she made people feel, even as they laughed, how Logos itself becomes impossible in a regressive atmosphere overruled by the Great Mother.

In *Sextette*, a final, dreadful film made in 1977 when she was eighty-four, West managed to self-destruct with élan. In the midst of the tedious farce, a knock comes at the door.

The man she is with cries out, "What's that?"

"It ain't opportunity," Mae drawls.

She was right: her audience had recognized the naiveté of its awe at the prospect of sexual pleasure. Her game of pointing it out was finally up.

Notes

[1] Gerald Clarke, "She Was What She Was," *Time*, December 1, 1980, p. 2. http://www.time.com/time/magazine/article/0,9171,924566-1,00.html (online).

STRENGTH

CHAPTER TWELVE

WILES

VIRGINIA APPERSON

Pride and Prejudice
(1940). Directed by Robert Z. Leonard.
Screenplay by Aldous Huxley, Victor Heerman, and Jane Murfin,
based on the play by Helen Jerome from Jane Austen's novel.

No one captures women at their resolute best and exasperating worst better than Jane Austen, especially in the story of hers that our culture never seems to tire of, *Pride and Prejudice.* If the women from Austen's novel command our interest, even with their dreadful eccentricities, it is because we do not have a clue as to how to bring these characters under control. Austen's women display elements within the feminine that have the capacity to go their own way from just about every angle imaginable, from insufferable busybodies to the admirable young woman most worthy of being emulated, Elizabeth Bennet. Intemperate women shape Austen's comedy in a way that reveals both the autonomy of the feminine and its remarkable potential for a non-moralistic integrity. If we can get past their melodrama and begin to appreciate their individual approaches to self-governance, we discover that Elizabeth is not the only female person in *Pride and Prejudice* we can profit from studying. From the privileged old battle-axe Lady Catherine to the insistently upward-mobile Mrs. Bennet and the two of her daughters that are most like her, harebrained Kitty and over-the-top and boy-crazed Lydia, the women consistently impress us with the force of their characters. To continue with the colorful list, Mrs. Bennet's oldest daughter, the indefatigably inoffensive Jane and the arsenic-tongued Miss Bingley form a pair of opposites in the feminine that might be termed "too nice" and "too nasty." Austen also includes the doll-like Georgiana Darcy, the inaudible Anne de Bourgh, the bookish Mary (the third Bennet girl) and the one who most knows her destiny is up for bid, Charlotte. Most are prose snapshots that catch women in unflattering poses, and most are unlikely role models for any female reader; yet, each of the female characters, in her own special fashion, holds herself apart from the expectations of others and in this way develops some facet of feminine self-control. Although I won't be able to highlight each of them with a lengthy analysis in this brief chapter, I would advise the reader to attend to the cumulative effect of encountering these characters, who together comprise a group portrait that might be termed "the faces of the feminine."

Austen's men are another story. They have long since squandered their feminine essence by projecting it onto available members of the opposite sex, and they respond both to the women's individual strengths and also to their various weaknesses in unhelpful and evasive ways—an understandable, but not very imaginative response to the baffling nature of the feminine. Mr. Bennet, a pretty much dowry-less father of five of the above-mentioned young ladies (Jane, Elizabeth, Mary, Kitty, and Lydia) copes with his lovely litter by hiding out in the library, while his daughters' potential suitors (Bingley, Darcy, Collins and Wickham) play cat and mouse games, approaching and avoiding the women by turns that bring home the arbitrariness of men in relationships. The penniless Wickham prospers from his fickle and opportunistic escapades, which always involve flirtations, until he is unable to squirm out of a dalliance with Lydia (who can more than hold her own with her husband when it comes to inconsiderate autonomous antics). Quite the opposite of Wickham is the benign Mr. Bingley, who feels great affection for Jane Bennet but has so little experience with love that he is not man enough to fight for her. And there is pretentious Reverend Collins, with his interminable name-dropping, who exceeds everyone in the novel when it comes to taking on airs and conveying absurdity. The ever-superior Mr. Darcy *is* superior to all these characters, but he fairly drips entitled masculine pride, when he first appears in his virtue to sneer down upon the Bennet clan and its not-polished-to-his-satisfaction community. It will take the whole novel for him to learn how to love outside the box of his comfort.

Austen's 1813 manuscript, brimming with dithering characters, has long been admired by directors, who have recapped her story in several films, two particularly well-regarded television adaptations, and a Bollywood musical.[1] It has also encouraged updated spin-offs, like *Bridget Jones's Diary*.[2] The production that has become canonical, however, is MGM's 1940 movie version, boasting an inspired cast that includes Greer Garson and Laurence Olivier and a script Aldous Huxley worked on. It is this version that I will rely upon to elucidate not only the mess that the feminine is capable of making, but also the unpredictable riches that live beneath the feminine's sometimes cockamamie ways. This production does justice not only to the impressive array of ditzy and disregardful characters that Austen was able to supply, but also to the way her tale can strike a collective nerve.

Jane Austen's famous first line that sets the stage for the story that unfolds, "It is a truth universally acknowledged that a single man in possession of a good fortune must be in want of a wife," is replete with the irony that this is an animus opinion, true only in the minds of the likes of Mrs. Bennet. If truth were really told about single men, it would be said that they often prefer not to get married too hastily while in the prime of their lives. The actual law that the women in the story live by, and which every character in the novel must choose either to honor or to resist, is revealed in the line that follows the first:

> However little known the feelings or views of such a man may be on his first entering a neighbourhood, this truth is so well fixed in the minds of the surrounding families that he is considered as the rightful property of some one or other of their daughters (1813, 1).

These words wryly reverse the traditional patriarchal view of women as the property of men, and though they are never actually spoken in the 1940 film, the idea is written into every page of the script. Now, as we watch at a significant distance from the cultural assumptions that governed the world of the movie, this second line of the novel helps us to clarify the ladies' agenda. When Jane Austen wrote, a woman's capacity for self-reliance was rarely seriously considered. Her women, that we get to see on the screen, understood that their world was so totally controlled by men's financial power that each one of them had to figure out what she had to do in order to exercise a measure of choice in the midst of such a controlling reality. In order to gain a spot in society, the ladies depended upon serious schemes and considerable compromise. Even the meek, clumsy, and less resilient of these young ladies figured out how to passively count on their awkwardness to successfully broker their way out of joining in. Austen's assemblage of characters, lovingly cast by MGM, does what is necessary with aplomb. By contemporary standards, the result is an embarrassing exposure of female manipulation, but even today no one can really fault these characters, when it is so clear that the discriminatory rule that governs their engagement with life is that they can have no economic standing of their own, apart from the men who agree to support them. If today we go beyond a literal viewing and consider Austen's women as if they represented parts of the feminine in all of us whose desperation comes from having to experience life as if it were ruled by the feudal law that makes chattel of anything feminine, then these characters' families are like social egos that have been developed to negotiate some sense of essential sovereignty for their daughters. That is the real point of Austen's saying that "a single man in possession of good fortune…is considered as the rightful property of some one or other of their daughters."

Considered in their historical context, we have to marvel at the ingenuity displayed by Austen's women. The hugely obnoxious Mrs. Bennet, for instance (whose annoying characteristics are played up by Mary Boland in the role) invades others' lives without compunction to create opportunities for her daughters to be exposed to eligible men. She comes by her connivances fairly—with five unmarried girls on her hands, what mother would not want her daughters to be nicely cared for, and who could deny her the fringe benefits of worrying intrusively over their futures? Although the contemporary audience that has rediscovered this film on DVD or on television is not living in Austen's England, it feels a kinship to Austen's world because the protocols that presently run middle class American lives are no less economically challenging. Today, ambition drives us in different but still ridiculously "all-consuming" ways, with our need for the latest fashion, technology and other status-giving stuff. Today's Mrs. Bennets are worrying about getting their daughters into the colleges that they have been told hold the keys to the jobs that young women must have to survive this modern madness of consumerism. A twenty-first century Mrs. Bennet wants her daughter to be prepared to benefit from the advanced freedom in the marketplace that women are enjoying. Furthermore, when it comes to marriage, these mothers know that two incomes are often necessary just to make ends meet. Enjoying much more social opportunity than the Bennet girls, young women of today are admirably delivering for their mothers, but at what cost? Once they have gone to college, today's fast-stepping women moving with confidence into the work force still have to consider when and how to have a child (and now whether to do so with or without a husband). They may have more choices than Austen's characters, but they too have little time to relax and enjoy their feminine autonomy, because they have become obsessed with scheming to support the trajectories of their lives. Men too are forced to join into the manipulation of the personal to achieve the contemporary goal called "getting a life." Perhaps it is the contortion of the feminine, as caricatured in Mrs. Bennet, that speaks to the sensibilities of contemporary people and makes *Pride and Prejudice* the quintessential comedy of manners of life under patriarchy that it is.

Like Signora Franco who teaches her daughter to be a courtesan in *Dangerous Beauty*, Mrs. Bennet knows what a woman has to do to find a place in patriarchal society that will grant her a measure of freedom from male control. Both mothers know all too well that in order for the feminine to achieve any such self-sufficiency, it will have to develop its capacity for cunning. As this cross-reference to a film set in 16th century Venice suggests, this conundrum confronted women, and the feminine, long before Jane Austen developed her characters. It would seem that in western society we have known the balancing act between masculine and feminine energies seems to be perpetually out of whack, and our imagination can easily put Austen's women and men, born in the late 18th century, into contemporary clothes and identities. (*Clueless*, Amy Heckerling's updated adaptation of Austen's *Emma*, passed muster with an American teen audience in 1995 that was totally unaware of its source).[3] Intrapsychically, the characters in *Pride and Prejudice* are even more consonant with contemporary identities, because they represent recognizable parts of ourselves that are present in the way we configure our personalities today, as the prides and prejudices of our complexes. None of us can claim immunity from the funny and appalling consequences of these parts of our psychology, shaped by social expectations, on our behavior. According to the Jungian notion of projection, whatever bothers us about the peculiarities of women today gives us a clue to the shadow that bedevils the feminine in all of us. The travails of Paris Hilton, Angelina Jolie, and Britney Spears are so interesting to us because they are a mirror of the desperation that has overtaken the feminine in all of us. And they are already foreshadowed by the uppity Miss Bingley and the flaky Kitty and Lydia. When we watch such women's lives, we discover that we cannot take our eyes off of them, a reliable sign of shadow projection.

Austen's continuing relevance suggests, therefore, that the same complexes that drive her characters are present in our own psyches. On the screen, her ladies, whose foibles we have come to know and love, have even greater resonance now than they did in 1940, because we are so much better schooled in the discourse of feminine power. Though we are apt to wince at the exaggerated presentation of the feminine in this golden-era Hollywood movie, we have to recall that the feminine has a past and admit to the way she remains distorted in our present times. *Pride and Prejudice*'s depiction of feminine wiles is timeless, closer to what our feminine sides are like than any of us care to admit. The one character in the movie that serves as a model for contemplating the feminine's covert strategies with appropriate empathy is Greer Garson's Miss Elizabeth Bennet. It is Elizabeth who sees the status of the feminine in a man's world for the artificial arrangement that it is, and it is Elizabeth who never abandons her belief in herself as a woman, as well as her feeling for her sisters and her friend Charlotte (even when she shudders at the methods they adopt in their effort to survive socially). Above all, Elizabeth never relinquishes her conviction that they all deserve more. Elizabeth's consciousness is informed by what Austen in her title calls a prejudice, an animus against the entitlement that men bring to their prerogatives, and the presence of mind that she brings to every situation is linked to the way she instinctively trusts her own heart. She has become an exemplary figure of the modern woman. In this regard, Austen's sense of a woman's right to trust herself is quite as radical as the insistence on women's prerogatives of her more contemporary, Mary Wollstonecraft, the founding mother of feminism.

Unlike the complexes of the other female characters in *Pride and Prejudice*, neither Elizabeth's self-assertive animus nor her vulnerable feminine side is attached to title or wealth; rather her confidence resides in her own judgment. She invariably speaks up for what she feels to be right (in this, she is similar to *Dangerous Beauty*'s Veronica Franco), and she becomes, in the process, a model of integrity. In his book *Integrity in Depth*, John Beebe discusses another Austen character, Anne Elliot, in *Persuasion,* noting that Austen's portrayal of integrity tends to be different from masculine depictions of this quality. Her signifiers of integrity, the extraverted Elizabeth and the introverted Anne, do not employ integrity "to advance ambition" (Beebe 1992, 10) for moral excellence; instead, they rely upon the more feminine approach of "constancy, amiability and self-knowledge" (ibid., 70) in order to achieve the right relations to others. What Beebe teases out about feminine integrity from Austen's characters extends our understanding of what the feminine can contribute to ethically sensitive living when she is at her best. Elizabeth excels in just this way.

Because Miss Elizabeth Bennett employs integrity so effectively in personal relations, she proves to be one of the most admired feminine figures in all of literary and film history. She speaks from a moral center all her own not only in her relationship with Mr. Darcy, but with everyone she comes across. She models for them (and us) how, as Beebe has put it, using contemporary psychoanalytic language, "to manage the chaotic world of internal object relations in a conscious and coordinated way" (ibid., 87). She does not simply rely on that more familiar sort of reflexive pride that immediately withdraws from relating to others when matters become a muddle. Although she does not always succeed in rising above a form of indignation, Elizabeth nevertheless shows us what it means to be a stabilizing force that hangs in there with people, even when she has to take issue with them. Her equilibrating strength is tested when she is hurt by

Darcy's initial disdain towards her family and her, and this ignites her prejudice towards his pride. This prejudice enables her to distance herself from his condescension, but it also blinds her, temporarily, to his underlying potential to engage. What is exciting, ethically, is to watch her own up to the animus into which her prejudice has led her, and to grow beyond her defensive distancing and recognize his actual interest in her. In this honest practice of moral trial and error, we get to see how her integrity really works. Once she steps back and responds to all of Darcy, rather than just his wounding, prideful side, she returns to the virtue that she knows so much about. Watching the interplay of pride and prejudice that is promised by the title is thus not just an interplay between characters but between parts of the self, within what Beebe calls the self's "moral process," which involves a kind of ethical learning. We, along with Elizabeth, learn that Darcy's pride (just like Elizabeth's prejudice) is not all bad, because it is an attempt at genuine honor. In the MGM movie we get to see Greer Garson's Elizabeth overcome the limits of her prejudice and Laurence Olivier's Darcy, the limits of his pride. Both actors convey the moral tension between these qualities, so that the movie audience is gripped by the intelligence of their engagement. By the film's finish, we are rewarded with the promise of a marriage that feels sustainable.

The film, like the novel, is finally about the feminine standing up for her own value and prevailing. Without Elizabeth's equanimity in maintaining her autonomy (which Garson conveys flawlessly with her restrained, yet passionate performance), Austen's tale would come unglued—swept away by the more garden-variety prides and prejudices of all the minor players who are constantly vying for position at the expense of others. This is not to deny that Garson's Elizabeth does not struggle with her own provincialism, but rather to marvel at how she realigns herself when she comes to understand the possibilities that lie beneath Olivier/Darcy's conceit. Once she has deployed her keen sensibilities to perceive the tangle of possibilities, her approach is surgical and healing: she cuts through the snarls of courtship to make possible a durable relatedness in at least two unions that we can respect, Bingley's with Jane, and her own with Darcy. The result is to fulfill her meddling mother's ambitions for her daughters in an ethical way. The story ends on a note of balance, creating a new cosmos in which neither men nor women are exclusively in charge of marriage, and both the masculine and feminine have learned to yield to the other in a spirit of cooperation.

There are, however, a few corners in the film that do not get neatly tucked away in this made-bed happy ending. These curious loose ends in the plot are there, I believe, to make sure that we do not forget just how irregular the feminine finally is. The first bit of loose sheet is an interesting departure from the book. It may have been added in the play from which Huxley and his cohorts shaped the movie's script, and it is an addition that is remarkably compatible with Austen's own style of irony. In the novel, Darcy's aunt, Lady Catherine de Bourgh, lambastes Elizabeth for daring even to entertain a proposal from her nephew Darcy. Lady Catherine's feeling is that Elizabeth should simply know she is not good enough to marry a nobleman. It is precisely because Lady Catherine, in her outrage, reports back to Darcy that Elizabeth "refused to refuse" such a proposal, that Darcy (who has already been turned down once by Elizabeth for the pride with which he offered himself) is emboldened to try again, and this time without all the pretension. So far, this is all, and quintessentially, Austen. But at just this point the film script deviates from Austen's plot line, to reveal something the novel leaves out: that Lady Catherine (the towering Edna May Oliver at her haughtiest) is in fact deeply impressed by Elizabeth's self-assurance and thus agrees to act as Darcy's "ambassador" in order to determine whether, after all, Elizabeth has had a change of heart.

There could be sentimentality in giving Lady Catherine such an accommodating and unsupercilious side, refashioning her as a positive mother figure. But not to worry, the writers have not done a complete makeover of this *grande dame*. In spite of showing an unexpected degree of willingness to give her social prejudice up once she has been confronted by Elizabeth's actual virtue, Lady Catherine does not completely abandon the cantankerous nature that is her signature. Huxley and his team must have understood the danger of sanitizing the disagreeable out of the feminine, recognizing that much of the charm and the power of the feminine lie in its obstinacy. But in their handling of the character, Lady Catherine's sparring skills carry the deep conservation of instinct that is a hallmark (again) of the feminine's autonomy. The same conservatism guides the way Greer Garson's Elizabeth does not so much forgo her prejudice towards Darcy in the course of the film, as use it wisely. As the film seems to near a graceful close, Elizabeth has won both Darcy's heart and Lady Catherine's admiration: the script has run the risk of a happily-ever-after conclusion that would appeal more to a masculine need for closure. *Pride and Prejudice* does not finish, however, on a Hollywood-tidy, perfectly clean note. Had it done so, it would not offer up such a realistic portrayal of the pluckier, but also more problematic side of the feminine (the side that can hold its own against masculine forcefulness at the cost of being a bit messy). The most unsavory aspect of the feminine that is left un-cleaned up by both the book and the film is revealed by the painful fact that the ever-loopy Lydia and her go-along sister Kitty are still on the loose. Lydia, towards the end of the film, has become even more ridiculous and less contained than at the outset. In a shocking denial of her mother's value of matrimony and money, which seem to come to Lydia as mere afterthoughts, she puts the entire family's respectability at risk by running away with Wickham, for what Lydia is really all about is the sport of merrymaking, and she cannot be bothered by details. As a thoughtful counter-balance, in one of his most redeeming moves, the transformed Darcy rescues Lydia (and the family he once scorned) by anonymously funding the basis for a marital commitment out of the up-until-now uncatchable Wickham. Though Lydia is plainly delighted with her handsome husband and newly found status, it is appallingly clear now that this morally dubious Bennet daughter (along with Kitty who eagerly awaits her own turn at disrupting middle class morality) has an unchecked appetite for diversion that marrying Wickham has barely whetted: no doubt many more larks are yet to come. Though Elizabeth's integrity is contagious, bringing out the best in such seemingly intractable characters as Darcy and Lady Catherine, there is no such hope that a comparable redemption will be cultivated in her youngest sisters. They remain beyond taming because they are a pair of persistent princesses determined to remain perched on their high horses. But Austen, for all her moral vision, is not, finally, a moralist. The last gesture of the film is vintage Austen, and a key to her understanding of the resources of the feminine, even at her most silly, is to recognize that when the feminine is on a joy-ride, perhaps the best thing to do is hop on with her and head to the nearest ball. The buoyant ending of *Pride and Prejudice* seems to probe our patriarchal natures with a question: what would living in this world be without a protective dose of feminine frivolity, to immunize us against the harshness of life?

References

Austen, Jane (1813/1981). *Pride and Prejudice.* Toronto: Bantam Books.
Beebe, John (1992). *Integrity in Depth.* College Station: Texas A&M University Press.

Notes

[1] The most recent have been: *Pride and Prejudice,* BBC television miniseries (1980). Written by Fay Weldon. Directed by Cyril Coke; *Pride and Prejudice,* BBC television miniseries (1995). Script by Andrew Davies. Directed by Simon Langston; *Pride and Prejudice: A Latter-Day Comedy* (2003). Screenplay by Andrew Black, Anne K. Black, Jason Faller, Katherine Swinger. Directed by Andrew Black; *Bride and Prejudice—The Bollywood Musical* (2004). Screenplay by Gurinder Chadha and Paul Mayeda Berges. Directed by Gurinder Chadha; and *Pride and Prejudice* (2005). Screenplay by Deborah Moggach. Directed by Joe Wright.

[2] *Bridget Jones's Diary* (2001). Screenplay by Helen Fielding, Directed by Sharon Maguire.

[3] *Clueless* (1995). Written and Directed by Amy Heckerling.

CHAPTER THIRTEEN

INTEGRITY

JOHN BEEBE

Monsoon Wedding
(2001). Directed by Mira Nair.
Screenplay by Sabrina Dahwan.

On the morning of September 11, 2001, citizens of New Delhi awoke to newspaper articles celebrating the news that a film by one of their own daughters about upper middle class Punjabi life had won a Golden Lion for the best picture at the Venice Film Festival. It was the first time a woman director had ever claimed the award, and for a film that seemed to have been thrown together in no time at all—just in time, in fact, to capture the happy spirit of international, postmodern, postcolonial culture before a new round of paranoid anxiety about the viability of that very culture would start to poison the party. Seeing *Monsoon Wedding* now, one can only marvel at the celebratory spirit of the pre-9/11 time that Mira Nair's movie recalls and preserves for us, like a jam made from summer fruit to get us through a prolonged winter.

The film, as the title makes clear, belongs to the genre of movie known as "wedding pictures," and Nair, a Professor of Film Studies at Columbia, knows her Vincente Minnelli, Robert Altman, P. J. Hogan (who struck gold in this genre twice), and Ang Lee well enough to have created a classic to stand beside *Father of the Bride*, *A Wedding*, *Muriel's Wedding*, *My Best Friend's Wedding* and *The Wedding Banquet*—and to trump her predecessors in getting at the deeper meanings of the marriage archetype. This motif, known to students of analytical psychology by its alchemical name, *coniunctio*, the "chemical marriage" of male and female opposites, is described by Jung in two charmingly arcane, if deeply clinical, works, "The Psychology of the Transference" and *Mysterium Coniunctionis*, and in such intuitive-thinking terms that it is possible to read these texts, with their endless symbolic explications, without ever grasping that what is being discussed is an emotional event. It is part of the achievement of Mira Nair's film to have delineated the *coniunctio* in feeling-sensation terms, so that we can experience the way it transforms lives.

That her own film comes together grants Nair the authority to instruct us on so deep a psychological matter, but she never neglects the surface in her approach to her *prima materia*, which is simply a Punjabi wedding. The director and producer has admitted that she wanted to capture on film what in New Delhi is called *masti*, "the singular life-loving spirit of Punjabi culture," and in this she succeeds handsomely. But the *masti* is also accompanied by *musti*, a spirit of mischief that subtly plays through the film like a trickster insinuating itself into the loving animus of the movie.

The convergence of these forces is symbolized at the outset of the film by an odd-couple marriage of convenience between incompatible characters who must cooperate in bringing the wedding off. The cost-conscious, upper-middle-class householder, Lalit Verma, is intent on seeing that his daughter's arranged marriage to Hemant, a Houston-based engineer, is celebrated properly as a suburban June wedding. To decorate the garden and set up tents that will protect the party from the impending monsoon downpours, he has hired the dubious P. K. Dubey, an extraverted intuitive tent contractor from the city who is trying to pass himself off as a wedding planner. Already, though, the marigold bower is disintegrating, and all *tentwallah* Dubey wants to do is munch on the falling marigolds while blandly insisting to the increasingly doubtful Lalit that everything will be all right.

Neither man seems at all close to any feminine figure at this point: Lalit's wife, Pimmy, has to hide her smoking from him, and Dubey has not yet noticed how Lalit's lovely young maid, Alice, is shyly eyeing him while she goes about her tasks in the background. But their less than animated face-off is nothing to the estrangement that looms at the heart of the arranged marriage itself. The bride, who in modern style has, like the groom, veto power over the arrangement if it proves to be unsatisfactory, has elected to marry in this traditional way only because the man she really loves, her married ex-boss, shows no sign of leaving his wife for her despite the unbroken intensity of their ongoing affair. Everywhere we look, a discordant note is struck. Only the bride's younger brother, plump, androgynous Varun (played with enormous charm by Mira Nair's own sixteen–year–old nephew, Ishaan) seems to sense the degree to which things are not as they should be—and his solution, to the exasperation of this conventionally homophobic father, is to want to cook and dance, as if to summon in his own body the feminine element that is missing in this heartless wedding.

The comedy of the wedding that is out of *tao* (to import yet another language into this polyglot movie filmed in English, Hindi, and Punjabi) is a convention of the genre of wedding picture, which belongs to an even larger class of films that the philosopher Stanley Cavell has called comedies of remarriage. The scenarios in such films move from lesser, unsatisfying conjunctions to greater, more permanent, ones, as if to suggest that at some point the false arrangements have to give way to authentic feeling, or there will be no individuation in our lives. Nair takes up this suggestion with surprising force in *Monsoon Wedding*, so that when the rains do catch up with the wedding party, they have been preceded by an inner *solutio*.

The film takes care of us throughout with an extraverted sensation panorama of contemporary India as it is, inviting us into the extended family of a vibrant emergent middle class. Although it makes no concessions to a colonial standpoint that would require a first-world audience to bear a burden of guilt for the continuing underdevelopment of yet another third world country, it does not lack a critical perspective in regarding its apparently privileged subjects. This goes beyond the documenting sociological contemplation with which Nair observed the suffering of India's homeless children in *Salaam Bombay*. In *Monsoon Wedding*, her scriptwriter Sabrina Dhawan has deepened her vision, for the film seems to be seen through the silent eyes of an author's introverted feeling. This point of view concerns itself, not with the inappropriate distribution of wealth and power, but with taking responsibility for what one has.

An insistence on integrity pervades the film, and is given a vivid personal face in the bride's cousin Ria, who has lived since childhood in Lalit's house because her own father, Lalit's brother, has died. Ria, an aspiring writer who is still unmarried, bears the twin resentments of the early loss of her father and the memory of subsequent childhood traumas. Her watchfulness qualifies the action of the film with hidden reservations—hidden, that is, until she suddenly challenges the conduct of a family elder. At this point, the film moves into extraordinary emotional territory. As head of the house, Lalit must decide what to do, and predictably, his first care is to maintain the appearance of harmony. But this is not a solution, and it does not hold.[1] When Ria has finally seen her paternal uncle choose integrity over continuity, her eyes burn with amazement. This is not the scenario feminism has prepared the modern woman for! The blaze of Ria's initiatory vision forges a new understanding of the patriarchal animus.

Around this spine established between the introverted feeling niece and the extraverted thinking uncle, the rest of the plots swirl into the kind of satisfying resolutions that echo the MGM musicals reprised in *That's Entertainment*. Aditi, the "bride with the guy on the side," comes clean to her groom, and they enter a truly enchanted space of love, while in the charming subplot P. K. Dubey courts Alice, who turns out to be just witchy enough to face down his tricksterish defiance and release his sincerity. She even succeeds in transforming his lemur face into a lover's ennobled visage. Dubey's assistants, puerile men who have been stealing a glance at Alice while she tries on some of her mistress's jewelry, end up apologizing to her. (This is a sly assertion by filmmaker Nair of the reform politics of the "gaze" in feminist cinema, which allows her to glance repeatedly throughout her film at the beauty of men.)

During one of the New Delhi street scenes, we get a glimpse of a statue of Shiva, the paradoxical Hindu god who brings both destruction and integration, so that in the religious background of the movie this god is presiding over the regeneration of the family. As the monsoon hits, and P. K.'s tent proves inadequate, the guests happily continue their dancing in the soaking mud, a dark fertility in which they have found their footing. Lalit asks his maid, now Mrs. Dubey, to dance, and with this union of high and low the comedy of integrity completes its revitalization of Ria's world. As Nair's expansive film comes to its buoyant close, it is as if India has taken the lead in getting the world's act together.

References

Cavell, S. (1981). *Pursuits of Happiness: The Hollywood Comedy of Remarriage*. Cambridge, MA: Harvard University Press.

Notes

[1] What seems to shift him is intimate contact, when he cannot sleep that night, with his wife Pimmy's body. Pimmy has come from dancing with other women, in a scene Virginia Apperson rightly emphasizes (in her chapter on *Monsoon Wedding*, which follows); they seem to be rallying libido for what will eventually be a defense of the feminine body against masculine aggression. I am indebted to Ann Alkire for first pointing out to me the importance of the scene of the women dancing, which speaks particularly to women viewers; it is indeed the key to the moral movement of the film.

CHAPTER FOURTEEN

A PROPER SOAKING

VIRGINIA APPERSON

Monsoon Wedding
(2001). Directed by Mira Nair.
Screenplay by Sabrina Dahwan.

A teacher in grade school, Mrs. Lynn, showed me how to meet a book. Instead of immediately and greedily flipping to page one, Mrs. Lynn taught us to ponder the title and start to imagine where the book's story might go. She wanted the narrative to come to life for her students and knew the sooner our imaginations were kindled, the more actively engaged as readers we would be. It is easy to extend Mrs. Lynn's approach beyond books to film, and especially one with the title *Monsoon Wedding* because it conjures all sorts of images about curious connections between weddings and monsoons. So without knowing a thing about the film but the title, I began to think how a torrential deluge might really upset a bride and groom's special day, capsizing all the meticulous preparations. Or maybe the heavy rains are simply Mother Nature's capricious way of contributing to such a man-made affair. More happily, I thought of a thoroughly saturated, but potentially jubilant occasion. Even if we normally prefer sunny, June days for weddings, perhaps, heavy winds and rain could turn out to be the uninvited guests that bring just the right gifts. With these random musings, it is not hard to imagine further that the feminine must be implicated in such a reclimatizing matrimonial melee. And so, after mulling over the title, it really did feel like I was well on my way to a richer and more engaged experience with the film, exactly the sort of start hoped for by Mrs. Lynn.

Monsoon Wedding did not disappoint these anticipations that were stimulated by its title. The talented Director Mira Nair and her first-time scriptwriter Sabrina Dahwan literally pour the blessings of their exquisite sensibilities over this delightful film. In the process, its very feminine energy manages to authenticate an arranged marriage, turning it into a genuinely renewing experience for all who are privileged to participate (including those of us watching). The feminine is not hard to spot throughout the film, as she is allowed to take the lead in a way that is quite satisfying, from the emotions that worm their ways into the more poignant scenes to the pudgy matrons' bodies jiggling beside the supple maidens, all of whom are simply rehearsing their joy. A feminine mystique, too, is certainly in charge of draping both the privileged and the commoners in the luscious colors and silky garments that Nair has used as a female *auteur*'s mise-en-scène. The feminine shows up in the sticky red Popsicle that tempts the wide-eyed bride-to-be, in the mischievous crones who honor the matrilineal tradition by spinning bawdy tales, and even in the fashion-restricted, Anglophile men that sport pastel pink turbans. Even the lively soundtrack (well-worth having purely on its own merits) combines mellifluous sounds of honeyed voices with Delhi's daily cacophony. In every single scene, the energy of the feminine is what drives the film forward and makes *the monsoon wedding* a grand and celebratory event.

Helping us around and about the film's Delhi setting, Mira Nair has a great ability to appeal to all of the viewer's senses, so that we feel like we can taste and smell as much as see and hear her motherland. Nair herself has observed that she employed "affection" as the movie's very "cornerstone," which helps us appreciate her greater gift, the way that she employs feeling in the sense of appreciative valuing.[1] Overall, *Monsoon Wedding* cannot help but be a moving picture, because it allows an unconstrained, throbbing, erotic femininity to emerge as its true star. Created in a thirty-day shoot with a cast that lived in close quarters from morning to night, including daily community yoga, Nair set out to make something "out of nothing...where [everyone] could make fools of [themselves] and tell the truth."[2]

As Nair clearly understands, a feminine sensibility is, too often, relegated in most films to a peripheral status out of deference to an audience that is more accustomed to high speed antics than the enigmatic twists and turns that are more feminine fare. In contrast to movies dominated by masculine themes, *Monsoon Wedding* allows the feminine to rule, beyond even the fondest expectations of its chastened central female characters: the bride, her best friend cousin and a housemaid. The older women who surround these young women have long since resigned themselves to subsidiary roles, but when the wedding occasion sets them all free, a femininity distilled from every one of them freely splashes about the screen, ultimately showing the characters and the viewers that "love transcends division."[3] Closer scrutiny of *Monsoon Wedding* reveals a subtle infrastructure of themes, which I would like to bring out in bolder relief, so that we might better understand the special ingredients that fuel the film's development.

Re-Arranging Arrangements

Arranged marriages are still to be expected in much of India, but a close look at the institution of marriage in general, even in the West, exposes behind the scenes maneuvers that work against the free will of the betrothed. Whenever a partnership is formed, an assortment of players offers opinions, mandates and feeling-judgments. In addition to the predictable intrusive parents conspiring for the most favorable match from the standpoint of what the family needs, there are powerful social pressures that create their own proscriptions on the couple's freedom, and every couple is driven to manipulate these in their own way. This dynamic is clearly evidenced in the films discussed in this book and makes you wonder if all marriages do not involve connivances to some degree. No apologies are made in *Monsoon Wedding* for such calculations, but then every character is given a chance to display a capacity to adapt and change. By the film's finale, *Monsoon Wedding* ends up telling the story of several pairs who step outside of the prearranged plan and strike their own bargains with each other, enriching their original culture in the process. One by one, each of the key characters in the film develops a confidence in his or herself and in their own union which gives the necessary fortitude to resist the urge to carry on pro forma.

The result is that a lot gets re-arranged. The most obvious transformation occurs in the relationship of the central couple, Aditi and Hemant. Initially, Aditi rather limply accepts the assignation set up by her parents. Looking like the archetypal unknowable bride who cannot really be seen, she obediently allows herself to be introduced to their intended for her. Aditi's own overt willfulness is not revived until a disappointing encounter with the man she thinks she loves. Only after her heart is broken by her lover does she decide to have a choice in this significant matter of marriage. With eyes finally alive and wide-open, she recognizes that Hemant is in fact the far more suitable swain. She chooses him, not because her parents told her to, but because she likes him. The film is replete with parallel subplots containing re-configured associations in which each individual in a couple allows him or herself to be infected by the other with refreshing and rehabilitative consequences. Other pairs where this deconstruction process occurs include: Lalit and Pimmy, the bickersome, but loving parents of the bride, Dubey and Alice, the droll and tricksterish wedding planner and the mostly reticent housemaid that he finally courts, and (though theirs is not a romantic relationship) Lalit and his niece Ria, who develop an unanticipated, but quite potent partnership around a desperate need within the family to actively defend the feminine at any cost. The consciousness that grows from each character's willingness to reshuffle their lives, resisting both the internal and external dictates that say how things are supposed to be, enables everyone to strike a better bargain for themselves, for their relationship and leaves their families with a far healthier legacy.

Masculine Overdrive

Even though *Monsoon Wedding* aims for a new standard in which male and female receive equal billing (where the feminine is able to hold her own), an irrepressible masculine desire to oppress still swaggers around the film looking for something to control. In the early reels, Lalit plays the indignant patriarch, as he periodically blusters about like a surly rooster— intolerant of his wife's concerns, his son's girlish ways, and his nephew's devil-may-care attitude. Lalit persists with such power plays as he micromanages the wedding extravaganza until it turns into a real pain in his neck rather than an eagerly anticipated occasion. All the while, his wife Pimmy unintentionally supports his tyranny with her conciliatory, avoidant behavior.

Numerous other examples of cocky male postures are sprinkled all over the film. While Dubey plans the wedding, he hides his marshmallow of a heart, bluffing his way through with a hilarious display of self-important conceit. The normally decently restrained Hemant, the primary groom, throws a brief macho tantrum when he learns of his fiancée's trysts. The slightly effeminate son Varun, after his father threatens to send him to boarding school, resorts to babyish bravado that only serves to keep him from what he loves most, enjoying the swishy dance number with his theatrical cousin. Each time the guys hide behind such self-reliant superiority, they never really prevail, but instead manage to postpone an authentic engagement with the feminine.

John Gottman and his wife Nan Silver, marriage and family research psychologists at the University of Washington, have addressed this male proclivity for eclipsing others in the name of self-assertion. Their research traces how men have been socialized to resist women's influence in order to develop a sense of their own independence. Such self-assertion serves to advance a man's autonomy, but when it becomes his hard-line in the face of conflict, it destroys his capacity to sustain relationship. Whereas women are socialized to consider men's offerings (the downside of this has been discussed at various points throughout this book), men shy away from the vulnerability that emerges when one defers to another. Gottman and Silver's work shows that successful partnerships, however, are ones in which a man lets down his guard long enough to be impacted by a woman's perspective (1999, 100).

This clinical research focuses on cultural factors conditioning men and women in their relationships. Though it is out of fashion to say so, their findings may also say something about the essential nature of masculinity and femininity (which we should always remember from an archetypal perspective are principles in both men and women). Certainly there is an archetypal aspect to the sadistic masculine inclination to dominate and impinge upon feminine territory and something equally archetypal in the masochistic feminine's nasty, self-sabotaging habit of playing along passively with the aggression. The researchers' conclusions show that the relationship between the genders can only succeed when the feminine partner brings herself to face her male partner and the masculine partner develops a greater receptivity to what his female counterpart has to offer.

Thankfully, the immoderate and unyielding masculine (that in another film leads to the feminine's demise) is scaled back to proportion, because in *Monsoon Wedding*, there is plenty of self-aware and confident feminine energy at the conjugal table. A sweet example is when the women have gathered round the bride to paint henna, sing ribald songs and share old wives' tales. These women are so grounded in themselves and so eager to share their goodwill that the effervescent spirit that they exude is positively contagious. Rather than reacting with disdain or feeling intimidated by the women's collective power, the men recognize where the real action is and eagerly join in. So though the film has plenty of exaggerated masculine energy that struts and frets, in the end such overbearing energy is not allowed to hijack the film. Rather, as John Beebe suggests in his review of the movie, supporting the feminine actually enhances their own integrity as men—a much handsomer solution.

Boys Must Be Boys

One of the most egregious directives of patriarchal culture is that boys should limit themselves to virile behavior. Such a manhandled campaign results in a determination that the feminine must be undermined for men to come into their own. Refusing to comply, Lalit's exuberant son Varun bristles at this patriarchal bridle and bucks his father's stereotypical ambitions for him, making it clear that learning to cook and perform Bollywood's boogie are more his cups of tea. After all, why should the girls have all the fun? Though, at times, he acts like a eunuch in a harem of family women with all his affectations and aspirations to be best-in-show, he is still the only male phallic enough to stand up to Lalit's top-heavy ways.

The Feminine Default

Wife Pimmy seems a bit edgy. Maid Alice appears to be thieving. Daughter Aditi is resigned to marry (while carrying on an affair on the sly). And Niece Ria is becoming hysterical. Repeatedly these women play into the hands of critics, making the feminine seem like a principle of dubious character. Each of them compromises herself by keeping her mouth shut—relying on deference rather than dispute, compliance over defiance and silence rather than open expression of outrage—all passive-aggressive assertions of their feminine prerogatives. Sometimes these strategies work, but ultimately they really only serve to evade a genuine confrontation of the masculine and help perpetuate a sick system. Here is how it plays out.

Pimmy puffs cigarettes on a toilet stool instead of getting huffy at her husband's anxious diatribes. It is just plain easier for her to swallow his outbursts and absorb his angst than to rebut him with her own authority. And because she keeps quiet, Lalit never has to question his own misdemeanors.

Little workhorse Alice, so attuned to everyone else's desires, momentarily allows herself a flight of fancy. Dazzled by her mistress Pimmy's jewels, she lets her guard down and tries them on, innocently playing at being a princess. The unimaginative dopes that catch her (Dubey's workmen) decide rather loudly that she is trying to steal the jewelry. Mortified, Alice frantically removes them and returns like a shamed Cinderella back to the ashes of her life.

Aditi has grown up knowing that her parents would some day plan her marriage because it would advance the social standing of the family. (The man they have carefully selected for her, Hemant, has gracious, upper class manners and a good job in America as an engineer.) Looking like a big, sad child who has not yet learned to be intentional about her choices, to be aware of her projections or to be accountable to her longings, Aditi goes through the motions of the engagement on autopilot. Dutifully acting as the family's collateral, she plays the good daughter. Since her own desires have never been sanctioned, and it is her nature to accommodate others, her passion has gone underground, expressed in the illicit affair with a married co-worker whom she confuses for the love of her life.

Ria's father died when she was young, which left his brother (the often-stretched Lalit) to support her. When she was little, her defenseless position was exploited by the Anglicized Uncle Tej who was surely aware that Ria felt beholden to the family's male powerbrokers. Ria understood that the family relied on Tej for prestige and finances, that she, too, was dependent upon this family structure, and that she had no other choice than to acquiesce to Tej's lecherous kisses and gropes. As a young adult, Ria still suffers in silence with the childhood abuse because she is convinced that no one in this aspiring upper middle class family would ever take her side against Tej. And up until now, no one bothers to get to the bottom of her temperamental nature.

The surprise of the movie is that all of the women find firmer footing as the film proceeds. Each, at the end, comes out with a stronger sense of what she has to contribute. Pimmy learns to assert herself with love. Alice dares to make her fantasy real, as she meets and holds Dubey's gaze. Aditi, having shattered all pretenses, gains Hemant's admiration, and Ria's willingness to expose what has happened to her in the family evokes a moral stamina from Lalit that redeems both himself and her. Like a fresh breeze, an egalitarian spirit that brings courage to the feminine wends its way through the film, and not only do the women finally take themselves seriously, but they are each met with appreciation and respect.

Little Petals of Desire

Few in any contemporary patriarchal country would disagree that possessing a masculine mindset ensures remarkable proficiency and efficiency in most of life's tasks. Deploying bold directives and employing unwavering discipline in the execution of these directives enables the masculine to cut to the core of most quandaries. Maintenance of this can-do spirit and single-minded focus requires, however, insensitivity thick-skinned enough to callously blast past anything that interferes with more important considerations. With logic as the guide, extravagant or even simple pleasures, especially desires of the heart, are the first to go.

Like in so many films, the ones in this book have not been short on depictions of desire. Wants pop up with ease, preserving them is what proves to be the greater challenge (as we sadly saw in *Wide Sargasso Sea*). Because desires tend to complicate, once they perplex, frustrate and interfere with a master plan, elimination of them makes perfect sense. As would be expected, since *Monsoon Wedding*'s subject is a drive toward marriage, desire abounds in the film but even better, the amorous and sybaritic urges that too often get thwarted, survive. So what is it in this film that protects the sweeter things in life?

It is the hapless Dubey, who fumbles upon the answer as he hustles around, pretending to make things happen. Hired to plan Aditi and Hemant's wedding, his ridiculous, but endearing pretense of upper class savoir-faire really only serve to impress his rather dimwitted assistants (the ones that falsely accuse Alice). But much more arises from Dubey than half-truths, and the underground element that propels Dubey's evolution turns out to be so small and seemingly inconsequential that one could almost forget about it. The unassuming change agent (that Dubey regularly snacks on) is none other than the common marigold. Hothouse-bred for the purpose of festooning the canopies under which the festivities will be held, this diminutive flower apparently feeds some hunger in Dubey that can only be understood by looking at the marigold's lineage.

The marigold ("Mary's gold") happens to be a particularly worthy representative from the feminine world since it originates from quite a royal matriarchal ancestry. Its archetypal pedigree reveals countless *Mari*an-related goddesses in just about every culture and religion imaginable including the Chaldeans, Jews, Persians and Christians (Walker 1983, 584-585). History helps us see that though male gods are far more familiar to our Western consciousness, they are actually relatively new divinities dating back to 2500 B.C.; whereas, female deities (from which the marigolds are descended) have been documented since 25,000 B.C. (Spretnak 1978, 26). As patriarchy took hold, matrifocal authority waned, leaving worship of the feminine practically an endangered practice. It is as if Dubey is righting this age-old imbalance by once more taking the feminine in, knowing on some level that his well-being depends upon a steady diet of marigolds.

The corrective tonic that the humble flower provides seems to do the trick as the driven energy that has guided and limited Dubey's life begins to change course. The blossom's subtle, integrating influence bears fruit when Dubey manages to catch the eye of the selfless and demure servant Alice. In spite of Dubey's coxcombry, Alice (who is clearly rooted in the marigold's tradition) is wise enough to look beneath Dubey's arrogant surface and to feel his capacity to love. Fortified by the flower's essence, he finally notices her sweet attention, and desire not only stirs but slowly transforms his narcissistic buffoonery. This time the more masculine approach does not get a chance to undercut the oblique efforts made by such earthly delights, since Dubey has been savoring and incorporating them, one petal at a time. And so, he and Alice both finally get a shot at love.

The False Father

The ultimate negative patriarch of the film, the slick and smooth Uncle Tej, feels (to this woman, at least) like a creep from the very beginning. Though it is hard to put a finger on what is amiss, coolness fills the air whenever he enters a room.[4] As the story unfolds, it becomes apparent that the family resources are locked in Uncle Tej's vault; so, in order to maintain their upper middle class appearance, the family is at his mercy. His largesse seems harmless enough on face value because of the game the family all understands: fawn over him shamelessly, shower Tej with praise, turn to him for advice and approval and be eternally grateful for his blessings. Tej relishes this purchased flattery and the privilege of bearing the mantle of paterfamilias. But behind this scene of ingratiating manners, Tej had his way with young Ria.

Exploiting his sanctified status, he forced Ria to accommodate to his desires, which of course carried the implicit demand that she stifle her own. The injustice of this is unconscionable. How can a man so revered engage in such malevolent exploitation? The answer seems to be that he does not see it as such. And here, we can find a painful home truth:

> [I]n the so-called real world it is still far too easy for men to conform to patriarchal stereotypes in an uncritical and unthinking way....Patriarchy has been a self-serving and self-perpetuating system, and it is difficult to stop what tradition and social structure have mobilized and upheld. (Tacey 1997, 193)

Ignorant of their good uncle's underbelly, the clan struck a bargain that was mutually satisfying to both sides. Since everybody seems to be fat and happy, benefiting from Tej's self-aggrandizement, there is no impetus for Tej to outgrow the family hero worship and own up to his indiscretions. It is in this chilling climate that the young feminine is recurrently sacrificed.

Tej's Achilles' heel is fairly easy for Mira Nair to expose. His sole focus has been maintenance of his patriarchal persona. When Tej's desires do emerge (the kind that the patriarchy has so little experience honoring), he can only respond in a juvenile way. What is repellent in the man is not his desire. It is his cold-hearted assumption that his entitled status automatically gives him carte blanche to do as he pleases, even if that includes taking his lust to a little girl. His other victim, which he unfortunately must have conquered at a very early age, is the feminine side of himself.

Ria Speaks Up

Tej dictated the terms of what he would accept from Ria, and Ria assumed that her voice would not be considered. Even long after the abuse, the internal wounds festered because Ria's only recourse was to hide the truth (and such isolation can never provide a cure). It is only when Ria suspects that Tej has found his next victim in her young niece Aliya (who looks to be about eight years old) that Ria gives voice to her own fury. Out of her suffering depths, her cry makes its long-delayed emergence, and she screams for him to let Aliya alone. Such a gutsy move, purely on behalf of the young feminine, provides the necessary catalyst that shatters the regime that has blindly supported such scurrilous behavior.

> If patriarchy is being gradually disrupted, it is because the rejected and excluded feminine forces are awakening to a new life, and demand to be heard. Any movement which blandly 'seals over' the cracks and fault-lines that are appearing in the fabric of patriarchy must therefore be construed as historically backward and regressive. The uprising feminine spirit must be allowed to create havoc within the comfort-zones of patriarchy (Tacey 1997, 192).

When the havoc of Ria's libido for justice is finally unleashed, Tej falls back on his negating paternalism to rebuke her, "she's mad; she's crazy." Ria responds with her only and very best defense, "You know I don't lie."

A Paternal Overhaul

Ria's denunciation of her uncle does not bring immediate results. Initially those within earshot of Ria stumble away from her in shock, having difficulty processing the indictment. Her accusations are especially reverberant within Lalit because he is so deeply indebted to Tej, both for financial and social standing. Accepting the reality of the abuse creates an unbearable dilemma that forces Lalit into utter despair. If he supports his beloved niece, the foundation of his world, which has been so nicely subsidized by Tej, will crumble. Thank goodness his wife awaits him at the bottom of his grief to accompany him through the oncoming night's unrelenting darkness. Their lovemaking is perhaps one of the loveliest images captured on film of a woman comforting her man. It is not certain that Lalit could have survived his tortuous state or found his own power base without her modulating presence. One senses that she mostly serves to get him to feel, as fully as possible, the magnitude of his pain which includes his shame at having bought into a system that would perpetuate such abuse. Living into his misery turns out to be the necessary act of penitence that enables him to loosen his paternalistic grip and allows his heart to open.

Lalit responsibly suffers through the excruciating angst and comes to an understanding that in order to share Ria's burden, he must surrender his dependence on Tej and relinquish his own false bravado. Lalit takes his role as father to a new plane, recognizing that he:

> serve[s] the spirit of the father best by challenging and criticizing his established traditions. If the father's traditions are to maintain integrity and not be allowed to lapse into parody or corruption, they must be updated, reconstructed, and revived (Tacey 1997, 191).

In order to truly be a father to his dead brother's precious daughter, Lalit must die to his upward-mobile world and return to the bedrock of his feeling for his family. Since he is now nicely connected to the anima, Lalit can effectively facedown Tej. First, he tenderly invites Ria back into the fold and then firmly insists that Tej leave his house. This is not patriarchy: it is what one does as a good father.

The Splendidly, Corporeal Feminine

The revelation that Uncle Tej is a pathetic, self-serving man is a shocking moment in *Monsoon Wedding*, but the real power (and beauty) of the film comes from the other characters whose relationships evolve out of the labors that love requires. Watching individuals struggle with their own shortcomings, learn from his or her partner and become better for the challenges that result from consciously participating with love's experiment provide the viewer with lessons in how to make healthy joint ventures. And there is one final facet of *Monsoon Wedding*, with its exceptional rendering of feminine talent, that makes it a film that has much to teach our overly regulated lives: the way that the female body is featured in a rare ungirdled fashion. After all, what is the archetypal feminine without her fleshy abundance? In other movies mentioned in this book, the woman's body has been objectified, corseted, anesthetized and ravaged. In *Monsoon Wedding*, though, with the exception of Ria's plight, the corporal is given central billing in plenty of wonderfully unself-conscious poses.

One of the most fun and physical scenes occurs towards the end of the film (just prior to Ria's outburst). The scene is set at the bottom of an empty swimming pool that has an elaborate Gaudí-esque design. Like Venus arising out of the foamy sea, Lalit's provocative teenage niece, Ayesha, makes a dramatic entrance and boldly entertains the guests with her Bollywood gyrations. As if to create a responsive mindset for the upcoming revelations of Tej's abuse, Ayesha's fully embodied and electric performance makes a decidedly feminine statement within the pool's lavish depths. Backed by family and friends' enthusiastic approval, an appreciative space is made for the maiden's nubile sensuality. The absence of shame or lasciviousness with regards to her stimulating routine speaks to a genuine and natural regard for a vital aspect of the feminine archetype. Instead of a reactive reprisal for her exuberant and unabashed spirit, the fellow partygoers are inspired by Ayesha, so much so that they all join in, filling the pool, young and old, with twirling and gyrating and entwining bodies.

Dancing in our seats, the uniting ambiance empowers the audience, too, to embrace the ethic that basically guides the rest of the film. With such a public display of genuine receptivity, the full-fledged feminine is allowed to work her last bit of magic, granting Ria the wherewithal to speak on behalf of Aliya and by so doing to fully express concern for the susceptible feminine everywhere. It takes a crucible with this much body and heft to hold Lalit's pain and prideful denial of the shadow side of the patriarchy, the one that up until now has supported him. No longer ruled by a cynical patriarchal ego, and now nicely bolstered by his wife's loving embrace, he is able to assert virtues more appropriate to his role as the father of his family.

After the sobering exorcism of the fallacious-father uncle, all are now truly prepared to celebrate a wedding. When the actual matrimonial festivities begin, the merry movement resumes, companioned by buckets of rain that wash away the fears and anguish, the confusion and divisiveness that have burdened so many of the characters in the film. It is as if the force of the feminine has become incarnated in these torrential drops which benevolently christen the party. Finally recognizing the feminine gift that has joined them, everyone welcomes the disorderly and dispersive deluge. By the end of the final take, the entire cast is gliding and colliding to an erotic, amalgamating rhythmic beat. And then it is clear what a *monsoon wedding* really is: a joyful union of all the parts to each other and a celebration of the courage that is required to care.

References

Gottman, John and Silver, Nan (1999). *The Seven Principles for Making Marriage Work*. New York: Chiron Publishers, Inc.

Spretnak, Charlene (1978/1992). *Lost Goddesses of Early Greece: A Collection of Pre- Hellenic Myths*. Boston: Beacon Press.

Tacey, David (1997). *Remaking Men: Jung, Spirituality and Social Change*. London: Routledge.

Walker, Barbara G. (1983). *The Woman's Encyclopedia of Myths and Secrets*. San Francisco: HarperSanFrancisco.

Notes

---

[1] Interview with Mira Nair in *Monsoon Wedding* DVD, 2002.

[2] Ibid.

[3] Ibid.

[4] Ibid.

CHAPTER FIFTEEN

GETTING IT RIGHT

JOHN BEEBE

The Queen
(2006). Directed by Stephen Frears.
Screenplay by Peter Morgan.

The English film director Stephen Frears, though not usually recognized by critics as a master auteur, has long evidenced an instinct for what makes a cinematic subject and what it takes to bring it off. He has a capacity to bring out the best in actors (both leading players and those in supporting roles); a nice sense of timing; an ear for language and accent; a dramatist's feel for the affective rhythms that roll character into fate; and a sharp eye for humor. He always finds the comedy in tragedy, and the tragedy in comedy. Great actors and screenwriters love to work with him: the scripts and stars he chooses have more than once been selected for Academy Award nominations.

These qualities are on proud display in his perfectly proportioned new movie *The Queen*, which will doubtless make film lovers look once again at his earlier oeuvre—at *My Beautiful Launderette, Dangerous Liaisons, Prick Up Your Ears*, and *The Grifters*—and perhaps revalue his considerable psychological gifts. Here Frears treats, as if by divine right and with a royal touch, Queen Elizabeth II, miraculously impersonated, under the spell of his direction, by the fine actress Helen Mirren. As mediated by Mirren, the Queen faces Frears' camera bearing the commonest and most fearsome of human problems—the difficulty we all have in summoning feeling that is appropriate for the big events in our lives. Perhaps the film works so well because this role is that kind of event in Mirren's career.

In *The Queen*, the occurrence, both awkward and archetypal, that confronts Elizabeth is the death of Princess Diana. This public calamity has come only a year after the princess embarrassed the British royal family to its core by divorcing Elizabeth's hapless son, Charles, heir to a throne that Diana publicly declared him unfit to hold. Diana's death is being mourned in unprecedented degree by the public, which expects the Sovereign to preside over their wet display of spontaneous feeling, the one demand of her job the dry Elizabeth is just not up to.

As we contemplate Elizabeth's incorrigible stiffness, we find that we are not only embarrassed for her but with her. Most of us are more like her than we know in preferring to contemplate the archetypal moments of our lives in private. An archetypal intrusion, however, is an event in the collective unconscious with power to link us to others in the human group: we see that we will be judged by how we respond. One would not expect a commercial motion picture about Diana's death, which occasioned in England an outpouring of mourning so profound that it led even Jungian analysts to contemplate the phenomenon,[1] to be a comedy of manners, but that is just what Frears is able to shape his film to become. The way the Queen resists the human display that is expected of her, too, is irresistibly droll, but at the same time deeply moving. The one time she cries— alone—her back is to the camera. Her stalling is egged on by the attitudes of two powerful families—her own, which except for her callowly intuitive son Charles, fails to recognize the public relations problem she is creating by her insistence that this is a private matter for them; and the political family of the new Labor Prime Minister, Tony Blair, which is aligned with the people and against the monarchy. Blair's people—his teasingly insinuating wife Cherie, who thinks the monarchy should be abolished, and his satiric chief speechwriter and public relations officer, Alistair—do get how serious a gaffe the Queen's refusal to make any public sign or statement is, and they support Blair entirely in pointing that out to her; but they actually relish the Queen's image being tarnished by her choice of privacy over public confession.

The Royal Family's Scottish retreat, Balmoral, represents for the Queen a world of introverted feeling in which she can be comfortable, at least when she is entirely alone. Her family, to whom she instinctively turns in the difficult days after she receives the cumbersome news of Diana's death, is inevitably disappointing. Her husband Philip, the Duke of Edinburgh, can think of no better consolation for the boys who have lost their mother (if the monarchy survives, one of them will be a future King of England) than to distract them with "stalking" a prize stag that has appeared on the partially forested slopes of the estate. Her "mummy" (The Queen Mother, also an Elizabeth) confines herself to reciting the norms of royal protocol, for which Diana's death offers no precedent. The Queen's son, the nervous Prince Charles, whose adulterous liaison with Camilla

Parker-Bowles had been revealed to all the world by Diana as the basis for her divorce, thus seriously qualifying his right to succession, takes this opportunity to remark to his mother that whatever Diana had been like to them she was a wonderful mother, never afraid to show her feeling for her sons, even in public. The three Job's comforters are poisonously rendered by expert character actors, but Mirren's Elizabeth is armed with an antiserum: as the Sovereign, she recognizes that she must choose her own counselors and make her own path.

Mirren's Elizabeth, though carrying the stony bland stare that the real Queen Elizabeth II is so famous for (in my experience, the only time America's greatest comedian, Bob Hope, wasn't funny was during a command performance in Washington when she sat in the front row), is a master of disguise. She likes to cloak herself in what looks like introversion and to argue dryly for the necessity of handling feeling in private, but she is neither an introvert nor without a capacity to convey feeling. The Queen's problem, as Mirren's psychologically literate performance makes clear, is intuition. She is miserable and stony in the first days after the tragedy because she has not really connected with what Diana's death means, and that is the real reason she is not prepared to meet a public that is so obviously—if uncomprehendingly—moved by the tragedy.

While the Queen, struggling to trace her own sense of it all, drives herself around the Balmoral estate in her old Range Rover, a far more public version of the drama is unfolding in London. There Tony Blair, just a couple months in office, is hyper-conscientious about keeping abreast of the public's feeling. He sees it as the Queen's duty to attend to the grief of her people, and his, as her Prime Minister, to advise her to do so. His grasp of the magnitude of the event has already given him the stature of a Churchill in the press: in a prescient elegy crafted the day after the death by his scriptwriter Alastair, he calls Diana "the People's Princess," and he follows that lead in trying, with the Queen, to become the People's Prime Minister. He keeps phoning Her Majesty to advise her to make the right extraverted feeling moves to secure her standing with her subjects—to fly the royal standard at half-mast over Buckingham Palace (the Queen refuses because it would break with protocol to use it for anything but as a signal that the sovereign is in the palace); to end her silence by making a public statement to lead the people in their grief ("THEIR grief," she exclaims)[2]; and to come to London to be with the mourners ("If you're suggesting I drop everything and come down to London before I attend to two boys that have just lost their mother you're mistaken"). From a Jungian point of view, he epitomizes the introverted thinking hero who has decided how a feeling matter must be handled: the more Tony Blair experiences rebuke from the Queen's refusal to take up his suggestions, the more convinced he becomes that his definition of the situation is the right one.

The history the film records (still fresh in the memories of many of its viewers)—how Elizabeth is finally forced to yield to all of Blair's demands by making, at the end of the week, the gestures he has asked for all along—would seem simply to support him, but the film, like its subject, is deceptive. Blair learns at least as much about timing, and political survival, from the Queen. By waiting, and even drawing the ire of her subjects, the Queen is all the more effective when she finally appears in their midst. This only happens once her private mourning is complete, punctuated by two private audiences with the stag her husband and grandsons have been rather mindlessly hunting. The stag, a medieval allegory of Christ, and also of Christian *superbia* (the pride one can take in ruling one's human instincts, for instance), seems in the film to represent divine right, the archetype that is passing away in the age of easy access to the masses through the media that Diana and Blair (and Frears) under- stand so well. The mystery of the divine in transformation is to be experienced, not explained, but from a psychological point of view we can say without spoiling the effect that her scenes with the stag represent the moments in which the Queen, from her own extraverted sensation standpoint, finally connects with the introverted intuition she needs to realize that the time for *superbia* has passed for the royals. Asserting divine right is no longer the way to carry her authority; rather, she has to have the humility to be a Presence, even if an unpopular one, in the midst of her subjects. When at last she encounters firsthand a throng of mourners outside Buckingham Palace, the scene renders convincingly her confrontation with collective emotion. Blair, watching on TV (in a sequence that deserves comparison to the one in *Schindler's List* of Schindler watching the little girl in red move through the chaotic liquidation of the Krakow ghetto), suddenly finds his own uncalculated extraverted feeling and sees what the royal touch really means for a country. Blair's smart, feminist wife, who suspects her husband of a "mother thing" with Elizabeth, and of being one more Labor prime minister to go gaga for the Queen, cannot follow the development of his feeling with her extraverted thinking, nor can the tricksterish speechwriter who is caught in limning the Queen's insincerity. Blair turns on the latter with appealing ferocity, in one of the great movie speeches: "You know when you get it wrong, you REALLY get it wrong!" Just as Elizabeth, with her irrational process, has connected with her intuition, he, through the force of his reason, has connected with his feeling.

When prime minister and queen meet again in the fall, it is before a fountain in the palace gardens that presents itself, seen from above, as a stately English mandala. For a Jungian, this familiar symbol of wholeness reflects the psychological design of the film, denoting the integrity of consciousness, achieved by the crossed union of opposite psychological types on both the rational and irrational axes. Blair's union of high and low, achieved by extending himself beyond his superior introverted thinking to arrive at authentic and no longer insecure extraverted feeling, is crossed, as it were, by the link that the Queen has been able to make between her reliable extraverted sensation and her newfound introverted intuition. Her insight parallels the discovery made by the Prime Minister (whom she will now be able to helpfully advise) that rule is never a right, but rather a responsibility to care for people. She has surpassed the role of sovereign to find her more embodied authority as the mother of the country, a needed balance to patriarchal rule.

References

Beebe, John (1998). Review of *When a Princess Dies: Reflections from Jungian Analyst*. In *Harvest* 44/2, 158-164.

Haynes, Jane & Shearer, Ann (1998). *When a Princess Dies: Reflections from Jungian Analyst*. London: Harvest Books.

Morgan, Peter (2006). *The Queen*. New York: Hyperion.

Notes

[1] See Haynes & Shearer (1998) and Beebe (1998).

[2] Specific lines from the film are given as they appear in the published screenplay by Peter Morgan (2006).

CHAPTER SIXTEEN

AFFIRMING THE HUMAN

JOHN BEEBE

Rhapsody in August

(1991). Written and Directed by Akira Kurosawa.

The opening of Akira Kurosawa's twenty-ninth film offers a clear blue
sky over the mountains outside Nagasaki, where, in the summer of 1990,
wonderfully white clouds can still suddenly echo the shape of the nuclear
explosion that occurred forty-five years before. The image of this sky
announces the filmmaker's conscience, which is buoyantly clear even in
the face of a lifetime of war-inspired visions, ready at last to take up the
hardest of cinematic subjects for a director who has specialized in
depicting conflict, the return to normal conditions that can follow
abnormal events. The ninety-seven minutes that follow do not disappoint
this promise of a fresh perspective: this is perhaps the least heavy-handed
film Kurosawa has ever made. *Rhapsody in August* stands alone in his
work for the ease and command of its feeling for people in a peaceful
situation. The scenes are casually but aesthetically defined as groupings of
relatives or friends arranging themselves spontaneously in relation to each
other.

The movie takes as its theme the everyday problem of trying to get the
feeling between people right—a theme that is epitomized by seventeen–
year–old Tateo's "absolute" determination to fix his grandmother's out–
of–tune Kawai organ during his summer vacation before starting college.
(He and his sister, and his uncle's son and daughter, are visiting
grandmother's farm on the other side of the mountains from Nagasaki,
while his mother and uncle pay a visit to a wealthy great-uncle in Hawaii.)
He wants to be able to play Schubert's *Heidenröslein*, a setting of one of
Goethe's early lyrics:

And the boy a rose did see
A rose standing in the field
Blossoming in all innocence.
The sight then to him revealed
A never-ending fascination
For the crimson color
Of the rose standing in the field.[1]

The rose, the organ, and the echo of Goethe's musical verse point to an extraverted feeling everyone can delight in—precisely the feeling that modernity and the culminating catastrophes of World War II made suspect.

Grandmother, whose husband, a Nagasaki schoolteacher, was killed in the August 9, 1945, bombing, carries feeling of another sort—a deep introverted feeling that pleases itself with love for her grandchildren and passionate support for the values she would like to see survive. These she expresses in traditional meals for her young guests (they shame her into letting them take over the cooking, switching from pumpkin and kidney beans soaked in soy sauce to spaghetti) and in her outbursts at their parents for their greedy eagerness to insinuate themselves into the good graces of the wealthy relative in Hawaii. She sits in silent colloquy over tea with another widow of the bombing, and chants through long Buddhist prayer services in memory of the dead: the high point of her year is the annual memorial service on August 9.

This year, however, grandmother is challenged to alter her routine: the relative her son and daughter have gone to meet turns out to be her only surviving brother, whom she has not seen since 1920. He is thoroughly Americanized, with a son by an American wife and grandchildren who do not look Japanese at all. This older brother is ill, and would like to see his sister once more before he dies. To fulfill his request would require that she travel to Hawaii, and this the grandmother finds hard to conceive: she says she cannot even remember the brother, one of at least ten siblings who have died or disappeared. (She is also suspicious of the motives of her children in urging her to go to see this man: it is obvious they are currying favor to try to win jobs for themselves in his international business.)

The challenge to the old woman's extraverted feeling is brilliantly conveyed by the eighty-six year old veteran stage actress Sachiko Murase, in a great cinematic performance. As the children draw her out, trying to convince her to accept her older brother's invitation, she responds by teasing them with long-buried memories of her other brothers, all of whom had names of metals embedded in their names, chosen by her somewhat peculiar father. The stories are wonderful and frightening at the same time—a shoemaker's apprentice who ran away with the shoemaker's wife and set up housekeeping in a forest hut near two trees struck by lightning that looked as if they had committed a double suicide; a weak-minded brother who never recovered from the shock of seeing the explosion, and would draw pictures of a terrible eye he beheld over the mountains as the bomb exploded that day.

This eye is revealed, in a great surreal image, as a human consciousness magnified to take in an intolerable red dawn, perhaps a pitiless demand to awaken to the possibility of total planetary destruction. Yet the same brother, who like grandmother, was forced to witness that eye, was also saved from drowning by a water-imp. Shinjiro, the youngest grandchild, masters his fear of the eye by dressing up as the water-imp, a figure that implies resilience—and a healthy relation to water.

Water is used throughout the film as a visual metaphor for feeling— most effectively in one scene where three of the children, visiting a fountain monument to the victims of the bombing who were parched with thirst, instinctively wet the dusty marble with water. And splashing each other by the waterfall where grandmother's weak-minded brother used to go to bathe is the way the littlest boy makes friendly contact with Clark, the American nephew who comes to call on grandmother on his dying father's behalf.

Clark, beautifully played in phonetic Japanese, and a more expansive Hollywood English, by Richard Gere, whose trademark discomfort with expressions of feeling works perfectly here, has the difficult task of apologizing to his aunt for the family's neglect of the memory of her husband. In fact, his cousins (grandmother's son and daughter) have gone to lengths to keep from him the fact that their father died in the bombing. They worry that the news will be "awkward," will kill the deal they are trying to bring off, and they are angry at the children for sending a telegram saying grandmother will come to Hawaii after the annual memorial for the Nagasaki victims. But when they learn that Clark has come to apologize to grandmother, they quickly realize their mistake, accepting their shame in a charmingly awkward way which elicits feeling for them from us as we watch the film. The families come together at the playground of the school where grandfather died.

This is the second visit to this site in the film. The first, an elegiac set piece, moves on to a memorial park, where monuments on the theme of mother and child have been raised by various countries of the world. Many of the sculptures come from the onetime Soviet bloc, but there are also ones from Holland and Brazil. The littlest boy notes that the United States has no monument there: "They dropped the bomb," he is reminded. This time, Clark's presence performs the American acknowledgement. The schoolyard memorial looks like an enlarged drooping section of barbed wire. One of the most succinct and poignant central images in any film, the tangled iron structure, which simultaneously evokes nuclear explosion and concentration camp—both kinds of holocaust—gradually reveals itself as a melted jungle gym. Associations accrue as the camera contemplates it. One recalls grandmother's brothers, who all had metal in their names, and then a time when world leaders themselves took names like Stalin, man of steel. As children appear on the playground to use their new white painted jungle gym standing in the background, one suddenly realizes that other children were actually playing here when the bomb exploded. Because it is the time of the August memorial services, surviving classmates of the children who died on the day of the blast, some of them blind, come to tend the memorial, to wipe clean the stone slab that reads "1945 8.9 11:02" and to replenish the flower bed that surrounds the jungle gym.

Clark goes on to the house of his father's sister, where the little boy witnesses his grandmother's reception of Clark's apology. He realizes he has "seen something wonderful." By now, the organ has been repaired, and the children sing the Schubert lied about the boy who saw a rose. Soon after, at the memorial service, the little boy does get to see a rose, in a scene which carries the essence of this film's view of human individuation as a path toward appropriate feeling. That the moment is so carefully prepared in no way dilutes the intensity of the beauty that is revealed.

But this static introverted epiphany is but a preparation for the extraverted feeling *satori* with which the film concludes. Events make it plain that grandmother has also neglected her American brother, and now it is her turn to apologize, and to face the tightness of her own introverted feeling. An inverted Lear, she starts to go mad because she has asked so little of the world and realizes that she owes it a more expansive caring.

In the history of cinema, no one has done weather as well as Kurosawa, and he gives us a thunderstorm that half convinces us to believe the grandmother when she says that a new explosion has occurred. But in her grief, grandmother is giving in to a delayed post-traumatic reaction. She runs off into the storm, and all the family run comically after. They are beyond pulling her back into her ritualized life of denial of her fear of nature. As they catch up to her, her umbrella is torn inside out and a smile of gratitude begins to show on her lips. She is moving in nature, with full acceptance of its changeable force. The bomb itself is but one manifestation of that force, and she has opened herself to all of nature's possibilities. In this culminating image of his own individuation as an artist, Kurosawa follows Shakespeare and Goethe in collapsing the distinction between a normal and an abnormal fate. And like his great predecessors he reveals himself as a poet of nature for whom affirmation of the human is consistent with love of nature itself.

References

Goethe, J. W. (1983). *Selected Poems,* Christopher Middleton (ed.). London: John Calder.

Jung, C. G. (1946/1966). "The Psychology of the Transference." In *Collected Works,* vol. 16,

— (1955-56/1963). *Mysterium Coniunctionis. Collected Works,* vol. 14.

Notes

[1] The complete text of the poem, in the original German, can be found in Goethe (1983, 16).

ANIMA FIGURES

CHAPTER SEVENTEEN

THE ANIMA IN FILM

JOHN BEEBE

The anima in film is much like the anima anywhere else:[1] a confusing, deceptive presence with the capacity to engender inner transformation. In film, as in dreams, there is the advantage that the archetype is visible as well as effective. For that reason, I have frequently turned to movies to understand better the typical role of the anima, and my hunger, as a clinician, to get a clearer sense of the functioning of this unconscious feminine presence has not gone unsatisfied. What I will offer here is a guide for exploring the anima through film, as well as an indication of some things film has helped me to discover about the anima's function in relation to other archetypes of the psyche, most particularly the persona.

I do not think it is appropriate to call every woman in film an anima figure, although the luminous representation has the important charac-teristic of turning a human being into an image that can be manipulated to aesthetic effect by a supraordinate creative personality, the film director. The director's role in making a film is already, therefore, not unlike that of the Self in creating dreams. In dreammaking, the Self seeks to achieve the goals of the total psyche by affective stimulation of the ego, using images that are not so much representations of reality as feeling-toned complexes of unconscious life. These complexes are, however, often made to simulate conscious reality and especially significant persons so that consciousness will take heed of the "home truths" they are there to convey. Of these feeling-toned complexes that mediate, in the regulation of psychic balance, between Self and ego, none has such a memorable effect as the anima. (This is why so many women are not content with Jung's insistence that their mediating figure appears as a male, the animus.) In a movie, the importance of the female image in stimulating emotionally relevant fantasy is obvious. One has only to point out the heavy emphasis the motion-picture medium has always placed upon its leading actresses.

Not every leading female character in a film is an anima figure, but often there are unmistakable signs that an unconscious, rather than conscious, figure is intended. It may be useful at the outset to specify some of these signs:

1 Unusual radiance (e.g., Garbo, Monroe). Often the most amusing and gripping aspect of a movie is to watch ordinary actors or actresses (e.g., Melvyn Douglas and Ina Claire in *Ninotchka*) contend with a more mind-blowing presence—a star personality who seems to draw life from a source beyond the mundane (e.g., Garbo in the same film). This inner radiance is one sign of the anima, and it is why actresses asked to portray the anima so often are spoken of as stars and are chosen in large part for their uncanny presence, whether or not they are particularly good at naturalistic characterization.

2 A desire to make emotional connection as the main concern of the character. One of the ways to distinguish an actual woman is her need to be able to say "no," as part of the assertion of her own identity and being.[2] (Part of the comedy of Katharine Hepburn is that she can usually only say no, so that when she finally says "yes," we know it stands as an affirmation of an independent woman's actual being.) By contrast, the anima figure wants to be loved, or occasionally to be hated, in either case living for connection, as is consistent with her general role as representative of the status of the man's unconscious eros and particularly his relationship to himself. (Ingrid Bergman, in *Notorious*, keeps asking Cary Grant, verbally and nonverbally, whether he loves her. We feel her hunger for connection and anticipate that she will come alive only if he says "yes." His affect is frozen by cynicism and can only be redeemed by his acceptance of her need for connection.)

3 Having come from some quite other place into the midst of a reality more familiar to us than the character's own place of origin. (Audrey Hepburn, in *Roman Holiday*, is a princess visiting Rome who decides to escape briefly into the life a commoner might be able to enjoy on a first trip to that city.)

4 The character is the feminine mirror of traits we have already witnessed in the attitude or behavior of another, usually male, character. (Marlene Dietrich as a seductive cabaret singer performing before her audience in *The Blue Angel* displays the cold authori-

tarianism of the *gymnasium* professor of English, Emil Jannings, who manipulates the students' fear of him in the opening scene of the movie. Jannings pacing back and forth in front of his class and resting against his desk as he holds forth are mirrored in Dietrich's controlling stride and aggressive seated posture in front of her audience.)

5   The character has some unusual capacity for life, in vivid contrast to other characters in the film. (The one young woman in the office of stony bureaucrats in *Ikiru* is able to laugh at almost anything. When she meets her boss, Watanabe, just at the point that he has learned that he has advanced stomach cancer and is uninterested in eating anything, she has an unusual appetite for food and greedily devours all that he buys her.)

6   The character offers a piece of advice, frequently couched in the form of an almost unacceptable rebuke, which has the effect of changing another character's relation to a personal reality. (The young woman in *Ikiru* scorns Watanabe's depressed confession that he has wasted his life living for his son. Shortly after, still in her presence, Watanabe is suddenly enlightened to his life task, which will be to use the rest of his life living for children, this time by expediting the building of a playground that his own office, along with the other agencies of the city bureaucracy, has been stalling indefinitely with red tape. He finds his destiny and fulfillment in his own nature as a man who is meant to dedicate his life to the happiness of others, exactly within the pattern he established after his wife's death years before, of living for his son's development rather than to further himself. The anima figure rescues his authentic relationship to himself, which requires a tragic acceptance of this self-sacrificing pattern as his individuation and his path to self-transcendence.)

7   The character exerts a protective and often therapeutic effect on someone else. (The young widow in *Tender Mercies* helps Robert Duvall overcome the alcoholism that has threatened his career.)

8   Less positively, the character leads another character to recognize a problem in personality that is insoluble. (In Nicholas Ray's *In a Lonely Place*, the antisocial screenwriter played by Humphrey Bogart meets an anima figure played—with a face to match the cool mask of his own—by Gloria Grahame, who cannot overcome her mounting doubts about him enough to accept him as a husband. Her ambivalence is a

precise indicator of the extent of the damage that exists in his
relationship to himself.)

9   The loss of this character is associated with the loss of purposeful
    aliveness itself. (The premise of *L'Avventura* is the disappearance of
    Anna, who has been accompanied to an island by her lover, a middle-
    aged architect with whom she has been having an unhappy affair. We
    never get to know Anna well enough to understand the basis of her
    unhappiness, because she disappears so early in the film, but we soon
    discover that the man who is left behind is in a state of archetypal
    ennui, a moral collapse characterized by an aimlessly cruel sexual
    pursuit of one of Anna's friends and a spoiling envy of the creativity of
    a younger man who can still take pleasure in making a drawing of an
    Italian building.)

Simply recognizing a character in a film as an anima figure does not
exhaust the meaningfulness of what an analytic approach to cinema can
unlock. The true interest of this approach comes when, through it, the
dynamics of a cinematic experience of the anima are revealed and one can
see how the figure herself changes in relation to the character whose life
she affects. In life, we know the anima mostly as moods, impulses,
symptoms, and as a shape-shifting fleeting personage in our dreams—if,
indeed, we can remember them. In film, we can see the anima figure and
follow her behavior as she mediates the fate of a protagonist.
    A way to understand a film psychologically is to take its various
characters as signifying complexes, parts of a single personality whose
internal object relations are undergoing change.[3] These object relations are
represented by the interactions of the characters, who usually include a
figure representing the anima. Because the relation of the anima to other
complexes is of particular interest to a therapist, I have often
recommended to therapists that they use the movies they view in their
leisure time to train themselves in visualizing the internal relationships
involved. In addition to increasing their own enjoyment of films, those
who have followed my advice have often found that their sensitivity,
within analytic work, to dream and associative material is greatly
improved. This exercise, following in the Jungian tradition of having
analysts-in-training engage in the interpretation of fairy tales, has the
advantage that the material studied for archetypal comparison to clinical
material is drawn from the same culture as our patients. It also draws a
therapist deeper into what is essentially a new ritual context for the
immersion into visionary archetypal experience.

Filmmaking, at least in the hands of its acknowledged masters, is a form of active imagination drawing its imagery from the anxieties generated by current concerns, and film watching has become a contemporary ritual that is only apparently leisure.[4] Going to movies has achieved, in this country, almost the status of a religious activity. As a teacher, I have found that seminars built around the showing of a movie rich in imaginal material have been more successful in getting students to enter into a dialogue with images than my similar efforts to work with materials drawn from a more remote culture form, and I think this is because the viewing of films is numinous for us. Few myths impact contemporary Americans the way the films of Spielberg, Coppola, and Lynch do.

I would like to examine here the work of a different triad of American directors, mainstream Hollywood *auteurs* who have particularly concerned themselves with the anima.[5] Both in their obsessive devotion to certain female stars and in the seductiveness of their ability to make good scripts built around movie formulas come alive enough to seem real, George Cukor, Alfred Hitchcock, and Peter Bogdanovich belong to the culture of anima, so much, in fact, that it sometimes feels as if the anima chose these directors to make her presence visible to us in our time.

In what follows, I will address films by these directors—*A Star is Born, Vertigo,* and *Mask*—that express the extreme of their inspiration by the anima archetype, films that I would call masterpieces of the anima. They are also exercises in personal filmmaking. In each of these films, the neurosis of the *auteur,* or at least that of his creative personality, is painfully evident.[6]

Each takes as its starting point a major malfunction of a hero's persona that threatens permanently to impair this male character's ability to work or find love. Each of these films, as is characteristic of movies about the anima, engages this wounded character with an anima figure who is symbolic of a deeper aspect of his suffering and who attempts to move his psyche beyond it. However, in these films, she fails. None of the films lead to an enduring, happy connection with the anima or to genuine transformation. The function of the anima here is significantly more tragic than therapeutic: her presence serves to deepen our sense of the hero's suffering, and to make us, and him, accept it as his fate.

These films were released in America between 1953 and 1985, but they share the distinction of finding special favor with critics and audiences grown sophisticated enough to appreciate their imaginal power at a particularly self-reflective moment in the history of film watching, 1983 to 1985, when the sense of a lull in the general level of current American films combined with the first availability of American movie classics on videocassette led a mass audience to undertake what until then only cinema buffs had been able to pursue—a basic reexamination of the corpus of the American cinema. This kind of reflection on an aesthetic tradition is itself an anima activity, one that the archetype will insist upon at times when its further evolution in life or in art seems blocked by an excessive insistence upon persona values. The period just before and just after Reagan was elected to his second term was such a time, when a one-sided interest in what the hero "can do" was in evidence. It is not unfitting that, at this point in our history, the great American warhorses of anima disappointment, *A Star is Born* and *Vertigo*, films about what the hero could not do, would be re-released in their restored or rediscovered wide screen formats and that they would generate in theaters the kind of interest that is usually reserved for new films. It is more surprising that Peter Bogdanovich, whose early career had involved him in the role of American film appreciator celebrating our *auteurs* of the hero archetype, Ford and Hawks and Welles, would be able to break through with *Mask*, a great new American film putting forward so solidly the anima theme of the hero's failure. Bogdanovich's film is in the tradition of the hard-boiled sentimentality and macabre kitsch of his earlier masters, who could satirize heroic aspirations, but it is less macho in its assertion that an ideal relationship to the anima on the hero's terms is not an American possibility and more gracious in its acceptance of the necessity for the defeat of the hero.

A Star is Born

George Cukor's *A Star is Born* draws explicit life from the assumption that its audience will be steeped in Hollywood culture. It begins with the crackling of carbon arc lights coming alive to illuminate the skies of Hollywood for a premiere; much later in the film we will hear Judy Garland's electric voice cry out "lights!" as she begins to pantomime a production number she has been rehearsing for the cameras.

The story is about the birth of the star portrayed by Garland, but in Cukor's handling the real theme is the culture of film turning a searchlight upon itself. Judy Garland, as a band singer pulled into a new career in the movie business, becomes the image of a bewildered creative conscious-ness assimilating the many ironies of filmmaking itself. These ironies are presented as pitfalls of the studio system, but it is clear that the resonance is to the introverted problems of the creative process as well. Filmmaking is, above all, what Andrew Sarris has called "a very strenuous form of contemplation" (1968, 37), and in many films a leading actress becomes the personification of the director's meditative stance toward the materials of story, acting, photography, and music.

In *A Star is Born*, Garland becomes the image of Cukor's approach to creativity. The person she is here could not have been the prototype for any actual woman initiating a career: she is far too reactive to the man in her life and to Hollywood itself. Moreover, she is not particularly good at shaping herself even to these expectations. As a comeback vehicle for Judy Garland the movie was a disaster, despite its excellent critical notices and its part in securing her niche as cinema legend; but as a depiction of the middle-aged Hollywood artist's anima, the demonic energy, the androgyny, the slightly worn and worried look, and the now puffy, now beautiful head of Garland, and even the grandiosity and tiresome intensity of this fascinating but self-destructive star, all work to the director's advantage. Making everything too much is a hallmark of the anima, and Garland indelibly conveys the intensity of the Hollywood *auteur* in imposing meaning on a commercial film. The frightening aspect of this dark film musical—and not just its plot, but the murky tones of its Technicolor qualify it as a true color *noir* film—is the way the anima of the filmmaking totally overtakes the persona, so that reasonable proportions give way to overproduction and melodrama. This is the subtext of Vicki Lester (Garland) supplanting Norman Maine, the Barrymore-ish star who discovered her. By the time of Maine's suicide, Vicki Lester is able to present herself accurately to her public as "Mrs. Norman Maine."

Throughout Moss Hart's script, a grandiose Hollywood possibility is followed by a grim Hollywood reality (for instance: "the wedding to end all weddings" ends up getting held in a county jail, to avoid the press), but Hart's jokes at the expense of the Hollywood persona have for Cukor the larger meaning that the persona is losing control to another archetype. The songs of the score—most particularly "The Man That Got Away"— reemphasize the loss of masculine identity (protested for most of the movie by James Mason as the doomed Norman Maine) in favor of the archetypal emotionality represented by Garland. In the end, the movie's command of voice and dialogue and gesture (as ably defended by Mason's performance) give way to an overwhelming presence, mood, and intensity, as personified by Garland, whose unconscious energy is more interesting than her conscious skill at character portrayal. Yet Mason and Garland are in vivid relationship to each other. To watch Garland lust after James Mason's mastery, and Mason appreciate and envy Garland's magnetism, is to participate in a mystery at the core of cinema experience, the interplay between movie star and actor expressing a reciprocal tension between anima and persona. Cukor's appreciation of the neurotic dynamics of this relationship in the work of cinema artists is what make this movie great, especially in its mad moments, like the one where Norman Maine walks into the midst of his wife's Academy Award acceptance speech to make a drunken pitch for a job and ends up smacking her in the face with the back of the hand he stretches out to make a point.

A Star is Born is not the only movie where a director works out of the tension between a command of style that is losing ground and a capacity for creative expression that is still vibrant (Federico Fellini's *Ginger and Fred* has exactly this theme), but I think it is by far the greatest one, raising this peculiar problem to the status of creative tragedy. In *A Star is Born*, Cukor delivers one of Hollywood's seminal lessons: even though movies are nothing without stars that can act, stars are finally more important than actors to the emotional effect of a screen experience. This is a truth that the actual Academy Awards loves to obscure, with its frequent honoring of thespians like F. Murray Abraham, Geraldine Page, and Jessica Tandy, and its slighting of authentic movie stars, like Chaplin and Garbo and Garland, and of *auteur* directors, like Hitchcock and Spielberg, who understand how to turn actors into images. (Look at *The Prince and the Showgirl* and watch what happens when Laurence Olivier is pitted against Marilyn Monroe.) What Monroe and Garbo and Garland understand with their star acting (which, despite their occasional ambitions, was never of the Broadway or London variety) is that film, unlike the stage, is not a medium of actors, but of actors' images. The actors are not up there on the screen, their images are; and this translation of person into image is crucially important psychologically, because it moves film past the personal and into the archetypal realm of psychological experience.

When, in the first decade of this century, Griffith adapted the new "trick photography" effect of the close-up and projected gigantic "severed heads" of actors upon the screen, cinema became a medium for our direct engagement with archetypes. A cinematic close-up is analogous to an aria in opera, a moment when a timeless dimension of human experience can be caught and contemplated (Balázs 1985). But once the archetypes are summoned, they take on their own life. The magical moment in *A Star is Born* where Garland (entertaining Mason) looks out at us and says, "Now here comes a big fat close-up!" framing her face with her own panning hands, is extraordinary not just because it reveals the role of the anima in creating the close-up, but because the anima wrests control of her own image away from the director. It is in the nature itself of the anima to use a medium to create images of herself and to concern herself with the style of these images. This relationship between the anima and the image of herself that she creates is corollary to the intense interaction between anima and persona.

Perhaps the most telling example of this dynamic comes as a silent monologue played out on Judy Garland's face, as the band singer is being readied for her first screen test. While the make-up men recite possibilities for dealing with the lack of statement in her visage, Garland, staring into a make-up mirror, tries on the arched look of "the Dietrich eyebrow" and puffs her lips to get the fullness of "the Crawford mouth." Then, for a fleeting moment, she stares in despair at her own trapped and suddenly shapeless face, the personification of an anima without an image, wondering if she will ever find one.

Vertigo

That this anxiety lies at the core of the anima archetype is made even clearer by Alfred Hitchcock's *Vertigo*, where an unknown, and perhaps unknowable, woman, working to convince a detective that she really does not know who she is, becomes trapped by the fiction she has created. The movie turns on the slightly malicious question, "Who is Kim Novak?"—a question that becomes more frightening, and unanswerable, once the secret of her character's dual identity within the film is revealed.

The deluded detective is not really able to get to the heart of the conundrum, which deepens in accord with his self-deception. The initial sequences, for all their beauty in summoning up the enchantment of the anima archetype, belong to a familiar-enough theme in psychology and art–the man as victim of seduction. We even feel that the fall of James Stewart's character Scottie into "acute melancholia complicated by a guilt complex" is what he deserves from biting into this familiar apple. Indeed, the cumulative kitsch elements of the romance—the staginess of the exposition of the preposterous plot; the tourist's view of San Francisco in the long, languishing silent sequence; the poor quality of the "museum painting" of the nineteenth-century woman Kim Novak is supposed to be obsessed and perhaps possessed by; the monotonous unreality Novak brings to the reading of her lines; and James Stewart's ponderous earnestness as Scottie becomes her victim—all have a wearying effect, much like the depression of co-addiction.

But when the trickster beneath all this gnawing at the bone of hopeless love is exposed to us, and we see both characters know that it was all a trick, the film develops a wildness in which anything could happen. Stewart's solution—to precipitate the total loss of his object in the fever pitch of his disillusionment—is a truly shocking finale, forcing the audience to the conclusion that the premises of romantic love have themselves disappeared. If *Vertigo* has, as Royal S. Brown (1986) argues, the form of an Orphic tragedy, a story of the romantic artist's need to gaze murderously upon the illusion-based love at the center of his creative impulse, then the irretrievably lost Eurydice within this poet's film is the anima herself as we have known and used her to support the image of ideal romantic love. At the film's end, a bell tolls for the loss of the archetype.

The film's extraordinary poignancy turns upon Kim Novak's uncanny ability to make us care what happens to her, despite the palpable deceptiveness of her many guises. She is presented initially as Madeleine Elster, the impossibly elegant wife of a San Francisco shipbuilder. Later we learn that Novak is really Judy Barton, a San Francisco shop girl from Salina, Kansas, who had been coached to impersonate Madeleine by Madeleine's husband while he disposes of his actual wife. Novak's Madeleine is a classic 1950s woman, who confines her body within a gray tailored suit, her hair close around her head like a man's, except for the elegant feminine knot behind the head. Her image is the extreme of compliance to the demands patriarchy makes upon the feminine, to be voluptuous and pleasing within a masculine mold. Like a fourth-century BCE marble bust of Aphrodite, Novak-as-Madeleine is a personification of the goddess as patriarchal anima, asleep to her other feminine possibilities and almost Apollonian in the balance of her contours.

Later, when she appears, in shocking contrast, as Judy, Novak is painted in a hard Dionysian style, like a vulgar theater mask. She is incapable of getting Stewart's Scottie to find any taste for this more florid, and angry, assertion of femininity. Instead, Scottie forces her to recreate the Apollonian image for him by redoing her make-up, her hair, her clothes, and even her nails in the image of the former, illusory Madeleine. We realize to our horror that, for all the cruelty and male chauvinism of his project, this is the only style through which Novak's soft femininity can express itself. We pity her the more because we love her this way, recognizing that we, too, are fatally attracted by the patriarchal anima style. There can be no happy outcome, but the fall from grace of this presentation of the feminine at the end of the picture is nevertheless an occasion for pity and dread. The film that might have left us mourning for this unattainable anima image upsets us more at the end with the repulsed sense that, like Scottie, we have seen the end of any basis for all our illusions about love.

This cynicism is a sign of the emergence of the senex archetype once the anima disappears.[7] We can read *Vertigo* as the initiation of a vulnerable man into the psychological senescence produced when the anima is irretrievably lost. Jung has given this classic description:

> After the middle of life . . . permanent loss of the anima means a diminution of vitality, of flexibility, and of human kindness. The result, as a rule, is premature rigidity, crustiness, stereotypy, fanatical one-sidedness, obstinacy, pedantry, or else resignation, weariness, sloppiness, irresponsibility, and finally a childish *ramollissement* [softening of personality] with a tendency to alcohol (Jung [1954] 1959, 147).

Vertigo defines the process by which the anima is sacrificed in a man destined to assume the senex character, making clear the role the anima plays in her own withdrawal from the psychological scene. The anima that seduces a man into permanent disillusionment with the feminine is under the spell of a malignant father complex, so that her energy is infected by the demands of the complex and ceases to serve the total personality. This is the shadow of the process that therapists more usually imagine the anima to be catalyzing for a man in midlife, which is normally the discovery of the value of his aliveness to him. In the dark variant depicted here, the anima is a tragic accomplice to a form of negative initiation, by which the man is denied an inner life in favor of a hollow victory over his emotions.

There are two sequences in this movie that are organized around the unexpected and uncanny experience of Madeleine/Judy staring directly into the camera.[8] In both cases, Novak's face is frozen with the unhappiness of her unfree condition, disclosing to us her tragic foreknowledge of the role she will be forced to play in Scottie's psychological demise. The first of these direct gazes occurs in the car just before she and Scottie reach the mission at San Juan Bautista where she will meet her accomplice, Gavin Elster. This gaze is transposed to the livery stable of the mission, where she sits in an old carriage rather than the car. She keeps staring for a long time, then begins to move to join Elster, who is set to throw his real wife's dead body from the top of the tower and make it look like a suicide.

The second of these direct gazes at the camera occurs when Judy sits in her hotel room, her face a mask of tragedy, and recalls what actually happened when she did reach the top of the bell tower ahead of Scottie. As before, the actress's gaze prefigures further actions that will lead to the completion of the project—which Elster set in motion and which Hitchcock, as director, will finally use her to complete—to destroy any basis Scottie, or the film watcher, may have for believing that a healthy connection to the feminine is possible.

Scottie's vulnerability to such control by a cynical complex is the vertigo of the film's title, visualized as an acrophobia that affects the way he sees the base of the bell tower's stairwell when he looks down.[9] Its square geometric shape is a Self-symbol that recedes further away from him as he contemplates its enlarging possibility: we are looking at a man's terror in the face of the depths of his own being. It is this terror that the father complex represented by Elster can successfully manipulate: since the anima promises connection to the Self, the complex moves the anima to convince the man that he must discard her for her own survival and mastery of his fear.

Mask

If the anima in *A Star is Born* overtakes a failing persona, and is lost in *Vertigo* to a hollow persona, *Mask* suggests the healing of a wounded persona by an anima neither too strong nor too weak to do her real job of protecting the personality. Like *A Star is Born* and *Vertigo, Mask* is set in California, but twenty-five years later, in the matriarchal, counterculture California that had grown up to one side of the freeway, and the film is only superficially about a tragedy within patriarchy. Part of the fun of the film is to watch the resilience of a personality that could never get by if it played according to the patriarchal rules set for persona and anima behavior that the films from the 1950s delineate. The hero, Rocky Dennis, collects Brooklyn Dodgers cards from 1955, and some of his mother's biker friends tell him that that seems like yesterday, but clearly we have entered another system of values. His mother, Rusty Dennis, is a beautiful queen of the counterculture, permanently estranged from her critical Jewish father, and, as played with perfect ease and authority by Cher, who looks like a dark Aphrodite in this movie, she can oppose her own authority to anything that patriarchy can dish out to stand in her son's way. The film opens on a day when she has to take him to be enrolled in a new junior high school, and it will be a problem, because he was born with craniodiaphyseal dysplasia, a rare condition that causes him to deposit calcium in his skull at an abnormal rate. His face looks like a Halloween mask, or, more precisely, the long, bent facial shield of a Mycenaean warrior. His mother's defiance of doctors (who told her he would be retarded, blind, and deaf) and of school principals who don't think he can fit in (he gets along well with the other kids and is in the top five percent of his class) has become legendary, and her verve in defying their authority makes almost anything seem possible. When his head aches (they've been told that because of the pressure on his spinal cord he may have only a few months to live), Cher's Rusty can get him to talk himself out of it; when she puts her hands against his head, the pain goes away. Rocky is, in turn, Rusty's conscience and her moral support, forcing her to look at her serious drug habit and urging her on to a stable relationship with one of the nicer bikers.

This is the naive condition of the mother complex in the junior high school period when it is most hopeful, humorous, and aspiring, when a son and mother living without a father can truly be two against the world. The boy, who is, in fact, hopelessly unadapted to the patriarchal world, gets by as a charming and poignant exception to the usual patriarchal expectations, and, for a time, it is possible for him to make a successful adaptation, as Rocky does. In a brilliant sequence that takes the movie down to the level of the myth involved, Rocky wins his class over with his retelling of the Trojan War. This choice is not accidental: like Achilles, who calls weeping to his mother for help when his girl is taken from him, Rocky is a mother's hero. He will not be able to outgrow fixation at the awkward developmental stage he epitomizes for everybody else.

Girls are a particular problem for Rocky: they admire him, but he cannot attract them. His mother brings a prostitute home for him, but that is no solution because Rocky needs to find out if he is lovable on his own. As this sequence makes clear, the anima is an archetype that the mother complex cannot deliver to a man; she must be found outside the mother's sphere of authority and as a consequence of his own initiative.

Pushing himself away from his mother with the excuse that she won't do anything about her excessive use of drugs, Rocky accepts a summer job as a counselor's aid at a camp for the blind, where he meets a beautiful blind girl his own age. Her name is Diana Adams, and, with his interest in mythology and the milky radiance Laura Dern brings to the part, Rocky is quick to associate her to the White Goddess whose name she bears.[10] When she asks him what he looks like, he tells her that he looks like the Greek god Adonis and then the truth about the condition deforming his face. She runs her hand over his features and tells him he "looks pretty good" to her. They fall in love, but she is a daughter of careful, protective, upper-middle-class parents from a southern California suburb, and when they come to pick her up her father takes a pained look at Rocky and whisks her away in the family station wagon. Rocky tries to telephone Diana but her mother intercepts his messages. It is evident that he will never be able to make a permanent connection with any patriarchal anima figure.

Bogdanovich appears to tell this true story naively, as if it were a docudrama enlivened only by the extraordinary naturalness of his direction, which gives the film the look of life. Yet everywhere, seamlessly introduced into the smooth cinematic narration, is his sense of the archetypal background of this strange but charming matriarchal constellation. In one scene, Rocky, teaching the blind girl how to associate to visual adjectives gives her some cotton balls to feel and tells her, "This is billowy." The movie reverses this process, giving us images that bring us as close as a visual medium can to the texture of a mother complex, a secret sacred marriage between mother and son that finally excludes all other loves. Like Diana, we are given a first-hand grasp of the soft intractability of Rocky's mother complex.

In this set-up, the anima's contribution is an acceptance of the insolubility of the problem. Rocky goes to find Diana once more and learns that she is being sent away to school. His headaches are getting worse, and he will have to go back home to die. Caught between the feelings of her own parents and the powerful sway of Rocky's irresistible fate, Diana can only console Rocky with her acceptance of him and of his limited access to her. Beautiful as she is, she must return him to the still more beautiful goddess who is his mother and to the archetypal pattern of the son-lover who dies young. This brief connection with the anima is enough, however, to enable him to accept his fate. Rocky is able to move on within his myth and to objectify it for us, so that when he dies and his mother becomes the grieving goddess, we experience the completion of his pattern and the sense that there has been an individuation.

The film itself does not step outside the frame of reference of the mother complex; it is not afraid to be sentimental or defiant. Yet Bogdanovich somehow achieves objectivity by letting us see the entirety of Rocky's situation, in both its personal and its mythological aspects. I suspect that this rounding out is an effect of the anima. Within the mother complex that cannot be overcome, the anima can sometimes find opportunities lacking in a patriarchal pattern of development for establishing the wholeness of the arrested personality.

In contrast to *A Star is Born* and *Vertigo*, which are patriarchal in their premises and narcissistic in their pathology, *Mask* is neither hypomanic nor depressed, although it is equally concerned with the emotional relationship between persona and anima. The film's even feeling-tone echoes the surprising resilience Rocky displays in the regulation of his self-esteem, a benefit, it would seem, of not having a father's expectations to live up to. In *Mask*, again in contrast to *A Star is Born* and *Vertigo*, neither the persona nor the anima has very much to lose. Without a fantasy of patriarchal success, there is no expectation of ideal apotheosis for either pole of the adapting self and, therefore, no liability to titanic disappointment. Instead of tragedy, there is pathos in the anima's disappointment and a humorous humility in the face of the persona's shortcomings. Within this matriarchal pattern, the anima can play only a limited role in extending the range or the health of a personality, but she can satisfy other needs of the psyche: for self-acceptance, integrity, and love.

It remains for us to ask what it does for a cinema *auteur* to reflect his anima problem so directly on the screen. It is clear that these films concern themselves with fatal constellations and reject the hope of heroic healing. One likes, nevertheless, to imagine that these directors healed themselves, or at least resolved tensions in their creative personalities, with these films. I have observed, following Jung, that it is therapeutic simply to visualize the anima with such clarity. Jung often expressed the opinion that the way for a man to analyze his anima is to get to know her better. In this process, as these films make clear, a man will come to experience not only her style and her nature, but also her autonomy as a factor that stands behind his ego in shaping his destiny. This independence, which promises an endless creative capacity for self-renewal, is sharply restricted by the nature of the other personality complexes with which the anima must contend. The film medium allows the director to articulate the limits of his anima's freedom in shaping his creative life.

We who are interested in psychological creativity may understand from the urgency with which these cinema masters have attended to the fate of the anima that the anima's vicissitudes refer to an imagination struggling to keep alive its capacity for psychological connection to itself. It would not be wrong to infer that this desirable outcome is by no means a guaranteed inevitability.

References

Balázs, Béla (1985). "The Close-up." In *Film Theory and Criticism* (3rd ed.), G. Mast and M. Cohen, (eds.). New York: Oxford University Press, 255-264.

Brill, Lesley (1988). *The Hitchcock Romance: Love and Irony in Hitchcock's Films*. Princeton, NJ: Princeton University Press.

Brown, Royal S. (1986). "*Vertigo* as Orphic Tragedy." *Film/Literature Quarterly* 14(1): 32-43.

Graves, R. (1960). *The Greek Myths*. New York: Viking Penguin.

Cavell, Stanley (1997). *Contesting Tears: The Hollywood Melodrama of the Unknown Woman*. Chicago: The University of Chicago Press.

Harrison, Barbara Grizzuti (1990). "Peter Bogdanovich comes back from the dead." *Esquire* 114(2): 146-156.

Hillman, James (1975). *Re-Visioning Psychology.* New York: Harper & Row.

—. (1985). *Anima: An Anatomy of a Personified Notion.* Dallas: Spring Publications.

Jung, C. G. ([1906] 1973). "Association, Dream, and Hysterical Symptom." In *Collected Works,* vol. 2: 353-407.

—. ([1954] 1959). "Concerning the Archetypes, with Special Reference to the Anima Concept." In *Collected Works,* vol. 9i, 54-72.

Kael, Pauline ([1973] 1994). "Everyday Inferno." In *For Keeps.* New York: Dutton, 505-511.

Rothman, William (1988). "*Vertigo:* the Unknown Woman in Hitchcock." In *The "I" of the Camera.* Cambridge: Cambridge University Press, 142-173.

Sarris, Andrew ([1968] 1971). "Directors, how personal can you get?" In *Confessions of a Cultist: On the Cinema, 1955/1969.* New York: Simon & Schuster, 360-365.

—. (1968). *The American Cinema.* New York: Dutton.

Notes

[1] The most succinct general description of the ways the anima manifests herself can be found in Hillman (1975, 42-44). A critical examination of the concept of the anima in analytical psychology is given in Hillman (1985).

[2] I am indebted to the Jungian analyst Beverley Zabriskie for first making this distinction for me.

[3] This is the basic principle, as well, of Jungian dream interpretation (see Jung [1906] 1973).

[4] See my recorded seminar, "Film as Active Imagination," C. G. Jung Institute of San Francisco, October 10-11, 1981.

[5] See Sarris (1968) for a discussion of rank and *auteur* in regard to Hollywood directors.

[6] It is best to resist the temptation to draw conclusions about the personal psychology of a director from his films, but the notion of "personal filmmaking"—a term Pauline Kael ([1973] 1994, 505) coined for her *New Yorker* review of Martin Scorsese's *Mean Streets* in 1973—does open up the psychology of the director's *creative* personality to critical inspection. See also Sarris ([1968] 1971).

[7] Hitchcock supplies an exact personification of the senex archetype in the figure of the coroner who presides over the jury called to determine the cause of Madeleine's

death after the first bell-tower episode. The coroner's tone in delivering the verdict of suicide insinuates that Scottie is at fault, which becomes the attitude Scottie assumes toward himself in his subsequent depression.

[8] A particularly lucid account of the first of these moments can be found in Rothman (1988), who invokes Stanley Cavell's "melodrama of the unknown woman." See Cavell (1997) for the latter's own development of this conception, which helps to amplify the anima in film by establishing the movie genre in which the archetype has most characteristically made her appearance.

[9] Lesley Brill, in his careful analysis of the camera's movement in *Vertigo* (1988, 202-206), points out that a geometric spiral is implied in this figure.

[10] Robert Graves's use of this term for Diana/Artemis is well known (1960, 85-86). Peter Bogdanovich revealed to Barbara Grizzuti Harrison that he was reading Robert Graves's *The White Goddess* in 1981, just after his lover, Dorothy Stratten, was killed (Harrison 1990).

CHAPTER EIGHTEEN

MIRRORING THE MASCULINE

JOHN BEEBE

Letter from an Unknown Woman.
(1948). Directed by Max Ophuls.
Screenplay by Howard Koch and Max Ophuls,
from the story by Stefan Zweig.

Were it not for its patriarchal frame story, which concerns the arrangements for a duel, *Letter from an Unknown Woman* might be taken for a woman's picture.[1] The masculine contextualization, together with the fact that the woman is seen and heard only through the mind's eye and ear of the male recipient of her letter—who cannot remember the identity of the sender—points us toward the recognition that the heart of the film emerges out of the man's anima. This is peculiar, because the man is portrayed as unconsciously heartless throughout most of the picture.

By contrast, the woman who has remembered him for most of her life, glows with attentiveness to every detail of their few contacts, recalling his carelessly discarded past in the letter that reaches him when it is too late for him ever to meet her again. In a sense, this movie is the opposite of what occurs to Macbeth to say after learning the news of Lady Macbeth's death on the battlefield by Dunsinane Castle: "It is a tale told by an idiot, full of sound and fury, signifying nothing." *Letter from an Unknown Woman* is a tale told by a feminine figure gifted with emotional intelligence, made of quiet reflections, signifying everything.

These opposed feminine and masculine sensibilities are brilliantly realized, as if dreamed onto the screen, by the master director Max Ophuls. His signature style, with its lingering tracking shots and swooping swirling camera movements that seem immune to a sharp angle or a jarring, cutaway from the developing mood, can fairly be called "feminine."[2] What is less often recognized is the contrasting, almost crude, masculinity revealed in Ophuls's penchant for buffoonish comedy and melodramatic gallantry, and in his acceptance of the idea that reality, as opposed to fantasy, is finally dictated by the patriarchal system.

Ophuls couldn't have succeeded so well as an auteur had he not been able to work with stars of the patriarchal system of his day. He was ahead of his time in enlisting their services without a studio in America or Europe to back him up. Joan Fontaine as Lisa Berndle, the "unknown woman" author of the letter, and Louis Jourdan as Stefan Brand, the celebrated Vienna roué who receives it, lend their Hollywood immortality to the luster of the film.

What results is a remarkable evocation of archetypes, Fontaine as the anima who more or less tells the story, and Jourdan the *puer aeternus* who must take it in if he is to recover his humanity from jadedness and addiction to seduction. The movie turns upon Stefan's ability to experience the guilt of what he has done to Lisa by being so oblivious to her. Psychologically, it is about the role the anima can play in awakening a man's feeling, an awakening which can only come as the corollary to the man's recognizing that the anima cannot really have an impact if her capacity for relationship is not appreciated.

There is another man in the film, who has already helped Lisa achieve the respectable fiction that passes for normal life, her husband, Johann. It is part of the crazy integrity of Lisa as anima figure—what the character's real life Viennese contemporary Freud would have called her masochism[3]—that she cannot sustain her marriage when she encounters Stefan again, even though she knows the limitations of his emotional staying power. Johann functions in the film to enforce what Lacan has called "the law of the father." Despite his kindness to Lisa and her son, most contemporary Jungians would identify this patrician husband as a senex figure: the crossed swords alongside his dueling pistols on the wall of his own are archetypally linked to Saturn's sickle.

The psychoanalytic and feminist film critic Robin Wood has made the case that the film contains, as a subtext,

> the possibility of a film *against* Lisa: it would require only a shift of emphasis for this other film to emerge. It is not simply that Ophuls makes it possible for us to blame Lisa for destroying her eminently civilized marriage to a kind (if unpassionate) man, and the familial security he has given her and her son; it is also *almost* possible to blame Lisa, and her refusal to compromise, for Stefan's ruin.[4]

The moral ambiguity that adheres to Lisa belongs to the anima archetype and illustrates the difficulty a man may experience in trusting the anima, even in the midst of abundant evidence that his life amounts to little without her.

Stefan, on the other hand, embodies the archetype of the puer aeternus, a mythologem first brought to the attention of English-speaking people by Jung in *The Psychology of the Unconscious* (which he later revised as *Symbols of Transformation*), where we read his citation from Ovid[5] as translated by Frank Justus Miller in the Loeb Classical Library's edition of the great Latin poet's *Metamorphoses*:

> For thine is unending youth, eternal boyhood: thou art the most lovely in the lofty sky; thy face is virgin-seeming, if without horns thou stand before us (Miller, I, 181).

Thanks to the pioneering work of Marie-Louise von Franz, who seems to have harbored an animus toward the type of man who remains overly identified with this figure, Jungian analysts have learned to recognize as a clinical problem the man who is a sort of "eternal promissory note," addicted to diversity in his love life, yet haunted by the possibility of an immortal ideal love that no actual woman can live up to. Jourdan, with his astonishing pretty features (he was to go on to light up the screen in Vincente Minnelli's *Gigi*) rather perfectly captures the image of such a man and the way he can seem to a woman like someone no other man can measure up to.

What is most remarkable in Jourdan's performance is his rendering of Stefan in middle age, when his eternal youth has gone rancid, like the picture of Dorian Gray (Albert Lewin had filmed Oscar Wilde's upsetting story just a couple of years before Ophuls commenced work on *Letter from an Unknown Woman*). One senses that there is something Faustian in the bargain Stefan has struck with life, which has caused him to abandon a promising career as a concert pianist to concentrate on his increasingly desperate and dissolute womanizing. The film does not cause him to infect Lisa (she catches the cholera that kills her, just after her son succumbs to the same disease, from a contaminated train carriage) but he looks unhealthy, like someone who might have syphilis. This hint of him as a doomed figure even before Lisa's husband challenges him to a duel suggests that Lisa may represent his own soul, come to claim him in lieu of Mephistopheles, enforcing the contract he made in trying to prolong his youth.

Stefan, surprisingly, ends the film as a sympathetic figure, at least to the degree that he takes the letter seriously enough to care at last about Lisa's fate, and to be stirred to a greater integrity than he has shown before. But it is still hard to see him as other than an unconscious participant in a strange, neurotic scenario that he barely comprehends. Virginia Apperson's perceptive essay, which follows, enables us to feel our way into the dynamics of the "puer" neurosis depicted in the letter's retrospective picture of Stefan's emotional career, and to see as well the other human values he has slighted and offended. If the film puts the feminine in the unenviable position of mirroring masculine shortcomings, Apperson's essay shows that the same mirror can reveal masculine strengths. She recognizes Ophuls as more than the greatest director of women's pictures, calling our attention to his masterful manipulation of the viewer's own ambivalent reactions to his story.

References

Jung, C. G. (1916/1947). (Beatrice Hinkle, trans.) *Psychology of the Unconscious: A Study of the Transformations and Symbolisms of the Libido.* New York: Dodd Mead.

Kael, Pauline (2008). http://www.geocities.com/paulinekaelreviews (online).

Mercer, John and Martin Chingler (2004). "The Woman's Film." In *Melodrama: Genre, Style, Sensibility.* London: Wallflower.

Miller, Frank Justus (ed. and trans.) (1976). Ovid. *Metamorphoses, with an English translation.* Cambridge: Harvard University Press.

Sarris, Andrew (1968). *The American Cinema.* New York: Dutton.

Wood, Robin (1986). "Ewig hin der Liebe Glück." In Virginia Wright Exman and Karen Hollinger (eds.). *Letter from an Unknown Woman*; *Max Ophuls, director.* New Brunswick, NJ: Rutgers University Press.

Notes

[1] Indeed, the film has usually been so taken by film critics and historians. Pauline Kael said that it "is probably the toniest 'woman's picture' ever made," and John Mercer and Martin Chingler, in their analysis of the broad genre of film melodrama, class it under "The Woman's Film" subcategory (2004, 121).

[2] I am using this term here in the sense of a holistic sensibility that serves the values of continuity and relatedness, and implying that it appears in Ophuls style as an approach that opposes the bold, separative moves that define what I would call the more typical "masculine" standpoint in the history of cinema. This more incisive style was from its earliest days shaped by the innovations of male directors—for instance, the montage of Eisenstein's *Potemkin* or the surrealist cuts (and shocking images of cutting the eye) in Bunuel (and Dali's) *Un Chien Andalou.* But it is possible to claim that Ophuls develops his own masculine

standpoint using camera movement. The great critic of directorial sensibility Andrew Sarris wrote, "The Ophulsian view is never feminist, like Mizoguchi's, or feminine like Bergman's and Antonioni's" (1968, 70).

[3] As Kael (2008) puts it, "Joan Fontaine suffers and suffers, but so exquisitely in this romantic evocation of late-19th-century Vienna that one doesn't know whether to clobber the poor, wronged creature or to give in and weep."

[4] Robin Wood (1986, 233). The other essays in the same book provide a good cross-section of the critical response to this film.

[5] Ovid's Latin lines, as quoted by Jung and translated by Beatrice Hinkle, are:

> Tu puer aeternus, tu formosissimus alto
> Conspiceris coelo tibi, cum sine cornibus astas,
> Virgineum caput est

[Thou boy eternal, thou most beautiful one seen in the heavens, without horns standing, with thy virgin head] (Jung 1916/1947, 373).

CHAPTER NINETEEN

THE "SYMPATHETIC" FEMININE

VIRGINIA APPERSON

Letter from an Unknown Woman.
(1948). Directed by Max Ophuls.
Screenplay by Howard Koch and Max Ophuls,
from the story by Stefan Zweig.

As the melodramatic plot thickens in *Letter from an Unknown Woman*, it becomes achingly apparent that the problem of love that the film presents is insoluble. Something is dreadfully out of sync, not just at the personal level between the protagonists, but if the film is understood as a myth of our time, also between the archetypal personalities that this woman and this man personify. The backdrop of the film is Vienna at the turn of the twentieth century, but the setting matters little (except that interestingly enough, it takes place at the very time and place that Sigmund Freud was developing his revolutionary ideas on the unconscious and would soon be in contact with C. G. Jung in Zurich). The movie (elaborating Stefan Zweig's short fiction of the same name) tells the story of Stefan Brand, an apparently well-known man about town who had gained some early celebrity as a promising concert pianist while really giving himself over to the id that rules his life, his never-ending search for the perfect woman. His personal life is a calendar of assignations that is perpetually full. The steady flow of lavishly adorned and adoring ladies has become a satisfactory replacement for the effusive applause that once fed his egoism and now has all but died out. The reality of his fate is told through a letter he receives from Lisa Berndle, who is the true subject of the film. The letter serves to finally bring the hitherto "unknown" Lisa to the forefront, though this belated attention is far too little, far too late.

Lisa starts out as an awkward adolescent, the sort of girl who at fifteen is fetching in a shy, mousy sort of way and grows into a lovely, personable, but incredibly sad figure (she fits the self-defeating image of "the eternal girl" as described by the Jungian analyst Linda Leonard (1985) in *The Wounded Woman*). Early on in the film, her purpose in life is revealed to her: it is to devote herself utterly and unconditionally to the worldly-wise, ridiculously inconsiderate Stefan Brand, who through most of the film makes no attempt to really know Lisa, even during the short, magical time that he is wooing her. Over the course of the movie, while the unseen Lisa is making every effort to monitor every move he makes, Stefan darts from one thing to the next, barely aware of anyone but himself. He simply assumes that others will be there to cater to his whims. In the early reels of the film, when Lisa is persistently lurking around the corners of Stefan's life, he is flitting from one diversionary tryst to the next—making the two of them a classic depiction of the man's marginalization of the feminine, in which the man's ego, the right hand of his psyche, has little interest in what his left hand, the anima is doing. The peculiar form of Stefan's dissociation from the feminine, however, goes beyond egoism: it belongs to the psychic territory that Marie-Louise von Franz (1970) maps out in her classic book, *The Problem of the Puer Aeternus*, about the neurosis of a man who, insisting on being an eternal youth, refuses to grow up. This is an archetypal pattern in which a kind of oblivion protects the man from the anxieties that come with connection and makes him lazy in relationships, which are finally too much "bother." Beyond Stefan's near-schizoid detachment from others behind his mask of charm, an even more profound separation from emotional integrity exists within himself and keeps him out of touch with his own relational potential.

As the story unfolds, Lisa's well-concealed, but compulsive monitoring of Stefan's comings and goings eventually pays off. Her early adolescent dream of standing by his side comes true, and when she is around twenty she gets penciled into his life. While the two are together for a brief, ephemeral affair, Lisa is in heaven and Stefan is happily amused, soaking in her earnest attention. Had the Freud of 1914 (when he wrote "On Narcissism") been consulted and told the story of Stefan's need to be center stage and his inability to sustain either his career or any long-term relationship (except with his mute servant John), he would have been understood by the psychoanalyst as a case of fixation at the stage of infantile omnipotence and its later elaboration, adolescent narcissism. (As played by Louis Jourdan, Stefan is not unlike the Narcissus of mythology, a gorgeous adolescent who lived by, and eventually for his own reflection). Present-day Self-psychology expands Freud's theory and shows us that this unhealthy form of narcissism is usually driven by a longing to make up for countless unmirrored moments from early life. In such a person, negative introjects take the place of a positive parental experience, and the narcissist who emerges compensates for the self-undermining energy that batters from within by becoming quite masterful at seducing attention out of others. The Jungian analyst Nathan Schwartz-Salant (1982) has demonstrated how a Jungian archetypal perspective can advance this pessimistic understanding of a narcissist's psychic structure and offer the possibility that the reality of the narcissist's indifference to others can be slowly transformed into an attitude of acceptance and compassion, if the anima is found and accepted within. But Schwartz-Salant explains rather clearly why this task is so difficult:

> Because the conscious ego of the narcissistic character anticipates no inner support and has no confidence in its own inner resources, it avoids introversion and imaginal activity except of the most passive wish-fulfillment kind (ibid., 28).

Though Stefan's life story represents the extreme, artist's version of such externalizing narcissism, many less obvious versions exist in people who simply do not know how to relate to anything beyond their own self-absorbed state. Ophuls's movie speaks to all of us by asking, "How can the feminine get through in such a psychological set-up?"

First of all, the role of any woman seriously interested in getting through to Stefan would have to be that of enabler. Comfortably fitting into Stefan's need for a sycophantic accomplice, Lisa provides the quiet, attentive reflection that Stefan lacks and sorely needs, but in an "echoistic" way, a pattern of behavior that Timmen Cermak (1986) recognizes as a dangerous form of co-dependence. Lisa becomes the nymph-like Echo who iconizes Stefan by softly prattling back his own conceit. Nothing, however, can solidify between them because Stefan is too shrouded by his puerile defense to let life in and allow his heart to be effectively touched by Lisa's oblations. Within two weeks of the affair that leaves her pregnant (she says later in her letter that she did not turn to him for help because she "wanted to be one woman you had known who asked you for nothing"), Stefan's fecklessness has led him to relapse into his philandering ways. He simply forgets about her, no longer remembering even her name. Before the film comes to its bitter end, after a final brief encounter more than a decade later, we are forced, with her, to realize that though Lisa has had all the love in the world to offer him, she has not even begun to breach the barrier that exists between him and the feminine. The reason is plain: female adulation only enables Stefan's endless narcissism. So, Lisa, the lady who is forever paying him unconditional attention, is the one who is most easily forgotten.

After their initial whirlwind affair (in which neither can seem to get enough of the other), Stefan disappears, leaving Lisa alone with a child to plan for. We hear about these years, very briefly, in the soundtrack narration of the letter, which sounds a bit like a radio play, but we do not get to see Lisa during the period when she is temporarily shaken out of her stupefying rapture and forced to be sensible. From her voiceover narration, we learn that she accepts the hand of Johann, a career military officer who, though she does not love him romantically, is in a position to provide handsomely for her and her son. Johann is dutiful and generous as her husband as long as she plays the proper wife, and Stefan Jr. is just starting to call him "father" when Ophuls's camera lets us see them. The visual irony is clear: Lisa's choice has taken her to the opposite end of the male spectrum, from the eternally boyish Stefan to the perpetually old Johann. The now properly Oedipal Viennese family of three carries on with maintaining a brilliant social persona, and for a while Lisa seems comfortable enough with a Stefan-free life: she looks quite composed in her role as mother and wife. Under the Saturnine shadow of her husband, who is alert to any lapse in his wife's self-control, her poise collapses when she encounters Stefan unexpectedly at the opera (the ultimate stage of melodramatic tragedy). Immediately, she is drawn right back into her addictive, tunnel-visioned fascination with him. Stefan takes the lovely, mature Lisa as a new, unknown woman that he has to seduce romantically. She, of course, is expecting a more vital connection. Just as he has little internal relation to the romantic ideal driving him (by now he looks dissolute and is little more than a sex and love addict), Lisa has failed to cultivate any incisive insight and can only relate to the masculine when it appears outside herself. Her calamitous choice is to forsake everything for the apparently ardent male, ignoring all she knows and has heard of his fly-by-night nature. (The latest warning is clearly given in gossip about him that she overhears in the Opera House.)

To better understand Lisa's character, we need to look at the man she ends up rejecting for Stefan. We need to look at her husband, Johann. Johann is very much a 19th century patriarch, living for his honor as a man and expecting his family to do the same. Freud might have identified him as a castration-threatening oedipal father, drilled in the didactic that one is bound by obligations. (This is the same, doomed force that at the time the film is set is galvanizing the Austro-Hungarian Empire that Johann is pledged to defend.) Johann's response to the infidelity between Lisa and Stefan is no less ruthlessly military—disavowal of his wife and vengeance against Stefan. Such a superego response has nothing to do with love; his feeling for Lisa is as callously cast aside as Stefan's was. Johann's ultimate response is about making the two pay for not playing by the rules. It works dramatically for contemporary, psychologically-minded viewers only because we would like to see Lisa and Stefan finally called to account for their lack of internal development. When this film is screened for a Jungian audience, Johann is readily identifiable as the personification of the senex archetype (senex being the Latin term for "old man"—conceived as the archetypal opposite, and often antagonist of the puer). The senex aspect comes through in the steadfast-to-a-fault husband's intolerance for any form of marital transgression. Johann's role in the film is to sternly insist on enforcing the marriage archetype, clearly his image of personal integrity. Stefan, who up to now in the picture has successfully insulated himself from censure, has met his shadowy match in Johann and is finally being called to account when challenged by him to a duel. Fighting it out to the finish, though, even if it might seem to restore Stefan's honor by showing him standing up for Lisa's memory, will only give the final victory to the more disciplined Johann and perpetuate the loveless conundrum of Lisa's marriage, which has deteriorated into a death-trap.

In all, the tragic scenario establishes three archetypal dynamics, beautifully visualized by the actors who portray the archetypes involved. Together, these dynamics work to mastermind the relational demise that is the uncanny psychological subject of the film:

1. A puer aeternus psychology that chooses self-centered flights of fancy over relational grounding.

2. A too-nice anima, a representative of the feminine all right, but one who is so busy supporting the puer that her own identity and authority remain blurry and marginalized.

3. A senex figure who is aligned against both the puer and the values of the anima, in such a way that integration of different sides of the masculine archetype (senex and puer) and engagement with the feminine (integration of the anima) are effectively blocked by a patriarchal ego-defense.

Despite the Viennese setting, this is more complicated than a Freudian Oedipal triangle; it involves the nature of creativity and personal striving. The tragic aspect in this telling scenario that Ophuls and the screenwriter Howard Koch have created is that these dynamics conspire to insure that the feminine will remain "an unknown woman" to the masculine. Only Stefan's mute servant John carries the continuity of her identity throughout the film in his mind. It is hard not to read Ophuls's film as voicing anything other than a deep doubt that an effective correspondence between a living man and woman is possible. In that sense, the film works to deflate romantic expectations.

To better understand the entropy of this unhappy film, I will tease out the circumstances that have resulted from these three archetypal determinants.

1. Stefan has lived his life on the prowl. Disinterested in learning from his experiences, he has taken what suits him and carelessly proceeded onward towards his next conquest, burning his candle at both ends in a brilliant, but self-consuming way. His "puer aeternus" approach to the erotic is to keep unearthing new women who can inspire him, but not let any of them close-in enough to disturb his own sense of primordial feminine perfection. The hopefulness in this strategy is expressed cinematically in Louis Jourdan's winsome face and voice, which convey the "angelic hermaphroditic quality where masculine and feminine are so perfectly joined that nothing else is needed" (Hillman 1979, 25). Its shadow is complacency, an attitude of self-sufficiency captured by Jungian analyst James Hillman who notes that for such a man there is:

> [N]o need for relationship or woman, unless it be some magical puella or some mother-figure who can admiringly reflect and not disturb this exclusive hermaphroditic unity of oneself with one's archetypal essence. The feeling of distance and coldness, of impermanence…can all be seen as derivatives of this privileged archetypal connection with the spirit, which may burn with a blue and ideal fire but in a human relationship may show the icy penis and chilling seed of a satanic incubus (ibid.).

The film never shows us Stefan dealing with a woman in any real way, outside his reading of Lisa's letter, where we do see some belated glimmer of appropriate feeling. Rather, we see him always in the act of departure, which seems to suit his self-confessed role as the Viennese bon vivant, but reveals, instead, the perpetual adolescent concerned above all with his own freedom. As well he should be; he is caught (and suffering) in a Sisyphean trap. He is desirous of something that only a woman can give him, but he refuses the work that a real relationship requires. By the end of the film, Stefan's chronic resistance to relationship has worn him down, and his look has deteriorated from the debonair man-about-town to a washed-out, cynical has-been.

2. As an aesthete who is intolerant of attachments, Stefan has entertained beautiful women throughout his youth and early middle age, freely moving from one to the next without consequence. What then is the lingering draw (and its final purchase on his soul) of Lisa's constant gaze (so exquisitely personified by Joan Fontaine in a performance that is like one long worshipful look at her beloved)? It is not simply that she mirrors him. There is something in her that haunts him through the reading of the

letter, until he can summon the memory of her at last on his own. Possibly it is her complexity (and Ophuls has made her a most complex figure) which compensates and oddly comforts the part of him that avoids anything that might complicate his life. Possibly he sees in her (as she in fact hopes he will) all the hoped-for devotion that she wants to provide. Or perhaps he thinks that her capacity for devotion will finally bring together the missing pieces of his life (quite as she does in her letter, making a meaningful narrative out of these shards of his wasted life) without bothering to draw him out of himself. Whatever the lure for this narcissistic man, Lisa's ingenuous wiles do touch his soul. Temporarily, they share the hopeful sense of embarking on a genuine journey through life together (that this is an illusion is poignantly conveyed by the little cinema-like Hale tour they take together at an amusement park, watching scenes of Europe pass by through the window of a stationary coach made to look like a railroad car, while the owner of this concession mechanically turns a wheel containing the images of different cities to create the impression of going somewhere). Unfortunately, in this particular enchanted scenario, Lisa gives herself away, while Stefan takes and takes and takes. Ultimately, his and her conspiracy not to look too hard at the life they are actually denying backfires into mortal catastrophe. Neither Echo nor Narcissus sees that the mirror image she is able to give back to him (which suits to a T his sense of who he is) is fundamentally flawed. Her approbation cannot possibly fill his bottomless pit because it misses the point of his shadow. By the time that Lisa is old and experienced enough herself to comprehend the sleaziness of Stefan's formulaic promiscuity, she has lost much of her own soul and thrown away the masculine potential in herself that might have roused her to more than an accommodation to life. The payoff is a dying of that potential. As the film nears its close, Stefan's youthful face has hardened into a death mask, and her son by him, Stefan Jr., has contracted typhus.

Lisa, by this time is the portrait of a psyche that has succumbed to, rather than discriminated, the promises of the puer aeternus. In this way, she speaks to a well-nigh universal neurosis within patriarchy—the attempt to sneak past the problem of the denied authority of the feminine. Speaking of the effect of "puer psychology" on the personality, James Hillman has said:

> It is to the puer that psyche succumbs, and just because it is psyche's opposite; the puer spirit is the least psychological, has the least soul. Its "sensitive soulfulness" is rather pseudo-psychological.... It can search and risk; it has insight, aesthetic intuition, spiritual ambition—all, but not psychology, for psychology requires time, femininity of soul, and the

entanglement of relationships. Instead of psychology, the puer attitude displays an aesthetic point of view: the world as beautiful images or as vast scenario. Life becomes literature, an adventure of intellect or science, or of religion or action, but always unreflected and unrelated and therefore unpsychological. It is the puer in a complex that "unrelates" it, that volatizes it out of the vessel—that would act it out, call it off and away from the psychological—and thus is the principle that uncoagulates and disintegrates. What is unreflected tends to become compulsive, or greedy. The puer in any complex gives it its drive and drivenness, makes it move too fast, want too much, go too far...because the world can never satisfy the demands of the spirit or match its beauty (Hillman 1979, 25-26).

The puer, therefore, is one more agent of patriarchy. His duel with the senex is really over which has the right to put down the feminine. Though the placable Lisa experiences a chronic gravitational pull towards Stefan, his impersonal and insatiable personality repeatedly obscures her very existence. Lisa, as the compliant anima, refuses to acknowledge his spurious side, while she remains mesmerized by his shallow gallantry. Lisa is the embodiment of a lady-in-waiting aspect of psyche in its masochistic form, one that merely exists to unwittingly feed this toxic cycle where the puer is given carte blanche to repeatedly seduce her, use her and leave her. The fact that Lisa plays the part of the pushover so well eventually leads to catastrophe for all involved, male and female alike. And yet, under the circumstances, she makes it all seem inevitable.

3. To be fair, Lisa comes by her zeal for the puer honestly. In her world, there are two kinds of men. The first is the stable, reliable type (her mother's petit-bourgeois second husband, the serious young officer who unsuccessfully courts her, and the older officer she eventually marries so that her son will have a father). The second is the type of man she favors in her choice of Stephan (and there is a hint in the script that her father was this kind of man). This is the entertaining ne'er do well who never grows beyond the appealing buoyancy of his youth, his eternal boyhood bought at the expense of neglecting any obligation save the one to seem charming. To Lisa, her penny-pinching stepfather, her stiff soldier suitor, and her predictable husband stultify her with their fussy respectability. Lisa clearly prefers the careless spontaneity of the puer (until she learns that that is a formula too). To me, not one of the film's men feels like he would be a very satisfying mate, although I could imagine that the right combination of them might make Lisa a pretty good husband. As it is, all the various sides of the masculine are quite dissociated from each other (seeming almost to belong to different pictures), and the men who are Lisa's husband and lover devolve psychologically into pathetic caricatures of

senex and puer, an engram of the split of the masculine in the psyche of modern people that the feminine cannot succeed in resolving on her own.

It is sometimes hard to see senex and puer as sides of a common cultural complex. Since patriarchy insists on responsibility (as Lisa's grim senex husband Johann makes clear), it seems to have little in common with the puer's insistence that life be a series of escapades. However, the disastrous interaction that regularly occurs in modern love scenarios between a puer and a woman is but a shadow of the patriarchal devaluation of the feminine that we find in the senex. Both the older-man by-the-book senex and the adolescent by-the-seat-of-his-pants puer share the inability to grant the feminine the status of an enduring reality to which attention must be paid. A similar narcissism exists between Stefan's dashing Epicureanism and Johann's shriveled traditionalism, both men stubbornly refusing to value Lisa as an entity separate from themselves. Given that she is faced on both sides of her split with such self-absorbed energy, it is hard to fault Lisa for not even trying to reveal herself (until the bombshell of her letter, which brings forward in a shattering way the impact of what she has suffered). Not only do the two sides of the masculine archetype fail to support and complement one another, their single-minded insistence on being true just to themselves abnegates the viability of the feminine, too. The rift between the puer and the senex undergirds the way the film puts our sympathies in a double bind. Should we side with the at-odds-with-itself masculine, which is infirmed, or the feminine that is overlooked? We cannot decide which archetype is most at fault, because all are suffering in this set-up. This is the double bind that Lisa finally breaks when she writes the letter that tells Stefan who she is and forces the much needed revaluation of her by everyone, including herself, that is at the heart of the problem.

James Hillman has written that the polarization of the masculine and the subsequent split of each of the warring parts from the feminine is "the psychological foundation of the problem of history" (1979, 8). Ophuls's film (released in 1948) makes it the stuff of modern tragedy. *Letter from an Unknown Woman* serves to this day as a cautionary tale, showing us how: "The division into mutually indifferent or repugnant polarities is tearing the soul apart" (Hillman 1979, 14).

Perhaps it is for this reason that as a woman who has tried to move beyond modernity in her own life and work within a new tradition of facing and healing such splits, wherever they are found, I react with such allergy to the idea that the double bind Lisa lives in has to be accepted as her fate. I find it horrifying that she so eagerly tries to embrace this series of neurotic splits as if they were the seeds of her destiny as a romantic heroine. Indeed, despite my recognition of this picture as an exquisite work of film art, and its accuracy as an anatomy of psychopathology, I find this film infuriating. Every time I watch it, I leave feeling mad: mad at Stefan, mad at Johann and mad at Lisa. Intellectually, I know that what is most maddening is the unimaginative and unregenerate patriarchal programming that has set Lisa up for a life of invisibility, that emboldened Stefan to believe that it was all right to live a life beyond reproach, that offered Johann copious justification to put everyone back in their place, and that involves us as viewers in accepting this melodrama at face value. Few critics have suspected Ophuls of wanting to enrage us, and yet the film has failed, I think, to reach its potential until we consider this possibility. The maddening truth it conveys (and no wonder so many have killed the messenger simply by ignoring Ophuls's work) is that each of us carries some piece of the worst of these three protagonists within ourselves. This piece is the introject of patriarchy that has afflicted all our romantic lives. The sound of Lisa's voice, as rendered by the knowing Joan Fontaine, is insinuating because it knows we have been raised by a similar system to hers, and that most of us have complied with it somewhere quite as much as she did in her life.

In a way, *Letter from an Unknown Woman* is the antithesis of the goal of this book of meditations on the feminine in film because it destroys its cinematic subject: when Lisa becomes a specular ghost in the entrance of Stefan's flat, her own identity has disappeared into the anima that Stefan will now sentimentalize. She remains, indeed, an image of the anima, but as John Beebe and I have argued in other places in this book, as long as the feminine is reduced and limited to an anima role, some aspect of her identity will remain poorly differentiated and only partially expressed, and the masculine who needs her will stay untransformed. Ophuls is too great a master not to note this lack of substance in his feminine character: indeed, it is her absence of substance that makes the film so maddening, so haunting, and so frightening. Perhaps the hardest lesson of the film can only be found in the hindsight recognition of what the movie does *not* show but that the still unknown woman's letter to the next generation nevertheless conveys—if the feminine is to be effective and realize her animating potential, she must challenge the limits of her masculine partner and risk revealing herself.

References

Cermak, Timmen L. (1986). *Diagnosing and Treating Co-dependence: A Guide for Professionals Who Work with Chemical Dependents, Their Spouses and Children.* Minneapolis: Johnson Institute Books.

Freud, Sigmund (1914/1959). *On Narcissism: An Introduction.* In *Collected Papers*, (trans. supervised and ed. by Joan Riviere). New York: Basic Books, vol. 4, 30-59.

Hillman, James (ed.) (1979). *Puer Papers.* Dallas, Texas: Spring Publications, Inc.

Leonard, Linda Schierse (1985). *The Wounded Woman: Healing the Father-Daughter Relationship.* Boston: Shambhala.

Schwartz-Salant, Nathan (1982). *Narcissism and Character Transformation: The Psychology of Narcissistic Character Disorders.* Toronto: Inner City Books.

von Franz, Marie-Louise (1970). *The Problem of the Puer Aeternus.* New York: Spring Publications.

Soul of the World

CHAPTER TWENTY

THE NOTORIOUS POSTWAR PSYCHE

JOHN BEEBE

Notorious
(1946). Directed by Alfred Hitchcock.
Screenplay by Ben Hecht.

There is in the midst of the flow of active imaginative imagery that makes up the cinematic narrative of Alfred Hitchcock's *Notorious* a frame too fleeting in the actual movie to be experienced as an isolated pictorial event. Yet so many commentators on the film have selected the still of this frame for reproduction that it has become a kind of engram for the impact of the movie, and I follow that tradition by evoking it here. The image conveys the moment in the action when "Alicia (Ingrid Bergman) begins to realize that her husband (Claude Rains) and his mother (Madame Konstantin) are trying to murder her."[1] The frame reveals Alicia, still dressed, but having collapsed from the effects of the arsenic that mother and son have been putting in her coffee. She is lying on the bed in which she can now expect to be held prisoner; as the faces of mother and son leaning over her prostrate form start to cast shadows on her body, her own face studies their significant exchange of glances. It is a culminating moment of insight in the sophistication of her consciousness, a process that has been developing since her decision, after the war and her father's conviction as a German agent, to marry Alex in order to spy on his attempts to keep the Nazi cause alive in Brazil. She now knows that he and his mother have not only the desire but the power to extinguish her consciousness and her life. Too weak to take more in, and engulfed by the merging shadows, Alicia passes out.

Who is this Alicia, and what has she seen? Why is this moment in Ingrid Bergman's performance as Alicia so remarkable? I do not think we get very far by seeing her as an actual woman experiencing something personally discomfiting; the film then becomes another 1940s Hollywood woman-victim scenario, with the woman a passive and masochistic role model in a patriarchal fantasy that places the ultimate responsibility for her suffering on another (older and, because less beautiful, envious) woman. This idea that the film documents patronizing assumptions about female authority does not explain the satisfaction feminist critics have taken in this film[2] and damages the contemporary resonance of its imagery. Neither is the film simply a dreamlike psychosexual romance, as its somewhat formulaic plot might suggest. I think it is important to understand the film neither as conscious social commentary nor as unconscious dream, but as a spontaneous elaborated fantasy emerging out of the joint imaginative effort of its two extraordinary scriptwriters.

We are fortunate in knowing the circumstances of the creation of the story.[3] The scenario for *Notorious* emerged out of the collaboration of Hitchcock and Ben Hecht, who spent several months in intense conversation developing the story of Alicia. At the conscious level, these were specialists in emotional effects and close observers of people, who were capable of working out between themselves, and with extraordinary fidelity, the likely reactions of a character they had created out of nothing to inhabit a story they had found for her. From another angle, it is hard to see how the unconscious would not also have become activated between these men, and it is likely that Alicia reflects much about the shared emotional state of her creators at the time. About this we know at least something. The collaboration itself was their second (their first screenplay had been *Spellbound*), and at this time both men were anticipating the end of the war and examining their creative options. I think both men felt more successful than creative at just this moment in their lives and that both were mildly depressed. Neither really appreciated the interference in their creative lives of the producer David O. Selznick, even though he was paying their salaries and making suggestions for the scenario that were extraordinarily helpful. At first, the screenplay did not proceed smoothly: the heroine was an idea for a long time before she became a character. Only very late in the game did her own voice come. I believe that Hecht and Hitchcock could not avoid projecting into her some of their own uncertain mood and that one of the strengths of their character is the way she personifies that confusion.

The situation that I think was operating in the background both to frustrate their imaginations about the character they were trying to bring to life, and in the end to give her her particular relevance to postwar concerns, was the dawning postwar era itself. Neither Hecht nor Hitchcock knew what this period would hold, and the character of Alicia gave them a channel into which to pour their fears and hopes for it. She incarnates a passionate uncertainty about her role in life that almost perfectly conveys the unconscious ambivalence of those who had won the war. The collaborators must finally have recognized that their own present moment in history was in fact the point of departure for the screenplay, because the completed film starts with the legend, "Miami, Florida. Three-twenty P.M. April the Twenty-fourth. Nineteen hundred and forty-six."

At the time they were working on *Notorious, Spellbound* was "in the can" but unreleased, and director and playwright were looking beyond Hollywood for ways to increase the creativity and the relevance of their work. Hitchcock was involved in producing a documentary on the horrors of the Holocaust; Hecht, who had been profoundly disillusioned by the failure of Franklin Roosevelt to directly charge the Nazis with the murder of the Jewish people, was working on an anti-Roosevelt play. Both were in a state of moral recoil and felt more than a little personally guilty that they had not done more during the war to advance the human condition. The scenario that developed between them can best be described as a shared fantasy of ethical redemption. Their joint creative effort, though spurred by both dramatic and commercial pressures to produce a strong emotional effect, went far beyond the requirements of even a highly suspenseful romance[4] and served, I think, to heal a shared creative depression. Certainly, it unlocked their creativity. By focusing on the personality and reactions of Alicia Huberman, they managed to convey their intuition of the new tensions that the end of the war would bring. In delineating the twists and turns of her fate, they also managed to formulate for their fantasy figure the deepest concerns, needs, and possibilities of the postwar psyche. The greatest gift of *Notorious* to those who can approach it on its own terms as an imaginative achievement is the realization of its power as an initiatory drama, a ceremony of healing in which Ingrid Bergman's Alicia represents the postwar psyche in its greatest period of ethical trial. As the scriptwriters elaborate it, her ordeal becomes not just a test of the integrity of that psyche's vision, but a genuine opportunity for its initiation into another level of consciousness.

For an adequate understanding of the experience of the film, I have found it helpful to turn to the writings of a specialist in the symbolism of the psyche under pressure, C. G. Jung. Jung understood that an active relation to its fantasy can give the disillusioned soul a sense of the basis of its suffering and a glimpse of its possibilities for redemption.[5] Unfortunately, Jung's insights have been too rarely applied to the study of film. However, we have Hitchcock's own permission to invoke his authority here. In *Marnie*, Hitchcock's much later film about the healing of a soul, Marnie's employer and would-be husband and healer, Mark, offers the troubled heroine a copy of Jung's *The Undiscovered Self.* We may be able to do justice to Alicia Huberman's moment of discovery by following this lead and drawing from another book of Jung's written not long after *Notorious* was released. Indeed, Jung's help can allow us to see the implications of her drama for the healing of postwar consciousness.

In *Aion*, which was published in 1951, Jung writes in what could be a gloss for the look on Ingrid Bergman's face that "it is a rare and shattering experience . . . to gaze into the face of absolute evil."[6] And, in his very next paragraphs, Jung seems to make a Hitchcock-like connection between the evil that is suddenly, shatteringly perceived at such a moment and the negative mother complex that is uncovered when a therapeutic analysis reveals the basis of an individual's failure to live:

> If this situation is dramatized, as the unconscious usually dramatizes it, then there appears before you on the psychological stage a man living regressively seeking his childhood and his mother, fleeing from a cold cruel world which denies him understanding. Often a mother appears beside him who apparently shows not the slightest concern that her little son should become a man, but who, with tireless and self-immolating effort, neglects nothing that might hinder him from growing up and marrying. You behold the secret conspiracy between mother and son, and how each helps the other to betray life.[7]

But this is the scene from *Notorious!* In their different efforts to organize their perception of the fundament of evil in the postwar Western psyche, Hitchcock the artist and Jung the psychologist seem to have stumbled upon a common image: the mother and son conspiring to betray life. Coming to this image caps the sophistication of Alicia Huberman's consciousness.[8] The film has so far offered her a progressive initiation into the world her discredited father has left behind, revealing in Alex Sebastian's home a secret cult of the remaining negative mother of Nazism, still hard at work behind a persona apparently reconciled to the outcome of the war.

Hitchcock produced this image of an undeniably "negative" mother in his forty-sixth year, when as a filmmaker he was trying to break through the Selznick-style barriers to a truly psychological cinematic expression. Jung, similarly, chose the negative aspect of the mother imago to illustrate the insidious effect of an unrecognized archetype, citing as his clinical example the deep immobilization of a forty-five-year-old patient "who had suffered from a compulsion neurosis since he was twenty and had become completely cut off from the world [and] once said to me: 'But I can never admit to myself that I've wasted the best twenty-five years of my life.'"[9] As Jung puts it, describing this patient:

It is often tragic to see how blatantly a man bungles his own life and the lives of others yet remains totally incapable of seeing how much the whole tragedy originates in himself, and how he continually feeds it and keeps it going. Not consciously, of course—for consciously he is engaged in bewailing and cursing a faithless world that recedes further and further into the distance. Rather, it is an unconscious factor which spins the illusions that veil his world. And what is being spun is a cocoon, which in the end will completely envelop him.[10]

Jung goes on to imply that the unconscious projection-making factor running this kind of patient's life from within will be a mother imago who serves not life but death. Jung's choice of this image, like Hitchcock's, reflects both his personal psychology and the time in which he lived and worked. For Jung personally, the negative mother meant a paralysis of empathy, a problem that had affected the tone of some of his public statements prior to the war years and unjustly tarnished his therapeutic reputation. For Hitchcock the filmmaker, the image of the controlling negative mother probably represented the threat of creative stagnation in a career as an expert technician directing for other producers. In *Notorious*, he goes so far as to present her as a kind of alter-Hitler,[11] carrying forward the evil of the world even after the victory of the Allies over the Axis powers.

Notorious is interesting as an imaginative document of 1946, the first full year after World War II, because it links the unconscious, seemingly personal problem of the negative mother to the problem haunting the collective consciousness of its time—guilt for the war. The emotional tone of the film is oppression: the depressive anxiety of collective guilt nags at the characters like a shaming mother, and *Notorious* suggests through the development of its fantasy that the Western soul must face down its unconscious negative mother complex if it is ever to forgive itself and recover its morale. As played with contagious resonance by Ingrid Bergman, Alicia personifies the mood of the postwar European-American soul, burdened with the guilt of departed fathers for sins that had been punished but not atoned for. For the Western soul, the most conspicuous part of the departed fathers' dark undigested legacy was the nuclear bomb, the deployment of which suddenly linked Roosevelt and Truman to the ruthlessness of Hitler and Stalin.

Alicia's belief that she can heal herself through love—that her deepest longing is to connect with a stronger masculine spirit—marks her, from a Jungian perspective, as an anima figure rather than an actual woman who could find meaning in herself simply by saying no to the bad fathers.[12] Her troubled radiance suggests the ideal vibrancy of an archetype of life being poisoned by doubt and shame. The urgency of the peril posed by internalized collective guilt is brought home to us by Hitchcock's deft handling of his actress, Ingrid Bergman, whose performance creates strong sympathy for the soul that must carry the postwar dilemmas.

The opening scene of the film sets the theme—the postwar situation—by beginning with a date that is just about a year since Hitler's suicide. We watch the sentencing of Alicia's unrepentant father as newspaper reporters with flash cameras wait for her to emerge from the courtroom. What will Miss Huberman have to say for herself? (The implicit question is, what is the mood of the postwar anima?) She is unable to answer, but just by dint of association with her father (for she is not otherwise famous) she has become notorious, a new scapegoat for collective guilt. We find ourselves next at a party in her house, wanting to know more about her, and we are shocked to see how literally she has taken on the guilty role: in her own house the beautiful Ingrid Bergman is coarsely drunk and dressed un-becomingly in a cheap two-piece outfit with shiny black stripes that looks surreally like a convict's uniform. Her hair pushes up into messy peaks that resemble horns. She is crudely sexual and explicitly "available:" the strength of her self-loathing is heard in her every word.

As we watch her, the shadow of our unwittingly disapproving gaze seems to be depicted on the screen by the silhouette of a man's head, placed there roughly in the position the news photographers had occupied, and looking not unlike the head of someone in the theater sitting a few seats ahead of us.[13] Only gradually is the head revealed to belong to Cary Grant, who then takes up the role of doubter of Alicia's cynical stance; we start to evaluate him and his right to judge her. With his elegant impassivi-ty, he too feels less like a human being than an archetype. (These larger-than-life stars perfectly convey the numinous, goddess- and god-like qualities of personalities in the collective unconscious. Grant is even photographed upside down from Alicia's standpoint early in their scenes together, as if to suggest that for her too he comes in from below, in other words, that he is a figure in her unconscious life.) Like Jung's animus archetype, he appears in relation to the demoralized anima as a spiritual challenger. If he is at first the image of her own self-doubts (in the logic of the fantasy, the personification of collective judgment), he is also the agent of her redemption, creating the very scenario by which she may encounter and work through the basis of her doubts about herself. Their trip to Brazil is like a journey in a fairytale to the "other side," down into the un-conscious, the realm of the shadow and the mother, where Hitchcock's portentous plot device—the nuclear secret—lurks like a treasure hard to attain. In this unconscious realm Alicia must, like a fairytale heroine, accept a role as false bride in order to be true to the initiatory task set for her by her true lover.

As in fairytales, this lover, the animus of the anima, is a healer who enables the feminine protagonist to solve her spiritual problem. As played by Cary Grant, Devlin (the name implies engaging in diabolic activities) is more than a little like Hermes—a mysterious stranger, a trickster, a messenger, a thief, an interloper, and finally the only physician Alicia gets or really needs. He is a wounding healer, whose role is to educate the anima about evil and to increase her capacity to suffer this knowledge: Alicia's ordeal can be understood as the Western soul's development out of the naive glib despair of the postwar mood into a heightened ability to confront the problem of evil. No scene is more powerful in accomplishing this task of sophisticating the anima than the famous episode that begins with Alicia's theft of the key to the wine cellar. As the champagne is running out at the party upstairs (the postwar celebratory mood quickly fading as the tensions of the new era start to become clear), Devlin takes Alicia down into the wine cellar where a wine bottle topples in a pseudo-explosion that reveals dark metallic sand—sequestered ore that turns out to be uranium.

In dreams when something is where it should not be the usual reaction is shock. Here the disruption of expectations is pointed up by Hitchcock's camerawork and dramatic timing. Wine refers to a natural spirit[14] released by human effort from the fruits of the feminine earth; it is a staple of Western civilization in both its secular and religious forms. The unexpected appearance of dark metallurgic *prima materia* from the wine bottle is like an invasion of the primitive underground tradition of alchemy into the midst of this modern movie. Thanks to Jung, we find it easier to recognize that this esoteric tradition has surfaced in our time, both in its physical-chemical and in its spiritual teachings, perhaps in response to the postwar push for both nuclear energy and a consciousness that can handle its awesome power.[15] With the return via modern physics and chemistry of alchemy's practical concern with the transmutation of elements has come a remarkable new psychological attention to the dark side of the feminine that philosophical alchemy had projected onto matter and made an object of intense speculation.

It is hard to pinpoint the moment alchemical consciousness made its return into our midst, but the date bears upon our theme. Jung's speculations in this regard are well supported by Hitchcock's imagery in *Notorious*. The bottle that breaks open is dated 1934; the bottle that Devlin uses as a replacement to contain the revealed ore is dated 1940. Taking Alex's point of view as he investigates in the cellar, Hitchcock emphasizes the jarring intrusion of this particular year into the assumed sequence of vintage 1934s on the wine shelf. That the ore has been replaced into this newer bottle reveals Alicia to her husband Alex as an American spy. It is as if Alicia herself is the new bottle that has insinuated itself among the others. Psychologically, this association marks her for us as carrying a consciousness of the dark that belongs to a newer era, supplanting the 1934-vintage naivete about evil that could ignore a developing Nazi ascendancy.

Jung always felt that 1940 was a watershed year, and during it he wrote to a colleague:

> This is the fateful year for which I have waited more than 25 years. Although since 1918 I knew that a terrible fire would spread over Europe beginning in the North East, I have no vision beyond 1940 concerning the fate of Europe. This year reminds me of the enormous earthquake in 26 B.C. that shook down the great temple of Karnak. It was the prelude to the destruction of all temples, because a new time had begun. 1940 is the year when we approach the meridian of the first star in Aquarius. It is the premonitory earthquake of the New Age.[16]

Though Alex credits his spying wife with an emerging consciousness that could pose a threat to the era he is anachronistically trying to revive, the problem of the dark matter in the wine bottle is for Alicia at this point in the film a shocking and unexpected reality at whose significance she can merely guess. Like the meaning of the year 1940 for the intuitive Jung, the secret signified by this dark earth is still mysterious to her. What the discovery means in human terms becomes plain when she sees Alex Sebastian and his mother leaning over her bed, openly conspiring to find the best way to hasten her end. Now she knows she must fear for her survival, for the "mother" has ceased to function as the guarantor of the continuity of life and has in fact become its enemy. This is the changed meaning of nature in the atomic era: Nature's dark side has become so apparent that all of us must fear for our survival.

In her role as Alicia, Ingrid Bergman's face registers the emotional impact of the soul's entry into a new age, the postmodern era. In this new period of history, Enlightenment ideas of progress and perfectibility have been called back, since they can only find ground in an image of Nature's support for human development that is unrealistically positive. The everyday "banality of evil" is the reality that Alicia's new consciousness enables her to see behind the elegant facades of Alex and his mother, indifferent to her suffering. Reimagining the moving picture as a medium to capture the motions of the world soul, Hitchcock simulates on film an event in the collective unconscious. Confronting his beautiful star with the ugly reality of an everyday mother complex, Hitchcock records a moment of instinctive recoil, a movement that signifies an unconscious shift in basic assumptions about the safety of the world.

But if *Notorious* records the world's soul in recoil, it also shows it able to accept and survive its initiation into the postmodern condition. When Cary Grant's Devlin returns to the scene, he is newly animated, and in the fairytale logic of the fantasy[17] this revitalization seems a response to Alicia's achieved new consciousness. No longer does he seem the guilt-invoking bystander. Instead, he is motivated by empathy, which allows him to manipulate Alicia's rescue. In the final sequence of the film, all four characters descend the staircase together—Devlin, Alicia, Alex, and Alex's mother. This quartet of players acting in tight ensemble is one of Hitchcock's most satisfying effects. Instead of the opposition between betrayed and betrayers that has so far governed the placement of the characters, and the extreme idealism and cynicism that have marked their alternating points of view, the four principals now occupy a single frame, sharing the ground of empathy and anxiety. Collective guilt gives way to cooperation for survival, and they are forced into a spirit of recognized mutual dependence. Alex and his mother are pushed into paradoxical acts of sacrifice on behalf of Alicia, if only to prolong their own existence.[18] Yet this harmony is broken up again, once Alex's energy is spent in setting Alicia free. Alicia, leaning on Devlin, is just strong enough to sustain a consciousness of being outside the domain of the old regime of the negative mother; Alex is reabsorbed into the mother world. It encloses him within a vanquished past that our world has been brought safely, if tensely, beyond.

References

Deutelbaum, Marshall and Poague, Leland (eds.) (1986). *A Hitchcock Reader*. Ames: Iowa State University Press.

Hillman, James (1985). *Anima: An Anatomy of a Personified Notion*. Dallas: Spring Publications.

Jung, C. G. (1960). "The Transcendent Function." In *The Structure and Dynamics of the Psyche. Collected Works*, vol. 8.

—. (1968a). *Aion: Researches into the Phenomenology of the Self. Collected Works*, vol. 9ii.

—. (1968b). *Psychology and Alchemy. Collected Works*, vol. 12.

—. (1969). "Transformation Symbolism in the Mass," in *Psychology and Religion: West and East. Collected Works*, vol. 11.

—. (1973). *Letters: 1:1906-1950*. Princeton: Princeton University Press.

Leff. Leonard J. (1987). *Hitchcock & Selznick*. New York: Weidenfeld and Nicolson.

Modleski, Tania (1988). *The Women Who Knew Too Much: Hitchcock and Feminist Theory*. New York: Methuen.

Rothman, William (1975). "Alfred Hitchcock's *Notorious*." *The Georgia Review* 29 (Winter).

Simone, Sam P. (1982). *Hitchcock as Activist: Politics and the War Films*. Ann Arbor: UMI Research Press.

Spoto, Donald (1984). *The Dark Side of Genius: The Life of Alfred Hitchcock*. New York: Ballantine Books.

Truffaut, François (1983). *Hitchcock*. New York: Simon & Schuster.

Wood, Robin (1970). *Hitchcock's Films*. New York: Paperback Library.

—. (1989). *Hitchcock's Films Revisited*. New York: Columbia University Press.

Notes

[1] Wood (1970, 31).

[2] See Modleski (1998) and Wood (1989).

[3] The best account is in Leff (1987, 174-223). Hitchcock's own version as related to Truffaut (1983) is itself an active imagination that is challenged by Spoto (1984, 297-306).

[4] The final scenario has been concisely summarized by Leff (1987, 177) as follows: After the war, "American government agent T. R. Devlin (Cary Grant) recruits Alicia Huberman (Ingrid Bergman) to infiltrate a Nazi cell in Rio. Though she falls for Devlin, he seems uncertain of his feelings and wary of her reputation as a playgirl. 'This is a very strange love affair,' she tells him, because 'you don't love me.' Alicia meanwhile pursues her assignment to seduce Alex Sebastian (Claude Rains), the head of the secret German war machine in Brazil. When Sebastian proposes marriage, Devlin allows Alicia to accept. The Nazis openly welcome the new Mrs. Sebastian, but Alicia's spidery mother-in-law seems jealous and suspicious. Alicia soon learns that her husband has hidden something valuable in the cellar. During a tense search, she and Devlin find uranium in some wine bottles, yet their discovery leads to her exposure. At last expressing his love, Devlin rescues her from the Sebastian home and leaves Alex and his mother behind to face their vengeful Nazi associates."

[5] See Jung (1960).

[6] Jung (1968a, 10).

[7] Ibid., 11.

[8] James Hillman (via a personal communication in 1986) has offered "sophistication of the anima" for the process going on in *Notorious*; for a thorough discussion

of the anima concept in analytical psychology, including a discussion of anima development, see Hillman (1985).

[9] Jung, *Aion*, 10.

[10] Jung, *Aion*, 10.

[11] This connection is made by Simone (1982, 144).

[12] I am indebted to the Jungian analyst Beverley Zabriskie for first making this distinction for me in a discussion of Alicia.

[13] Renov (1980). This article is summarized in Wood (1989, 304-305).

[14] Jung (1969, 252-254).

[15] See especially Jung (1968b).

[16] Jung (1973, 285).

[17] Abel (1986) makes the fairytale structure of the scenario explicit in his essay "*Notorious*: Perversion par Excellence," which can be found in Deutelbaum and Poague (1986, 162-169).

[18] See William Rothman (1975) for a careful analysis of this transformation from a formal point of view.

CHAPTER TWENTY ONE

A PHANTOM FROM HISTORY

JOHN BEEBE

Beloved
(1998). Directed by Jonathan Demme.
Screenplay by Akosua Busia, Richard LaGravenese, and Adam Brooks.

The theme of *Beloved* is unsubtle abuse—an assault visited also on the audience in the early reels of the film. A rational horror story, it treats with the gothic apparatus of passion, bloodshed, poltergeist, and spirit-possession the unconscious impact of slavery. Sethe, a runaway slave, has murdered her infant daughter rather than let her be taken into slavery. Saddled with guilt and collective ostracism, she now endures the revenge of the child's ghost. After eighteen years, she has learned to ignore the vengeful incursions of the infantile spirit, but they imminently threaten her surviving daughter's chance to participate in African-American life during the Reconstruction era.

This is the time after the Civil War, when, a generation before Booker T. Washington's call for gradualism, black aspirations could still be informed by the progressive spirit of Frederick Douglass, the first national women's movement, and the welcoming attitude of former Abolitionists. A developing city like Cincinnati, in the former "free" state of Ohio, could seem, in 1873, like a bustling emblem of African-Americans' potential to prosper at last in the New World. Jonathan Demme is at his best in creating a gallery of nineteenth century African-American faces, and his mise–en–scène includes county fairs, hog markets, river crossings, and gatherings in support of racial pride. The effect is a cumulative portrait of growing black self-esteem.

Both Sethe and her resourceful daughter, Denver, would seem to be likely candidates to join this surge toward progress, but they are held back by an unsuspected consequence of abrupt emancipation. The crude intrusion of a ghost who was *cut off* from being a slave is nothing less than the return of the psychic force of the unmourned, interrupted slave identity itself. Beloved, as played by the Anglo-African Thandie Newton, is equally a revenant of the movie past—Prissy from *Gone With the Wind*, or Stepin Fetchit in *Steamboat Round the Bend*—a tricksterish caricature of what supremacist whites expect from blacks. But this is not comic relief: Newton's flailing Beloved acts out the notion that a black person, once released from the duty of slavery, is not suited for anything else, being hopelessly childish, only fitfully intelligent (in a brain-damaged way), and glaringly greedy—orally and sexually insatiable, with no respect for boundaries, private property, or morality. It is this damaging projection that comes to haunt Sethe and Denver, the men of the house having long since fled in fright. Its image of black inferiority soon serves to enslave Sethe once more.

Toni Morrison used as the jumping-off point for her visionary novel, *Beloved*, the true story of Margaret Garner, who really did kill her two–year–old daughter rather than see her return to slavery. Garner, who died a slave, became a heroic figure for abolitionists and a scapegoat for defenders of slavery in the decade before the Civil War.[1] Morrison's Sethe is a more complex and enduring power, an avatar of the oppressed survival of the former slaves after the Civil War. As played by a restrained Oprah Winfrey, Sethe combines alert immediacy with stubborn insistence on her own point of view. The most horrifying aspect of the film is not the materialization of Beloved herself (who appears, decked with insects, like an exhumed Ophelia in borrowed hat, dress, and shoes) but the undefended sincerity with which Sethe welcomes this vampire in.

Seeming not to notice Beloved's lighter skin and Caucasian features, Sethe accepts the feral young woman as the grown-up re-embodiment of her murdered daughter. Although Sethe takes the exotic Beloved for her "best thing," it is clear that the demon-child is an absolutely undermining presence. Beloved seduces Sethe's lover, the sweet Paul D. (Danny Glover), who finally gets his excuse to take off when the history of the infanticide is revealed to him. The lonely Denver is all too happy to have a sister, but more and more finds herself sidelined by the demanding Beloved. That the women welcome in this wraith represents more than their desire to reconstitute the family they have lost: it illustrates the insidious process of introjective identification by which a people can accept a distortion of their identity. As poltergeist, Beloved had shattered the family's mirror. With Sethe all hers, Beloved enters a malignant regression that drains Sethe's remaining resources. By charting Beloved's erosion of Sethe's hardworking reliability, the film conveys the split in will that can be introduced in even a survival-oriented self when such a destructive projection is internalized.

This disaster is counterbalanced by a miracle. The energy for an exorcism of Sethe's annihilated home rises unexpectedly out of the surrounding community of formerly ostracizing black women who come, in a strong image of group agency, to pray for Sethe. One of their number, a canny maid in the house of "good white people," also provides an opportunity for Denver to work and perhaps receive an education. Their good will is the beginning of a convergence of forces that drive Beloved to disappear.

In her last moment on screen, Beloved stands on Sethe's porch, naked, barefoot, and pregnant. It is a crazy, off-kilter image, racist and sexist, in which we see Sethe as she might have looked years before to the white youths on the Kentucky plantation, egged on by their "Schoolteacher" to "milk her like a cow." But the apparition is witnessed by a different kind of white man now. Denver's new employer, Mr. Bodwin, has come to pick her up to go to work. Delirious, Sethe confuses Mr. Bodwin with the plantation overseer come to fetch Beloved back. The good will of the black women is again required to drive out this counter-projection, but even though the target is wrong, Sethe's expression of anger is a sign that she is starting to rid herself of the learned helplessness that Beloved finally represents.

Played by Jason Robards, Jr. in a silent performance scarcely a minute long, Mr. Bodwin personifies a white gaze that is not focused through the assumptions of supremacy. His compassionate, troubled look comes as a shock: up to now the camera has largely shown us black characters from a black viewpoint, either directly or in memory, allowing us to feel we are seeing African-American life entirely from the inside. This complicating moment, when the white man scrutinizes the bizarre image of Beloved and sees that it does not fit the reality of the other black women, carries the force of a projection seen through. The film invites its mainstream audience to participate in this gesture with a withdrawal of projection that is also a victory for heart.

References

Weisenburger, Steven (1998). *Modern Medea*. New York: Hill and Wang.

Notes

[1] See Weisenburger (1998) for the life of this remarkable figure.

CHAPTER TWENTY TWO

THE EYE AT THE HEART OF THE WORLD

JOHN BEEBE

The Heart of the World
(2000). Written and Directed by Guy Maddin.

"Film is the art of seeing," a projector repairman is told by the owner of a movie theater in Wim Wenders' 1976 film *Kings of the Road*.[1] The Jungian critic is in a position to complicate this observation by noting that what is seen is not merely physical, not just a picture of "outer" reality, but also a perception of the reality of the psyche.

It is not hard to demonstrate that film is a medium for the recognition of the psyche. As I have discovered in a quarter century of writing and lecturing on movies from a Jungian standpoint, a satisfying movie regularly displays the complexes, archetypes, and types of consciousness that make up the phenomenological manifestations of psychological life. It lets us "see" them.[2] That is the art a film *auteur* practices. But what is the attitude that emerges through the practice of this art? The *auteur* directors—from Ford down to Wenders—have for the most part remained silent on this point, or changed the subject when an interviewer tried to bring it up.

It was the rise of the *auteur* theory that not only canonized the forebears of Wenders but also grounded his generation of filmmakers in what their own work might be about. The recognition of film as the objectified expression of a director's subjective psychology coincided with the development of the academic discipline of film studies (including those studies that have preferred to see film as the expression of a culture's, rather than just a director's, complexes). But an appreciation of how very psychological film can be does not, in itself, get us very far in understanding how the medium of film, a scientific breakthrough in the history of photography and (more generally) of the mechanical archiving of lived experience, came to take up the psychological standpoint that is so characteristic of it today.

Most contemporary Jungian critics—Berry, for instance—have approached this question through the synchronism of film's appearance on the cultural scene with the emergence of depth psychology.[3] Freud and the Lumière brothers made at the same time their demonstrations of what their new technologies could do, and we can say that the apparatus of psychoanalysis and the mechanics of filmmaking occupy a common position in history. Both emerged, it would seem, as a way to solve the same problem, that of reflecting about the experience of modernity. Without too much of a stretch, a psychological historian can say that both psychoanalysis and cinema offered modernity a way to see its own shadow.

But how do filmmakers themselves see their turn to psychology? What is cinema's myth of its own origin as a medium for psyche? An unusual film by the contemporary Canadian director Guy Maddin provides an interesting answer to these questions, advancing the understanding of the medium for his own generation to the same degree that Wenders was able to do thirty years ago.[4]

The Heart of the World (2000), originally made by Maddin to serve as one of the short film "Preludes" to the Toronto International Film Festival in honor of its 25th anniversary year, has a running time of just six minutes, and may be the only film of its length and limited first release to appear on the annual ten-best lists of the *New York Times* and the *Village Voice*. It is currently available from Zeitgeist Video on a DVD that also includes two full-length features in Maddin's seemingly-throwback expressionist style that I have described elsewhere as Canadian Surrealism, to convey the flat-footed quality of his melodramatic forays into the fantastic, and the emotional integrity of his uncanny evocations of silent and early sound cinema.[5]

Victoria Nelson, a knowing cultural critic of the art movements that can be seen to intersect in Maddin's work, has described the sensibility in which he participates, in common with other contemporary film directors with whom he can be said to share a "family resemblance"—Joel and Ethan Coen, Tim Burton, and Lars von Trier—as "New Expressionist." In her book, *The Secret Life of Puppets*, which is about the strange ways the Neo-Platonic transcendent has managed to survive in offbeat twentieth century literature, theater, art, and film, she lists the following as defining features of the New Expressionism that had emerged by century's end: (1) the inner is made visible in the outer; (2) a metaphysical dimension is present; (3) in contrast to the Old Expressionism found in German silent films like *Caligari, The Golem, Nosferatu,* and *Metropolis,* the supernatural is no longer only the grotesque, i.e., it dares to be not of the Devil; (4) a high-art edifice is constructed on a low-art foundation; (5) extreme melodrama does not alienate us; extreme action is essential for deep identification with the main character; and (6) cliché is likewise deliberate, nonironic, and serves a high purpose as allegory.[6]

All of these qualities are richly evident in *The Heart of the World* and made easily palatable by the energy and humor that Maddin brings to his work. As the first titles appear, the manic, propulsive soundtrack ("Time, forward!"—the climactic movement of Georgy Sviridov's score for a 1967 Soviet film of the same name, itself an echo of a famous Soviet realist novel that celebrated workers' attempts, under the first Soviet Five-Year Plan, to construct a huge steel plant in record time) has already started us on our wide-eyed ride through Maddin's agitprop scenario: chaos and misery will prevail unless a new world order is found. The immediate impression, heightened by the calligraphic style of the titles, exact replicas of the futurist fonts of the first decade of the Soviet Union, is a send-up of Russian silent propaganda film. Maddin's tricksterism in pre-empting (and thus getting us to distance ourselves from) our own disbelief is calculated to make us attend to the seriousness of his message, which is conveyed by the passionate face of his central character, "State Scientist" Anna, played by Lesley Bais, who as made up by Maddin somewhat resembles the young Gloria Swanson, though she is even more beautiful. She is the anima figure of the film who makes clear with the anguished sincerity of her eyes, the lids heavily outlined with kohl, that the matter that concerns her is urgent: the world is dying because it is losing its heart, and only the right kind of attention can save it. Anna's job, as an astronomer, is literally to keep her eye on things of cosmic proportions, and initially a female eye, presumably hers because it is widely flared as if peering into a telescope, is made to occupy a large part of each frame while the film proceeds to expose what is troubling Anna.[7]

As this is a silent film, except for the overheated soundtrack, much of the exposition is done through titles in juxtaposition with the telling, and almost ridiculously intense images that nevertheless (as in actual silent cinema) have enormous emotional force. They are melodramatic in their own right, however, and they tell us that there are "TWO BROTHERS... who love the Same... WOMAN," and she is revealed to be Anna, who "loves both brothers!" Already, Anna has assumed an anima role as co-conspirator in the brothers' competitive narcissism because she is the obscure object of their shared desire. We are drawn into wondering who she is, even as the film, hurtling forward in synch with the galloping soundtrack begins to take as its theme what she is going to do next, in the decision she has to make between the brothers. (The suffering they share is symbolized by "a wildly scrambled cardiogram" that appears "over the heart of each ...brother."[8]) But, as ever in melodrama, our curiosity about her is interrupted by a more urgent crisis to which she must turn her—and our—attention. Instead of looking into her own heart to resolve the problem of which brother she really wants to marry, she has, with the logic of the new expressionism, in which the inner is met as the outer, directed her telescope toward the earth's interior, where indeed a heart is beating fitfully. It is there that she finds, as the next titles tell us, that the heart of the world is dying!

This heart is one of Maddin's slyest visual achievements. It is, so to speak, an agitated prop, like something lifeless jiggled by a stage hand on the set of a Buck Rogers film. With its excess of tubes and ventricles resembling more a rubber toy octopus or spider than a human heart, it is a vile thing, aesthetically, that we want to be rid of as soon as possible and that's obscene to think of as the source of the vital pulse of our world. The comedy of its abject ugliness is that it is so literal an image, divorced from any possibilities beyond itself.

We cannot, however, shake the authority of the insistent titles: this is the heart of the world, and there is "NO" doubt that it is dying. Here the pathetic fallacy, the ascription of human traits or feelings to the entities of nature, with the hint of the hidden sympathy of all things, takes on a comic force in our conviction that this dilapidated organ of the world's plumbing is incapable of caring. The electrocardiogram we saw earlier has now become a signifier neither of the brothers' lovesickness nor of Anna's feeling confusion but rather of the moribund state of the world's eros. In his published script for *The Heart of the World*, Maddin says "the Heart has a rip in it," and this reference to a frank inner split is a clue to what he conveys cinematically in the finished film, that the world is becoming more hysterical because its real condition is schizoid.[9]

Anna takes up the role of oracle:

Now ANNA addresses a crowd of people gathered at her observatory, not just people, but proles, bowed and beaten from long years of punishing toil, meaningless grinding years going nowhere until this surprise culmination in crushing news. From the aerie of her perch by the eye-piece, ANNA, the great scientist orates and gesticulates to the stricken people. Overcome with emotion, she announces in super-imposed titles:
    Title: Cataclysm!
    The End of the World!
    Little Time Remains![10]

Crazily, the film goes back from this world crisis to the love problem of which brother to choose. As Anna turns her attention back to the brothers, Osip and Nicolai, the two try to win her with feats. Osip, the elder, has been playing Christ in a passion play, and as the more "spiritual" brother he now enacts the part of the Messiah with missionary zeal, exhorting sinners to change their ways, and healing the sick. Nicolai, a youth who is already a mortician, is the more "practical" of the brothers, but he is no less manic than Osip in the way he dresses the dead and places them on an assembly line into coffins, which he himself nails shut so as to better direct them into hastily dug graves. The film forces us into an allegorical reading in which Anna, the scientist with her telescope, stands as symbol for the new technology of seeing that is the science of cinema, and the brothers as choices with regard to the way that technology may end up being deployed. The clichés surrounding the brothers' displays of spiritual and practical prowess, however kitsch their presentation, are entirely serious at the level of signification. We come to recognize that they are used by Maddin (in accord with Victoria Nelson's criteria for a New Expressionist filmmaker) as allegory to point to an ambivalence at the core of filmmaking itself: whether this new technology will be used idealistically, to exhort and to heal; or realistically, to encapsulate lived experience into so many cinematic coffins, the documents of a now dead reality. Anna must decide which of these goals to ally herself with. Does she want the science of observation to nail reality or to revive it?

Maddin has set up the brothers as a pair of opposites that lead nowhere: archetypally, one can spot in Osip's messiah complex the heavy-handedness of a developing *senex* (though still a young man, he looks a lot more like Rasputin than Christ) and in Nicolai's grandiose craftsmanship the narcissism of the *puer*, and it is not hard to see why Anna cannot decide between them. In an inspired turn to the style of Fritz Lang's *Dr. Mabuse, the Gambler*, Maddin dips unexpectedly into the shadow to provide a third alternative for Anna's affections, one that shocks us not only stylistically, but ethically. This is the industrialist Akmatov—a stage-villain plutocrat that Maddin initially imagined as resembling "Mr. Monopoly from the Parker Bros. Game."[11] His excessive, rotund torso encased like sausage in a tuxedo, Akmatov exudes an unmistakably German air, with his straight-across-the-lip brush moustache and his open, Weimar-Republic lechery. As soon as she sees his money, Anna falls for him (surely, in the allegory, a demonstration of the seductive power of filmmaking for profit.) We are appropriately grossed out when they wed and an obscenely phallic cannon, previously constructed by Osip, ejects gold coins in celebration.

At just this point, the heart of the earth gives out. People panic, buildings lurch, and the dead that Nikolai has buried tear open their coffins. Anna awakens from her trance and finally realizes "the right course of action."

> She strangles the industrialist AKMATOV right in the middle of some apocalyptic love-making. Then she dashes to the top of her great inverted telescope, hefts open the glass manhole lid which is its eye-piece, climbs head-first into the cylindrical instrument as a girl entering some kind of Constructivist water slide, then hurls herself downward through the telescope and into the centre of the world, thus becoming its new heart. A human, a loving human, a naked human radiating great thermal and political and comradely warmth, is now the new Heart of the World.

> And a warm beam of light shoots from the glass eye-piece of the telescope! The telescope is now a movie projector! ANNA is its lamp! . . . ANNA pulses from the centre of her nimbus, limbs spread apart, her head supplying the fifth point to a great, powerful subterranean star.[12]

At this point, projected images begin to appear all over the world—first of Anna, and then, most significantly, of a dancing man who somewhat resembles Nijinsky. We recognize that the dance is in celebration of the birth of the new art form, cinema, with KINO, the word for cinema taken up by the early Soviet filmmakers, appearing in repeated exuberant titles.

This is a thrilling denouement, in which Anna's identity and romantic choice are resolved: she has become the anima of cinema itself, transforming the science of observation into a creative medium. At the same time, she consummates the melodrama of the unknown woman by emerging from a marriage that would have been a false identity to reveal her own expressive power.[13] To amplify Anna's final gesture in taking her position at the center of things, it is helpful, as a Jungian critic, to be informed by James Hillman's book *The Thought of the Heart & The Soul of the World*, which successfully pairs two lectures this mentor of archetypal psychology gave in different parts of Europe between 1979 and 1982, years in which aesthetic theory was striving to consolidate a postmodern standpoint. In the first of these lectures, Hillman discusses Henri Corbin's seminal work, *Creative Imagination in the Sufism of Ibn 'Arabi.*

> Corbin[14] states quite clearly that the heart's characteristic action is not feeling, but sight…The heart is not so much the place of personal feeling as it is the place of true imagining, the *vera imaginatio* that reflects the

imaginal world in the microcosmic world of the heart. Feelings stir as images move.[15]

This passage seems to me to clarify the ethic of the New Expressionist filmmaker who seeks to create emotion through the movement of images. Corbin (via Hillman) advances the discussion of "pure" cinema that began with Vertov, was revived by Hitchcock after his contact with the French New Wave, was thoughtfully probed in Germany and America by Wenders, and is so excitingly reprised in *The Heart of the World*. It was always the *vera imaginatio* that such filmmakers sought to project through their films. In the cinema, emotion that is authentic can only be created by filmmakers who have the integrity that comes from seeing from the heart, and we should look with a similar empathy when we try to understand their films psychologically. We have therefore to emend Wenders' landmark formulation: Film is not just the "art of seeing," but *the art of seeing from the heart*. The science of cinema becomes the art of film when it takes residence in the place of the heart—and we can only really see what it intends when we recognize from where the vision springs.

But we cannot stop with "the thought of the heart." We have as well to understand "the soul of the world," or we will miss something sacred about cinema. Anna's courageous, unexpected journey to the center of the earth has many echoes in contemporary Jungian thought: the descent of the goddess (Perera[16] and Meador[17] interpreting Inanna), the *anima mundi* or World Soul establishing the ego-Self axis (Edinger interpreting Robert Fludd[18]), and the "integrity in depth" that I have written about (interpreting Jung.[19]) The essence of this journey is the taking up of the psychological attitude itself.[20] As Anna assumes her new position, she becomes a star, and the new attitude is constellated for others, in an alchemical realization of heaven on earth—the heaven of captivating projected images, the language of cinema. Can there be any doubt, at the end of Maddin's creation myth of cinema, that what we are looking at is the birth of depth psychology's own medium, and that film's way of looking is the way to read experience with the heart so that the anima mundi can do her healing work?

Hillman, in the other essay in his indispensable little book, provides the rationale for the sane slowing of pace that follows on Anna's apotheosis as an *aesthetic* anima mundi, that is, her personification of a cinematic way of poesis. His argument helps us to understand why as her vision becomes more aesthetic, it also becomes more psychological:

Cultivation of the aesthetic response will affect issues of civilization that most concern us today and which have remained largely intractable to psychological resolution. First, an aesthetic response to particulars would radically slow us down. To notice each event would limit our appetite for events, and this very slowing down of consumption would affect inflation, hyper-growth, the manic defenses and expansionism of the civilization.

...Attention to the qualities of things resurrects the old idea of *notitia* as a primary activity of the soul. *Notitia* refers to that capacity to form true notions of things from attentive noticing.[21]

This returns us with a different understanding to Wenders' definition of film as the "art of seeing." Cinema, the aesthetic wing of the depth psychological edifice, is the *notitia* of our time, and we should read Maddin psychologically as serving notice that this is so. And notice that he returns us to the noticer, the kino-eye he borrowed from Vertov and gave to his central character, Anna. Maddin makes us see that the eye belongs to the anima and not to the modern filmmaker's ego for making movies. It is not the manic eye of the man with the movie camera, but the conscientious eye of the anima mundi, which through her present incarnation as cinema has managed to give the world, exhausted to the point of catastrophe by literal perspectives,[22] a new lease on heart.

References

Beebe, John (1992). *Integrity in Depth.* College Station: Texas A&M University Press.

Berry, Patricia (2001). "Image in Motion." In Christopher Hauke and Ian Alister (eds.), *Jung & Film: Post-Jungian Takes on the Moving Image.* Hove, England: Brunner-Routledge.

Craig, Robert (2002). "The Art of Seeing Rescues the Existence of Things: Notes on the Wenders Road Films and Henri Bergson's *Creative Evolution.*" http://www.horschamp.qc.ca/new_offscreen/artofseeing.html (online).

Cavell, Stanley (1996). *Contesting Tears: The Hollywood Melodrama of the Unknown Woman.* Chicago: The University of Chicago Press.

Corbin, Henri (1969). *Creative Imagination in the Sufism of Ibn 'Arabi.* Princeton: Princeton University Press.

Edinger, Edward F. (1973). *Ego and Archetype.* Baltimore: Penguin Books.

Henderson, Joseph (1984). *Cultural Attitudes in Psychological Perspective.* Toronto: Inner City Books.

Hillman, James (1992a). *"Anima Mundi*: The Return of the Soul to the World." In *The Thought of the Heart & The Soul of the World.* Woodstock, CT: Spring Publications.

—. (1992b) "The Thought of the Heart." In *The Thought of the Heart & The Soul of the World.* Woodstock, CT: Spring Publications.

Jung, C. G. (1968). *Aion. Collected Works,* vol. 9.

Maddin, Guy (2000). Script for *The Heart of the World.* In Caelum Vatnsdal, *Kino Delirium: The Films of Guy Maddin.* Winnipeg, Manitoba: Arbeiter Ring Publishing.

Meador, Betty DeShong (1992). *Uncursing the Dark: Treasures from the Underworld.* Wilmette, IL: Chiron Publications.

Nelson, Victoria (2001). *The Secret Life of Puppets.* Cambridge, MA: Harvard University Press.

Perera, Sylvia Brinton (1981). *Descent to the Goddess: A Way of Initiation for Women.* Toronto: Inner City Books.

Vertov, Dziga (1923/1970). "The Writings of Dziga Vertov." In *Film Culture Reader*, P. Adams Sitney (ed.). New York and Washington: Praeger.

Notes

1 See Craig (2002).

2 See Beebe, this book, Chapter Two, 17-25.

3 Berry (2001, 70).

4 Guy Maddin (writer, editor, photographer, and director), *The Heart of the World*, black and white 16mm film (Toronto International Film Festival, 2000 [available on DVD from Zeitgeist Video, 2002]).

5 See this book, Chapter Twenty-Three, 253-257.

6 See Nelson (2001, 215-217).

7 This image is appropriated from Dziga Vertov's *The Man with the Movie Camera* (1929), in which the eye of the filmmaker is seen fleetingly peering through the camera and thus made to symbolize the mechanical cinema eye itself. The 'kino-eye,' according to Vertov, is "more perfect than a human eye for purposes of research into the chaos of visual phenomena filling the universe" (Vertov 1923/1970, 356).

8 Maddin (2000, 149).

9 Ibid., 149. We recognize the schizoid "core" in the fantasy of world catastrophe, which we must understand not only clinically, but culturally. James Hillman has noticed how frequently people everywhere now fear a catastrophic end to the world, an end that he deliteralizes, prophetically, to mean the impending demise of the modern fantasy that the world is soulless (Hillman 1992a, 125-26). This imagined mechanical world—introduced to us in the 17th century, with William

Harvey's discovery that the heart's function in circulating blood is mechanistic—would have to be, like any machine, at risk of running down (Hillman 1992b, 18-25).

[10] Maddin (2000, 150).

[11] Ibid., 151.

[12] Ibid., 152. The sequence accords with the notion of the anima as "the projection-making factor" (Jung 1968, 13).

[13] Cavell (1996, 20).

[14] Corbin (1969, 221 & note, cited in Hillman 1992b, 28).

[15] Hillman (1992b, 28).

[16] See Perera (1981).

[17] See Meador (1992).

[18] Edinger (1973). Frontispiece.

[19] Beebe (1992).

[20] Henderson (1984, 79-86).

[21] Hillman (1992a, 115).

[22] Ibid., 201.

EMOTION

CHAPTER TWENTY THREE

ON KEY

JOHN BEEBE

The Saddest Music in the World
(2003). Directed by Guy Maddin.
Screenplay by George Toles and Guy Maddin,
based on the original screenplay by Kazuo Ishiguro.

On what basis does a movie presume to believe in its own emotional impact? After enduring several years of serious American films (from *American Beauty*[1] through *Mystic River*[2]) so confidently manipulative that I blush for the audiences that have been taken in by them, it feels good to have this question teased by the absurdist Canadian director and film critic Guy Maddin in his breakthrough movie, *The Saddest Music in the World*. Maddin, whose previous work includes *Tales from the Gimli Hospital*,[3] *Archangel*,[4] *Careful*,[5] *Twilight of the Ice Nymphs*,[6] *The Heart of the World*,[7] and *Dracula's Pages from a Virgin's Diary*,[8] is a favorite of film festival audiences throughout the world—in 1995, at thirty-nine, he was the youngest person to have received the Telluride Medal, for being "a master of postmodern expressionism"—but he was still almost unknown to most American moviegoers. *The Saddest Music* has helped to rectify that situation.

Boasting as its centerpiece the extraordinary acting of Isabella Rossellini (what she does here ranks alongside her work for David Lynch in *Blue Velvet*[9]), *The Saddest Music in the World* mirrors her performance by becoming a bravura exercise in deconstructive filmmaking. Throughout most of the film, as Lady Port-Huntly, a Winnipeg beer baroness of 1933 seeking a wider market for her lager as the end of Prohibition looms in the United States, Rossellini wears a platinum wig and sports a regal mien and accent that eerily summon the commanding presence of her real-life mother, Ingrid Bergman. At a crucial moment, however, the wig slips off, revealing Isabella's own dark hair and a mischievous, boyish look that is all her own—an imp masquerading as a goddess. And unlike her mother, she can actually play comedy—so that she successfully undercuts her character's emotions with irony.

Rossellini's arresting performance is wonderfully counterposed to that of Mark McKinney as the man she wishes she didn't love, the film's would-be hero, the scheming two-timer Chester Kent, whose look of cheesy B-movie star unreliability is matched by his insinuating radio actor's voice. Maria de Medeiros, as his other girlfriend, Narcissa, with her heart-shaped face, high and wide cheekbones, and large searching eyes, is made to resemble Marlene Dietrich in the von Sternberg films of the early thirties (the Dietrich of *The Scarlet Empress*[10]). As Chester's father, Fyodor, David Fox is a bit like Lewis Stone, who often played the father of the love interest in the Garbo films of both the silent and early talkie era. Finally, Chester's brother Rodrick (played by Ross McMillan), with his thick and near-ridiculous disguise as the competing Serbian cellist, Gravillo, and his habit of appearing vengefully as if out of nowhere, is—though he looks more like Lon Chaney, Jr. (who played the Wolf Man)—the sort of character Chaney Sr. loved to "do" in the twenties and thirties of the last century.

The Saddest Music in the World is deliberately archaic and, from the standpoint of contemporary digital technology (which in its cold, cheery brightness has its own corruption of image to worry about), visually challenged. The film, shot with a Super-8 camera and then blown up, achieves a weirdly snowy black–and–white (with a few, mostly funeral, sequences in Two-Strip Melancolour) that makes it resemble a bad copy of some hard–to–find classic. It was through bootleg prints that looked as bad as this that I first saw Griffith's *Intolerance*[11] and Jean Vigo's *L'Atalante,*[12] now routinely listed, by critics who were also introduced to them in this form, among the ten greatest films of all time. In the days before VHS and DVD, the classics came to us in grainy, bleached out dupes projected on bed sheets in improvised screening rooms by college dropout cineastes. Maddin's image also resembles the "snow" we used to get on TV sets in the 1950s—and this was another way the cinema classics were first made available to many. I had to see *The Saddest Music* twice to convince myself that Maddin's own images really do have an exactness that survives their deceptively fuzzy presentation. His odd process allows him to make daring forays into abstract filmmaking, so that he is able to dissolve his own dissolves into dancing points of light—the visual equivalent of the natural luminosity Jung discovered in numinous, archetypal images. Maddin also understands what Jung called the "play" of the archetypes—in which the possibility of new mythic patterns and previously unknown affects can emerge. Indeed, one leaves this picture feeling one has seen and felt differently: neither the situation nor the emotion it generates are quite what one expected throughout.

In a Maddin film, the stereotyped characters with their self-engineered, neurotic, and often incestuous suffering dissolve into archetypes of the anguish of being human, a very different thing from the kitsch he seems to start with. We begin to identify with their primitive emotional force. This time, the plot, skillfully developed by Maddin and his writing partner, the film historian George Toles, out of the bare bones of an idea left them by the Japanese novelist Kazuo Ishiguro, interlocks two scenarios of tangled kinship libido—a father/son and a brother-brother rivalry over different women. Interspersed are traumas and conditions of grief so hopelessly abject as to be pathetic and so unremittingly anguished as to become absurd. We can hardly believe that anything that develops can move us. But moved we are, particularly by Rossellini's Lady Port-Huntly, who is given a sour, fairy-tale fate to contend with (something along the lines of the Handless Maiden, but more brutal and more original). She meets it with the hauteur of the Snow Queen. Mark McKinney's Chester is, in his cynicism, like the boy that has a lump of glass in his heart in Andersen's fairytale, thereby binding him to the Snow Queen. And in homage to Jean Vigo's most striking image in the surreal masterpiece, *L'Atalante*, there is a broken jar, which had contained the heart of a boy who had died young. Perhaps the most telling image of *The Saddest Music in the World* comes in passing—the removal of a piece of glass from that pure boy's heart after the jar breaks.

The plot of the movie should not be told in full; that would spoil the charm of its unfolding. It involves—and this was Ishiguro's original, allegorical, political conception—a contest between representatives of different nations in a sort of Olympics of lugubriousness, to see which country can produce "the saddest music in the world." African, Canadian, Korean, Indian, Scottish, Serbian, and Spanish musicians all compete. But none can prevail against the early 1930s American movie musical sound, which in the midst of world economic gloom insists on being redundantly cheerful. As Chester labors to create his Busby Berkeley atmosphere of abundance (even, once he recruits the Indian musicians and others who have lost in the early rounds, anticipating contemporary Bollywood), *The Saddest Music in the World* begins to seem less like a compendium of moods out of Robert Burton's *Anatomy of Melancholy* (which the director, with his introverted thinking care at specifying affective states, studied before making the film) and more like a maniacal symphony of inferior feeling. By the end of the movie, with the covert familiarity of the uncanny, the manic defenses begin to crack apart. The film may be set in

Winnipeg in the Great Depression, but it is the truest evocation of the contemporary United States mood disorder that I have seen on any screen.

Where there is this kind of integrity in defining tones of soul, it can attract the grace of a healing vision, as happens here beyond, I think, what Maddin has managed to do before with his expressionistic Canadian surrealism. The miracle of *The Saddest Music in the World* is that it sees a false American self through to the end of its need to take appropriate revenge for the traumas it has suffered. This is what so sets this movie apart from the cycle of portentous films from our own country that are mostly distinguished by extraordinary actors miming what it's like to lose our moral bearings, as Sissy Spacek does, for instance, when insisting that her husband take revenge for the murder of their son in *In the Bedroom.*[13] Maddin's film invites Americans to contemplate themselves in a different way, leading us to something like the discovery of a forgotten other, our own *communal* selves. With the openhearted sincerity of her extraverted feeling delivery of "The Song is You," Maria de Medeiros actually breathes new expressiveness into Jerome Kern's classic of American popular song, to the point that a U.S. audience watching her rendition may feel that its own affective problem is being seen and addressed.

Sentimentality, however—according more feeling to a thing than is truly called for—is thoroughly undercut by the irony of the ensuing scenario, which ends the film in the gangster film *Götterdämmerung* that destroys even the possibility of self-pity. It's as if Maddin has elected to become some kind of Shiva, torching American excessiveness to make room for authentic sentiment. By movie's end, what he succeeds in releasing, as the film frees its woman characters from Chester's spell, augurs a new era of Canadian compassion. We experience a credible sense of the breaking apart of a cold self-interested egoism and the rescue of a consciousness capable of seeing the "American style" for the cynicism it is. From the reflective vantage that Guy Maddin attains as he surveys the country to the south that has supplied the emotional background for his own cinematic vision, *The Saddest Music in the World*, for all its dreamy humor, conveys the pity and dread of a horrified heart.

References

Auerbach, Nina and Skal, David J. (eds.) (1997). [Bram Stoker's] *Dracula: Authoritative Text; Contexts; Reviews and Reactions; Dramatic and Film Variations; Criticism*. New York: W. W. Norton.
Dubus, Andre (2002). *In the Bedroom*. New York: Random House.

Maroger, Dominique (ed.) (1955). *The Memoirs of Catherine the Great* (Moura Budberg, trans.). New York: Macmillan.

Notes

---

[1] *American Beauty* (1999). Screenplay by Alan Ball. Directed by Sam Mendes.
[2] *Mystic River* (2003). Screenplay by Brian Helgeland. Directed by Clint Eastwood. Based upon Dennis Lehane (2001). *Mystic River.* New York: William Morrow.
[3] *Tales from the Gimli Hospital* (1988). Screenplay by Guy Maddin. Directed by Guy Maddin.
[4] *Archangel* (1990). Screenplay by George Toles and Guy Maddin. Directed by Guy Maddin.
[5] *Careful* (1992). Screenplay by George Toles and Guy Maddin. Directed by Guy Maddin.
[6] *Twilight of the Ice Nymphs* (1997). Screenplay by George Toles. Directed by Guy Maddin.
[7] *The Heart of the World* (2000). Screenplay by Guy Maddin. Directed by Guy Maddin.
[8] *Dracula: Pages from a Virgin's Diary* (2002). Film adaptation by Guy Maddin of Royal Winnipeg Ballet production of *Dracula* (1998). Choreography by Mark Godden. Based upon the 1897 novel by Bram Stoker (see Auerbach and Skal's [1997] centennial edition.)
[9] *Blue Velvet* (1986). Screenplay by David Lynch. Directed by David Lynch.
[10] *The Scarlet Empress* (1934). Screenplay by Manuel Komroff and Eleanor McGeary. Directed by Joseph von Sternberg. Based upon the diary of Catherine II of Russia. (See Maroger [1995]).
[11] *Intolerance* (1916). Screenplay by D.W. Griffith. Directed by D.W. Griffith, with titles by Anita Loos, Walt Whitman, and Frank E. Woods.
[12] *L'Atalante* (1934). Screenplay by Jean Guinée, Albert Riéra, and Jean Vigo. Directed by Jean Vigo.
[13] *In the Bedroom* (2001). Screenplay by Robert Festinger and Todd Field. Directed by Todd Field. Based on the story "Killings," collected in Dubus (2002, 3–23).

CHAPTER TWENTY FOUR

EMOTION AND THE CINEMATIC FEMININE: A CODA

VIRGINIA APPERSON

Ponette
(1996). Directed by Jacques Doillon.
Screenplay by Jacques Doillon and Brune Compagnon.

The Lives of Others
(2007). Written and Directed by Florian Henckel von Donnersmarck.

The Namesake
(2007). Directed by Mira Nair.
Screenplay by Sooni Taraporevala.

For most of us, growing up demands that we learn to sacrifice spontaneous affective expression. As we mature, our gloom (not to mention glee) frequently is cast into the juvenile category, to be discarded as a social option. Like much that adults aim to outgrow, our emotions get left in the nursery or on the schoolyard. By the time we are adolescents, our aim is to be cool. Rather than tending to crummy or crazy moods, which only wear on others who are trying to put their own emotions behind them, we learn to button our feelings up and keep our miserable cards close to our chest. By the time we have successfully matured, we mostly have become adept at rallying our level-heads, at pasting on suitable facades and at dutifully marching through our appointed routines. We are so good at this repertoire of suppression because everyone we know has been similarly scripted to present themselves with even-tempers; that is the standard we have been asked to live by. We are sure we would be considered weak (and therefore replaceable) if any of our actual pain were to leak out and be made public. Meanwhile, as hearts silently throb and no one lets on that they were barely able to crawl out of bed today, depression is having its way with some of our best and brightest.

The one place that the tight reins on our emotions do not get checked is in the movie theatre. We have all heard it said; "I only cry in movies." But how do we reconcile the curb erected against that which stirs us, with this flood of feeling that wells up when we watch certain films. Were it not for this occasional release in a darkened movie house (one of the few remaining sanctioned places for emotional discharge), such censorship of our common sorrow in the midst of living would entirely reign. With the lights dimmed, we get to be alone with the characters on the screen who know how to let loose, and because they move us, our own emotional reticence recedes. Since no one sees our salt-stained cheeks, emotions begin to flow, still perhaps controlled, but not quite so severely. Or sometimes these feelings spontaneously rush in with such surprising intensity that our usual capacity for restraint is simply overwhelmed. Whether the aberrant outburst is provoked by watching Lassie or E.T. or Dorothy, all making their different ways back home, or sneaks up on us when Bond or the Beast gets the girl, or gushes at that heart-stopping moment when Oliver Twist requests more porridge, it is always a puzzle to us why a particular scene causes our veneer to crack and the tears to overflow.

Jungian analysts are not alone in considering the feminine the natural guardian of these poignant reservoirs of the soul that suddenly surface at the movies. Tending to emotions has long been thought of as women's work. Though many resent this traditional gender prejudice that consigns feelings to the feminine, contemporary lives *are* predominantly run by patriarchal values that render sorrow and grief immaterial, and it is, therefore, primarily to the feminine (and reflexively to women) that we continue to turn to for emotional instruction. Reliance upon the "fairer" sex for affective balance can disappoint, however, when forward-thinking women, in accord with the times, have become as proficient as their brethren at checking their feelings at the door of their careers, leaving our progressive culture chronically bereft of emotional experts. This trend informs movies like the *Alien* film series[1] and *G. I. Jane*[2] and the two parts of Quentin Tarantino's *Kill Bill*,[3] where the "Bride" is not a virgin but a vigilante who has trained herself not to let emotions interfere. Now, consistent with other cultural and developmental imperatives that have shifted us away from emotions, women are comfortably abdicating their customary duties as keepers of the feelings.

A common response to the liberation of women from hearth and home, and their pursuant development of the animus, has been to bemoan the fact that women on such a path have deserted their proper place and to express the hope that they will come back soon to their sympathetic senses. "Something has happened to women," that argument goes, "they have lost something, and they need to get it back." This contemporary version of the fall that requires Redemption suggests that only a regressive return to Eden will save us from the emotional wasteland of contemporary life. But if we put such wishful thinking aside, we can start to imagine others who could help arbitrate the feminine waters. Interestingly, and perhaps in a compensatory response to the rise of tough heroines, there seems to be a relatively new category of male expression on the screen, for which John Beebe has suggested the name the "wet masculine," which is preempting the old feminine prerogatives. Perhaps, as more and more men cultivate their emotive skills, a deeper masculine potential for emotion will join with the feminine and emotional privilege will be shared by both genders in and outside of the cinema. John noted this shift in men's consciousness as far back as *Kramer vs. Kramer*, calling it "the first men's weepie."[4] He has told me that he found Dustin Hoffman to be even more paradoxical (and fun) in *Tootsie*, which gave viewers in the 1980s an unprecedented model of the domineering male who wants to release his feminine spirit.[5] As we conclude this book, let us consider a few more idiosyncratic role models, to help us better identify the new form of feminine conscience emerging in contemporary film.

In the movies that we have chosen to focus on in the chapters of this book, John and I have exposed many examples of feminine values confidently (though not always successfully) asserting themselves, quite as if they had never been lost to our culture. Reviewing what we have written, it has been interesting to note that though most of the films we have chosen have come out of Hollywood, many have foreign born actresses and directors, subject matter that does not just feature women, and an emphasis on minorities and historical tensions. In hindsight, we can see that we have gravitated away from films that epitomize such masculine (and American) values as action and technical effects, in order to find the echoes of the feminine we wanted to record. Selecting films that feature powerful portrayals of feminine qualities has taken us out of the contemporary American mainstream. In keeping with this course, as we wend this book's way to a close, I will take a final divergent turn by examining less usual representations of the feminine in three films released in the past decade that (for the most part) were not made in America and do not focus on characters shaped by American models—one about a little French girl who has recently lost her mother, one about an East German playwright who is oppressed by an authoritarian regime, and one about a young Bengali-American man who has to make amends for his unconsciousness. Elsewhere in this book, like film watchers everywhere, we have mostly relied on grown-up actresses to convey the essence of the feminine, but consistent with our claim that women do not have exclusive rights to this mystique, these three protagonists have turned out to help along my understanding of what it really means to live a life informed by the values of the feminine. It is hard to imagine that anyone would leave *Ponette, The Lives of Others,* or *The Namesake* without noticing the respect for the feminine that is expressed by each of these movies. Perhaps a question to ponder as we meditate on the feminine one last time through the lens of these films is: What in these stories promises to restore our increasingly limited range of emotions? One answer may be to look at the films' central characters, each of whom has an idiosyncratic, but very strong, relationship with the feminine.

Ponette takes its title from the name of its little girl heroine, whose mother was just killed in a car wreck. Trailed by a camera crew that had to stoop to the little four year old's level to track her, Ponette (played with childish candor by Victoire Thivisol) trudges on, resolved to find her dead mother, in spite of the combined determination of her father, her teachers, her aunt, and her playmates to impose their narrow reality onto hers. Although some make genuine attempts to appreciate her grief, most become impatient with her visibly irrational search for her lost female parent. They just want her to accept her plight as a motherless child. Ponette, refusing to appease them, is unwilling to deny her despair or compromise her heartfelt investment in her mother. Though unable to explain herself, she follows her instincts, confident that somehow, some way her mother is still available to her. After searching high and low and listening to her broken heart, Ponette's receptivity to feminine resonances prevails, and she is able at last to meet her dead mother and absorb the essence of what she needs from her. This child's common sense has told her that life is not worth living without access to Mother, but she also teaches us that there is something more to Mother than a corporeal body.

A few years prior to the fall of the Berlin Wall, the protagonist in *The Lives of Others,* Georg Dreyman, an East German playwright who has believed in communism *and* a right to love *and* a right to creative expression was, unbeknownst to him, monitored by Stasi intelligence agents, who were of the opinion that his openhearted, individualized relatedness posed a threat to the state. In the film, this sweet, good man ultimately proves to be impervious to their efforts to ruin him because, like Ponette, he is governed finally by his own heart. Guided by both passion and compassion over which no one else has dominion, Georg becomes sensitized to the plight of a fellow artist whose work has been suppressed by the state. He and his friends in the intellectual community that remain in East Berlin realize that all they can do, in the face of such silent oppression, is to tell the story of their suffering. I am not sure that I have seen a more compelling example of a man holding onto his humanity while he and everyone he knows (especially his sweetheart) are pummeled by authorities who have sold their souls to the totalitarian devil. In an extraordinarily nuanced performance, Sebastian Koch, as the playwright, lets us see the feminine on his face (one of the great images in contemporary cinema). What seems to sustain Georg, in spite of the enormous suffering that he endures (and that, silently watching, we must endure with him) is a calm, though impassioned, containment that has the capacity to keep his friend's suffering from being completely in vain. Georg's empathic caring for the woman he loves (but cannot save from the same fate as his friend) seeps into and softens the cold stone heart of the very man who is orchestrating his and her surveillance. As the mole, Captain Gerd Wiesler methodically searches for incriminating evidence against Georg, whose rooms he has had bugged electronically. While listening in on Georg's rich emotional life, Gerd inadvertently experiences love for the first time. Gerd's defenses quietly dissolve while he is eavesdropping, and he becomes painfully aware that his commitment to scrutinizing others' lives has resulted in neglect and sacrifice of his own. On some level, he becomes aware that only a man like Georg Dreyman, with a healthy relationship to the feminine, really has the wherewithal to live up to his ideals and truly help others.

Finally, there is *The Namesake*'s Gogol (played with earnest fidelity to Jumpa Lahiri's character by Kal Penn), a young Indian-American who feels he has been dealt a bad hand by his provincial immigrant parents, who so hope to pass their traditions on to their son. Resistant to their unhip ways, Gogol looks for a love of his own choice in all the wrong places, that is until life deals him tough-enough lessons to move him to exchange pouting for a more authentic surrender to his actual life circumstances. Over the course of the film, Gogol labors through his life, resisting his roots and trying to fit into someone else's image of what a man should be in the contemporary world. He has enough ups and downs to wear him out (as well as his viewers), but they free him from his adolescent fantasies of what life should be like. The movie ends with a sense that Gogol at last is settling into himself. As he works through his illusions, a healthier anima is evolving, one that surely will continue to guide him to a lifestyle that suits him and a marriage that will stick. We have earlier in this book remarked on director Mira Nair's unerring eye in *Monsoon Wedding* for

the way the feminine emerges in a man's life. We watch through that eye
again in Nair's *The Namesake*, as Gogol develops an increasing comfort
living inside his own skin. The movie's charm and authority derive from
its capacity to gaze unblinkingly and yet lovingly at the egotistical young
man and to let life have its way with him until he yields to his own inner
wisdom. This is a wisdom that finds ground in respect for the feminine,
very like the instinct that informs the individuation of Ponette and Georg.

On first glance, Ponette, Georg and Gogol may not seem to have much
in common, but they are all exemplary role models for what it takes to be
faithful to feminine values. With reflection, we can see that their success
with today's filmgoers comes from eagerness on our part to be present in
the cinema to the world of feeling over which the feminine presides. The
strength of these three characters lies in their unembarrassed capacity to
care and their keen attunement to an interior drumbeat that beckons them
to their larger selves. Besides films that stimulate, distract and entertain,
we long for films that make a space to hear our own heart's requests as we
watch others pursuing theirs. That two men and a little girl are the
protagonists in these films proves that beautiful, legendary, or award-
winning actresses do not have exclusive dibs on the cinematic feminine.
They suggest that each one of us has the privilege of connecting with the
feminine in our own way. If I persist in calling the realm they inhabit
feminine, it is not to valorize my own sex, but to recognize some still-
sensitive core within all of us that is seeking something outside the
patriarchal system in which we presently live.

Notes

[1] *Alien* film series (1979, 1986, 1992, 1997). Screenplay by Dan O'Bannon et al.
Directed by Ridley Scott, James Cameron, David Fincher and Jean-Pierre Jeunet.
[2] *G. I. Jane* (1997). Written by Danielle Alexandra and David Twohy. Directed by
Ridley Scott.
[3] *Kill Bill:* I (2003), II (2004). Screenplay by Uma Thurman and Quentin
Tarantino. Directed by Quentin Tarantino.
[4] *Kramer vs. Kramer* (1979). Written and directed by Robert Benton.
[5] *Tootsie* (1982). Written by Larry Gelbart and Barry Levinson. Directed by
Sydney Pollack.

INDEX